The Tourist Gaze

Theory, Culture & Society

Theory, Culture & Society caters for the resurgence of interest in culture within contemporary social science and the humanities. Building on the heritage of classical social theory, the book series examines ways in which this tradition has been reshaped by a new generation of theorists. It also publishes theoretically informed analyses of everyday life, popular culture, and new intellectual movements.

EDITOR: Mike Featherstone, *Nottingham Trent University*

THE TCS CENTRE
The *Theory, Culture & Society* book series, the journals *Theory, Culture & Society* and *Body & Society*, and related conference, seminar and postgraduate programmes operate from the TCS Centre at Nottingham Trent University. For further details of the TCS Centre's activities please contact:

Centre Administrator
The TCS Centre, Room 175
Faculty of Humanities
Nottingham Trent University
Clifton Lane, Nottingham, NG11 8NS, UK
e-mail: tcs@ntu.ac.uk
web: http://tcs.ntu.ac.uk

Recent volumes include:

The Experience of Culture
Michael Richardson

Individualization
Ulrich Beck and E. Beck-Gernsheim

Virilio Live
John Armitage

The Sociological Ambition
Chris Shilling and Philip Mellor

Embodying the Monster
Margrit Shildrick

Critique of Information
Scott Lash

The Tourist Gaze

Second Edition

John Urry

SAGE Publications
London • Thousand Oaks • New Delhi

First published 1990

Reprinted 1991 (twice), 1992,1993,1994, 1996, 1997,
1998, 2000. **Reprinted 2002**

Second edition 2002

SAGE Publications Ltd
6 Bonhill Street
London EC2A 4PU

SAGE Publications Inc
2455 Teller Road
Thousand Oaks, California 91320

SAGE Publications India Pvt Ltd
32, M-Block Market
Greater Kailash - I
New Delhi 110 048

British Library Cataloguing in Publication data

A catalogue record for this book is
available from the British Library

ISBN 0 7619 7346 X
ISBN 0 7619 7347 8

Library of Congress control number available

Typeset by SIVA Math Setters, Chennai, India
Printed in Great Britain by The Cromwell Press Ltd,
Trowbridge, Wiltshire

'To remain stationary in these times of change, when all the world is on the move, would be a crime. Hurrah for the Trip – the cheap, cheap Trip' (Thomas Cook in 1854, quoted Brendon, 1991: 65).

'A view? Oh a view! How delightful a view is!' (Miss Bartlett, in *A Room with a View*; Forster, 1955: 8, orig. 1908).

'T[t]he camera and tourism are two of the uniquely modern ways of defining reality' (Horne, 1984: 21).

At least for richer households of the 'west': 'home is no longer one place. It is locations' (bell hooks, 1991: 148).

'For the twentieth-century tourist, the world has become one large department store of countrysides and cities' (Schivelbusch, 1986: 197).

'It's funny, isn't it, how every traveller is a tourist except one's self' (an Edwardian skit, quoted Brendon, 1991: 188)

'Since Thomas Cook's first excursion train it is as if a magician's wand had been passed over the face of the globe' (*The Excursionist*, June 1897, quoted in Ring, 2000: 83).

The tourist 'pay[s] for their freedom; the right to disregard native concerns and feelings, the right to spin their own web of meanings ... The world is the tourist's oyster ... to be lived pleasurably – and thus given meaning' (Bauman, 1993: 241).

'Going by railroad, I do not consider travelling at all; it is merely being 'sent' to a place, and no different from being a parcel' (John Ruskin, quoted in Wang, 2000: 179).

'The thesis of my book is that sightseeing is a substitute for religious ritual. The sightseeing tour as secular pilgrimage. Accumulation of grace by visiting the shrines of high culture' (Rupert Sheldrake, in *Paradise News*: David Lodge 1991: 75).

'Wow, that's so postcard' (visitor seeing Victoria Falls, quoted Osborne, 2000: 79).

Contents

Preface

I am very grateful for the advice, encouragement and assistance of the following, especially those who have provided me with tourist gems from around the world: Paul Bagguley, Nick Buck, Peter Dickens, Paul Heelas, Mark Hilton, Scott Lash, Michelle Lowe, Celia Lury, Jane Mark-Lawson, David Morgan, Ian Rickson, Chris Rojek, Mary Rose, Peter Saunders, Dan Shapiro, Rob Shields, Hermann Schwengel, John Towner, Sylvia Walby, John Walton and Alan Warde. I am also grateful to professionals working in the tourism and hospitality industry who responded to my queries with much information and advice. Some interviews reported here were conducted under the auspices of the ESRC Initiative on the Changing Urban and Regional System. I am grateful to that Initiative in first prompting me to take holiday-making 'seriously'.

John Urry
Lancaster, December 1989

Preface to the Second Edition

This new edition has maintained the structure of the first edition except for the addition of a new chapter (8) on 'Globalising the Gaze'. The other seven chapters have been significantly updated in terms of data, the incorporation of relevant new studies and some better illustrations. I am very grateful for the extensive research assistance and informed expertise that has been provided by Viv Cuthill for this new edition. I am also grateful to Mike Featherstone for originally prompting a book on tourism, and Chris Rojek who suggested this second edition as well as for collaboration on our co-edited *Touring Cultures*.

Over the past decade I have supervised various PhDs at Lancaster on issues of tourism, travel and mobility. I have learnt much from these doctorates and especially from the conversations about the ongoing work. I would especially like to thank the following, some of whom commented very helpfully on Chapter 8: Alexandra Arellano, Javier Caletrio, Viv Cuthill, Saolo Cwerner, Monica Degen, Tim Edensor, Hernan Gutiérrez Sagastume, Juliet Jain, Jonas Larsen, Neil Lewis, Chia-ling Lai, Richard Sharpley, Jo Stanley and Joyce Yeh. I have also benefited from many discussions with the MA students who have taken my 'Tourist Gaze' module over the past decade.

Lancaster colleagues with whom I have discussed these topics (some also making very helpful comments on Chapter 8) include Sara Ahmed, Gordon Clark, Carol Crawshaw, Bülent Diken, Anne-Marie Fortier, Robin Grove-White, Kevin Hetherington, Vincent Kaufmann, Phil Macnaghten, Colin Pooley, Katrin Schneeberger and Mimi Sheller.

Working on graduate matters in the Sociology Department with Pennie Drinkall and Claire O'Donnell has been a pleasure over the past few years.

John Urry
Lancaster, April 2001

1

The Tourist Gaze

Why Tourism is Important

> The clinic was probably the first attempt to order a science on the exercise and decisions of the gaze ... the medical gaze was also organized in a new way. First, it was no longer the gaze of any observer, but that of a doctor supported and justified by an institution ... Moreover, it was a gaze that was not bound by the narrow grid of structure ... but that could and should grasp colours, variations, tiny anomalies ... (Foucault, 1976: 89)

The subject of this book would appear to have nothing whatsoever to do with the serious world of medicine and the medical gaze that concerns Foucault. This is a book about pleasure, about holidays, tourism and travel, about how and why for short periods people leave their normal place of work and residence. It is about consuming goods and services which are in some sense unnecessary. They are consumed because they supposedly generate pleasurable experiences which are different from those typically encountered in everyday life. And yet at least a part of that experience is to gaze upon or view a set of different scenes, of landscapes or townscapes which are out of the ordinary. When we 'go away' we look at the environment with interest and curiosity. It speaks to us in ways we appreciate, or at least we anticipate that it will do so. In other words, we gaze at what we encounter. And this gaze is as socially organised and systematised as is the gaze of the medic. Of course it is of a different order in that it is not confined to professionals 'supported and justified by an institution'. And yet even in the production of 'unnecessary' pleasure there are in fact many professional experts who help to construct and develop our gaze as tourists.

This book then is about how in different societies and especially within different social groups in diverse historical periods the tourist gaze has changed and developed. I shall elaborate on the processes by which the gaze is constructed and reinforced, and will consider who or what authorises it, what its consequences are for the 'places' which are its object, and how it interrelates with a variety of other social practices.

There is no single tourist gaze as such. It varies by society, by social group and by historical period. Such gazes are constructed through difference. By this I mean not merely that there is no universal experience that is true for all tourists at all times. Rather the gaze in any historical period is constructed in relationship to its opposite, to non-tourist forms of social experience and consciousness. What makes a particular tourist gaze depends upon what it is contrasted with; what the forms of non-tourist experience happen to be. The gaze therefore presupposes a system of social activities and signs which locate the particular tourist practices, not in terms of some intrinsic characteristics, but through the contrasts implied with non-tourist social practices, particularly those based within the home and paid work.

Tourism, holiday-making and travel are more significant social phenomena than most commentators have considered. On the face of it there could not be a more trivial subject for a book. And indeed since social scientists have had plenty of difficulty explaining weightier topics, such as work or politics, it might be thought that they would have great difficulties in accounting for more trivial phenomena such as holiday-making. However, there are interesting parallels with the study of deviance. This involves the investigation of bizarre and idiosyncratic social practices which happen to be defined as deviant in some societies but not necessarily in others. The assumption is that the investigation of deviance can reveal interesting and significant aspects of 'normal' societies. Just why various activities are treated as deviant can illuminate how different societies operate much more generally.

This book is based on the notion that a similar analysis can be applied to tourism. Such practices involve the notion of 'departure', of a limited breaking with established routines and practices of everyday life and allowing one's senses to engage with a set of stimuli that contrast with the everyday and the mundane. By considering the typical objects of the tourist gaze one can use these to make sense of elements of the wider society with which they are contrasted. In other words, to consider how social groups construct their tourist gaze is a good way of getting at just what is happening in the 'normal society'. We can use the fact of difference to interrogate the normal through investigating the typical forms of tourism. Thus rather than being a trivial subject tourism is significant in its ability to reveal aspects of normal practices which might otherwise remain opaque. Opening up the workings of the social world often requires the use of counter-intuitive and surprising methodologies; as in this case the investigation of the 'departures' involved in the tourist gaze.

Although I have insisted on the historical and sociological variation in this gaze there are some minimal characteristics of the social practices which are conveniently described as 'tourism'. I now set these out to provide a baseline for more historical, sociological, and global analyses that I develop later.

1   Tourism is a leisure activity which presupposes its opposite, namely regulated and organised work. It is one manifestation of how work and leisure are organised as separate and regulated spheres of social practice in 'modern' societies. Indeed acting as a tourist is one of the defining characteristics of being 'modern' and is bound up with major transformations in paid work. This has come to be organised within particular places and to occur for regularised periods of time.

2   Tourist relationships arise from a movement of people to, and their stay in, various destinations. This necessarily involves some movement through space, that is the journeys, and periods of stay in a new place or places.

3 The journey and stay are to, and in, sites outside the normal places of residence and work. Periods of residence elsewhere are of a short-term and temporary nature. There is a clear intention to return 'home' within a relatively short period of time.

4 The places gazed upon are for purposes not directly connected with paid work and they normally offer some distinctive contrasts with work (both paid and unpaid).

5 A substantial proportion of the population of modern societies engages in such tourist practices; new socialised forms of provision are developed in order to cope with the mass character of the gaze of tourists (as opposed to the individual character of 'travel').

6 Places are chosen to be gazed upon because there is anticipation, especially through daydreaming and fantasy, of intense pleasures, either on a different scale or involving different senses from those customarily encountered. Such anticipation is constructed and sustained through a variety of non-tourist practices, such as film, TV, literature, magazines, records and videos, which construct and reinforce that gaze.

7 The tourist gaze is directed to features of landscape and townscape which separate them off from everyday experience. Such aspects are viewed because they are taken to be in some sense out of the ordinary. The viewing of such tourist sights often involves different forms of social patterning, with a much greater sensitivity to visual elements of landscape or townscape than normally found in everyday life. People linger over such a gaze which is then normally visually objectified or captured through photographs, postcards, films, models and so on. These enable the gaze to be endlessly reproduced and recaptured.

8 The gaze is constructed through signs, and tourism involves the collection of signs. When tourists see two people kissing in Paris what they capture in the gaze is 'timeless romantic Paris'. When a small village in England is seen, what they gaze upon is the 'real olde England'. As Culler argues: 'the tourist is interested in everything as a sign of itself … All over the world the unsung armies of semioticians, the tourists, are fanning out in search of the signs of Frenchness, typical Italian behaviour, exemplary Oriental scenes, typical American thruways, traditional English pubs' (1981: 127).

9 An array of tourist professionals develop who attempt to reproduce ever new objects of the tourist gaze. These objects are located in a complex and changing hierarchy. This depends upon the interplay between, on the one hand, competition between interests involved in the provision of such objects and, on the other hand, changing class, gender, generational distinctions of taste within the potential population of visitors.

In this book I consider the development of, and historical transformations in, the tourist gaze. I mainly chart such changes in the past couple of centuries; that is, in the period in which mass tourism has become widespread within much of Europe, north America and increasingly within most other parts of the world. To be a tourist is one of the characteristics of the 'modern' experience. Not to 'go away' is like not possessing a car or a nice house. It has become a marker of status in modern societies and is also thought to be necessary for good health (see Feifer, 1985: 224).

This is not to suggest that there was no organised travel in premodern societies, but it was very much the preserve of elites (see Towner, 1988). In Imperial Rome, for example, a fairly extensive pattern of travel for pleasure and culture existed for the elite. A travel infrastructure developed, partly permitted by two centuries of peace. It was possible to travel from Hadrian's Wall to the Euphrates without crossing a hostile border (Feifer, 1985: ch. l). Seneca maintained that this permitted city-dwellers to seek ever new sensations and pleasures. He said: 'men [sic] travel widely to different sorts of places seeking different distractions because they are fickle, tired of soft living, and always seek after something which eludes them' (quoted in Feifer, 1985: 9).

In the thirteenth and fourteenth centuries pilgrimages had become a widespread phenomenon 'practicable and systematized, served by a growing industry of networks of charitable hospices and mass-produced indulgence handbooks' (Feifer, 1985: 29; Eade and Sallnow, 1991). Such pilgrimages often included a mixture of religious devotion and culture and pleasure. By the fifteenth century there were regular organised tours from Venice to the Holy Land.

The Grand Tour had become firmly established by the end of the seventeenth century for the sons of the aristocracy and the gentry, and by the late eighteenth century for the sons of the professional middle class. Over this period, between 1600 and 1800, treatises on travel shifted from a scholastic emphasis on touring as an opportunity for discourse, to travel as eyewitness observation. There was a visualisation of the travel experience, or the development of the 'gaze', aided and assisted by the growth of guide-books which promoted new ways of seeing (see Adler, 1989). The character of the tour itself shifted, from the earlier 'classical Grand Tour' based on the emotionally neutral observation and recording of galleries, museums and high cultural artefacts, to the nineteenth-century 'romantic Grand Tour' which saw the emergence of 'scenic tourism' and a much more private and passionate experience of beauty and the sublime (see Towner, 1985). It is also interesting to note how travel was expected to play a key role in the cognitive and perceptual education of the English upper class (see Dent, 1975).

The eighteenth century had also seen the development of a considerable tourist infrastructure in the form of spa towns throughout much of Europe (Thompson, 1981: 11–12). Myerscough notes that the 'whole apparatus of spa life with its balls, its promenades, libraries, masters of ceremonies was designed to provide a concentrated urban experience of frenetic socialising for a dispersed rural elite' (1974: 5). There have always been periods in which the mass of the population has engaged in play or recreation. In the countryside work and play were particularly intertwined in the case of fairs. Most towns and villages in England had at least one fair a year and many had more. People would often travel considerable distances and the fairs always involved a mixture of business and pleasure normally centred around the tavern. By the eighteenth century the public house had become a major centre for public life in the community, providing light, heat, cooking facilities, furniture, news, banking and travel facilities, entertainment, and sociability (see Harrison, 1971; Clark, 1983).

But before the nineteenth century few people outside the upper classes travelled anywhere to see objects for reasons that were unconnected with work or business. And it is this which is the central characteristic of mass tourism in modern societies, namely that much of the population in most years will travel somewhere else to gaze upon it and stay there for reasons basically unconnected with work. Travel is thought to occupy 40 per cent of available 'free time' in Britain (Williams and Shaw, 1988b: 12). If people do not travel, they lose status: travel is the marker of status. It is a crucial element of modern life to feel that travel and holidays are necessary. 'I need a holiday' is the surest reflection of a modern discourse based on the idea that people's physical and mental health will be restored if only they can 'get away' from time to time.

The importance of this can be seen in the sheer scale of contemporary travel. There are 698 million international passenger arrivals each year, compared with 25 million in 1950 – with the total predicted to be one billion by 2010 and 1.6 billion by 2020. There was a 7.4 per cent increase in travel in the year 2000 alone (WTO, 2000a). At any one time there are 300,000 passengers in flight *above* the US, equivalent to a substantial city. There are two million air passengers each day in the USA (Gottdiener, 2001: 1). Half a million new hotel rooms are built annually, while there are 31 million refugees across the globe (Kaplan, 1996: 101; Makimoto and Manners, 1997: ch. 1; Papastergiadis, 2000: ch. 2). World-wide tourism is growing at 4–5 per cent per annum. 'Travel and tourism' is the largest industry in the world, accounting for 11.7 per cent of world GDP, 8 per cent of world exports and 8 per cent of all employment (WTTC, 2000: 8; Tourism Concern website).

This occurs almost everywhere, with the World Tourism Organisation publishing tourism/travel statistics for over 180 countries with at least 70 countries now receiving more than one million international tourist arrivals a year (WTO, 2000a; 2000b). There is more or less no country in the world that is not a significant receiver of visitors. However, the flows of such visitors originate very unequally, with the 45 countries that have 'high' human development accounting for three-quarters of international tourism departures (UNDP, 1999: 53–5). Such mobilities are enormously costly for the environment with transport accounting for around one-third of all CO_2 emissions (see the many accounts in *Tourism in Focus*). There is an astonishing tripling of world car travel predicted between 1990–2050 (Hawkin, Lovins, 1999).

Within the UK tourist-related services now employ about 1.8 million people; such employment having risen by 40 per cent since 1980 while overall employment has increased only marginally (Dept of Culture, Media and

Sport website). Tourist spending by overseas visitors to the UK is currently worth at least £13 billion (Dept of Culture, Media and Sport website). These figures reflect the many new tourist sites that have opened over the past two or three decades. There were 800 visitor attractions in 1960, 2,300 in 1983 and 6,100 by 2000 (Cabinet Office, 1983; Dept of Culture, Media and Sport website; Hanna, 2000). In 1987, 233 million visits were made to such attractions; by 1998 this had risen to 395 million (The *Guardian*, 12 December 1988; Dept of Culture, Media and Sport website). Apart from the Millennium Dome (with 6.5 million visitors in 2000), the most popular sites in Britain are Blackpool Pleasure Beach (7.2 million visitors), Tate Modern (5 million visitors), Alton Towers (2.7 million visitors), Madame Tussauds (2.6 million visitors), and the Tower of London (2.4 million visitors) (English Tourism Council, 2000/2001). However, the proliferation of new sites has meant that many struggle to attract sufficient paying visitors and there have been some closures of recently opened attractions (Hanna, 2000: A79–88).

There have been significant increases in personal travel. Between the 1970s and the late 1990s there was a 50 per cent increase in total passenger mileage within Britain; 6,728 miles are travelled each year (www.transtat.detr.gov.uk). Even by 1985, 70 per cent of people lived in households that possessed a car, while now one-quarter of households possess two cars.

Car ownership has permitted some increase in the number of domestic holidays taken in Britain, which rose from 126 million in 1985 to 146 million in 1999, although these mainly consisted of short and medium length holidays (Key Note Report, 1987: 15; English Tourism Council, 2000/2001). There has been a very significant increase in visits to see friends and relatives; this grew faster in the 1990s than any other form of domestic tourism, especially amongst young people. Business travel accounts for about one-eighth of all travel (English Tourism Council, 2000: F7–14).

At the same time there has been a marked rise in the number of holidays taken abroad. In 1976 about 11.5 million visits were made abroad by UK residents. By 1986 28 per cent of Britons went abroad, making about 25 million journeys, of which about a quarter were to Spain (Mitchinson, 1988: 48; Business Monitor Quarterly Statistics, MQ6 Overseas Travel and Tourism). And by 1998, UK citizens made 51 million visits abroad (BTA 2000: 52–3).

There has been an increase in the number of tourists coming to the UK. There were 11 million visits in 1976, 15.5 million in 1987, and 25 million in 1999 (Landry et al., 1989: 45; British Tourist Authority web site). The UK is the sixth most frequented tourist destination, following France, US, Spain, Italy and China, but only a little ahead of the Russian Federation, Canada and Mexico (World Tourism Organization website; the UK is fifth highest in terms of receipts).

Finally, spending by such visitors accounts for five per cent of the wider leisure market, much of it going on retailing expenditure (Martin and Mason, 1987: 95–6). Domestic tourists spend a lower proportion on shopping but even here the proportion is rising. Martin and Mason conclude: 'shopping is becoming more significant to tourism, both as an area of spending and as an incentive for travelling' (1987: 96). In 1998/9 household expenditure on transport had reached 17 percent of total expenditure, rising from around 14 per cent ten years earlier (Department of the Environment, Transport and the Regions/Transport Statistics website).

In the next section I briefly consider some of the main theoretical contributions that have attempted to make sociological sense of these extensive flows of people.

Theoretical Approaches to the Study of Tourism

Making theoretical sense of 'fun, pleasure and entertainment' has proved a difficult task for social scientists. In this section I shall summarise some of the main contributions to the sociology of tourism. They are not uninteresting but they leave much work still to be done. In the rest of the book I develop some notions relevant to the theoretical understanding of tourist activity, drawing on contributions discussed here but also connecting developments to debates on emergent 'globalization'.

One of the earliest formulations is Boorstin's analysis of the 'pseudo-event' (1964; and see Cohen, 1988). He argues, partly anticipating Baudrillard, that contemporary Americans cannot experience 'reality' directly but thrive on 'pseudo-events'. Tourism is the prime example of these (see Eco, 1986; Baudrillard, 1988). Isolated from the host environment and the local people, the mass tourist travels in guided groups and finds pleasure in inauthentic contrived attractions, gullibly enjoying 'pseudo-events' and disregarding the 'real' world outside. As a result tourist entrepreneurs and the indigenous populations are induced to produce ever more extravagant displays for the gullible observer who is thereby further removed from the local people. Over time, via advertising and the media, the images generated of different tourist gazes come to constitute a closed self-perpetuating system of illusions which provide the tourist with the basis for selecting and evaluating potential places to visit. Such visits are made, says Boorstin, within the 'environmental bubble' of the familiar American-style hotel which insulates the tourist from the strangeness of the host environment.

A number of later writers develop and refine this relatively simple thesis of a historical shift from the 'individual traveller' to the 'mass society tourist'. Particularly noteworthy is Turner and Ash's *The Golden Hordes* (1975), which fleshes out the thesis about how the tourist is placed at the centre of a strictly circumscribed world. Surrogate parents (travel agents, couriers, hotel managers) relieve the tourist of responsibility and protect him/her from harsh reality. Their solicitude restricts the tourist to the beach and certain approved objects of the tourist gaze (see Edensor 1998, on package holiday makers at the Taj Mahal). In a sense, Turner and Ash suggest, the tourists' sensuality and aesthetic sense are as restricted as they are in their home country. This is further heightened by the relatively superficial way in which indigenous cultures necessarily have to be presented to the tourist. They note about Bali that: 'Many aspects of Balinese culture and art are so

Figure 1.1   *The tourist gaze in Bali, Indonesia*

bewilderingly complex and alien to western modes that they do not lend themselves readily to the process of over-simplification and mass production that converts indigenous art forms into tourist kitsch' (Turner and Ash, 1975: 159; Bruner, 1995; and see Figure 1.1).

The upshot is that in the search for ever-new places to visit, what is constructed is a set of hotels and tourist sights that is bland and lacking contradiction, 'a small monotonous world that everywhere shows us our own image … the pursuit of the exotic and diverse ends in uniformity' (Turner and Ash, 1975: 292).

Somewhat critical of this tradition is Cohen, who maintains that there is no single tourist as such but a variety of tourist types or modes of tourist experience (see 1972, 1979, 1988, for various formulations mainly drawn from the sociology of religion). What he terms as the 'experiential', the 'experimental' and the 'existential' do not rely on the environmental bubble of conventional tourist services. To varying degrees such tourist experiences are based on rejecting such ways of organising tourist activity. Moreover, one should also note that the existence of such bubbles does permit many people to visit places which otherwise they would not, and to have at least some contact with the 'strange' places thereby encountered. Indeed until such places have developed a fully-fledged tourist infrastructure much of the 'strangeness' of such destinations will be impossible to hide and to package within a complete array of pseudo-events'.

The most significant challenge to Boorstin's position is that of MacCannell, who is likewise concerned with the inauthenticity and superficiality of modern life (1999; orig. 1976). He quotes Simmel on the nature of the sensory impressions experienced in the 'metropolis': 'the rapid crowding of changing images, the sharp discontinuity in the grasp of a single glance, and the unexpectedness of onrushing impressions' (MacCannell, 1999: 49). He maintains that these are symptomatic of the tourist experience. He disagrees with Boorstin's account, which he regards as reflecting a characteristically upper-class view that 'other people are tourists, while I am a traveller' (1999: 107; and see Buzard 1993, on this distinction). All tourists for MacCannell embody a quest for authenticity, and this quest is a modern version of the universal human concern with the sacred. The tourist is a kind of contemporary pilgrim, seeking authenticity in other 'times' and other 'places' away from that person's everyday life. Tourists show particular fascination in the 'real lives' of others that somehow possess a reality hard to discover in their own experiences. Modern society is therefore rapidly institutionalizing the rights of outsiders to look into its workings. 'Institutions are fitted with arenas, platforms and chambers set aside for the exclusive use of tourists' (MacCannell, 1999: 49). Almost any sort of work, even the backbreaking toil of the Welsh miner or the unenviable work of those employed in the Parisian sewer, can be the object of the tourist gaze.

MacCannell is particularly interested in the character of the social relations which emerge from this fascination people have especially in the work lives of others. He notes that such 'real lives' can only be found backstage and are not immediately evident to us. Hence, the gaze of the tourist will involve an obvious intrusion into people's lives, which would be generally unacceptable. So the people being observed and local tourist entrepreneurs gradually come to construct backstages in a contrived and artificial manner. 'Tourist spaces' are thus organised around what MacCannell calls 'staged authenticity' (1973). The development of the constructed tourist attraction results from how those who are subject to the tourist gaze respond, both to protect themselves from intrusions into their lives backstage and to take advantage of the opportunities it presents for profitable investment. By contrast then with Boorstin, MacCannell argues that 'psuedo-events' result from the social relations of tourism and not from an individualistic search for the inauthentic.

Pearce and Moscardo have further elaborated the notion of authenticity (1986; and see the critique in Turner and Manning, 1988). They maintain that it is necessary to distinguish between the authenticity of the setting and the authenticity of the persons gazed upon; and to distinguish between the diverse elements of the tourist experience which are of importance to the tourist in question. Crick, by contrast, points out that there is a sense in which all cultures are 'staged' and inauthentic. Cultures are invented, remade and the elements reorganised (Crick,1988: 65–6). Hence, it is not clear why the apparently inauthentic staging for the tourist is so very different from the processes of cultural remaking that happens in all cultures anyway (see Rojek and Urry, 1997). Based on research at New Salem where

Abraham Lincoln spent some years in the 1830s, Bruner distinguished various conflicting senses of the authentic (1994; and see Wang, 2000). First, there is the authentic in the sense of a small town that *looks* like it has appropriately aged over the previous 170 years, whether the buildings are actually that old or not. Second, there is the town that appears as it would have looked in the 1830s, that is, mostly comprised of *new* buildings. Third, there are the buildings and artefacts that literally *date* from the 1830s and have been there since then. And fourth, there are those buildings and artefacts that have been authorised as *authentic* by the Trust that oversees the 'heritage' within the town. Holderness (1988) has similarly described the processes in Stratford-upon-Avon by which the Shakespeare Birthplace Trust has come to exert a hegemonic role in the town, determining which buildings, places and artefacts are authentically part of 'Shakespeare's heritage' and those which are not so 'authenticated' (see Lash and Urry, 1994: 264–6). Bruner also notes that New Salem now is wholly different from the 1830s since in the previous period there would not have been camera-waving tourists wandering about in large numbers excitedly staring at actors dressed up as though they were residents of a previous and long-since disappeared epoch.

MacCannell also notes that, unlike the religious pilgrim who pays homage to a single sacred centre, the tourist pays homage to an enormous array of centres or attractions. These include sites of industry and work. This is because work has become a mere attribute of society and not its central feature (MacCannell, 1999: 58). MacCannell characterises such an interest in work displays as 'alienated leisure'. It is a perversion of the aim of leisure since it involves a paradoxical return to the workplace.

He also notes how each centre of attraction involves complex processes of production in order that regular, meaningful and profitable tourist gazes can be generated and sustained. Such gazes cannot be left to chance. People have to learn how, when and where to 'gaze'. Clear markers have to be provided and in some cases the object of the gaze is merely the marker that indicates some event or experience which previously happened at that spot.

MacCannell maintains that there is normally a process of sacralization that renders a particular natural or cultural artefact as a sacred object of the tourist ritual (1999: 42–8). A number of stages are involved in this: naming the sight, framing and elevation, enshrinement, mechanical reproduction of the sacred object, and social reproduction as new sights (or 'sites') name themselves after the famous. It is also important to note that not only are there many attractions to which to pay homage, but many attractions are only gazed upon once. In other words, the gaze of the tourist can be amazingly fickle, searching out or anticipating something new or something different. MacCannell notes that 'anything is potentially an attraction. It simply awaits one person to take the trouble to point it out to another as something noteworthy, or worth seeing' (1999: 192).

The complex processes involved here are partly revealed in Turner's analysis of pilgrimage (1973; 1974). Important *rites de passage* are involved in the movement from one stage to another. There are three such stages:

first, social and spatial separation from the normal place of residence and conventional social ties; second, liminality, where the individual finds him/herself in an 'anti-structure ... out of time and place' – conventional social ties are suspended, an intensive bonding 'communitas' is experienced, and there is direct experience of the sacred or supernatural; and third, reintegration, where the individual is reintegrated with the previous social group, usually at a higher social status.

Although this analysis is applied to pilgrimages, other writers have drawn out its implications for tourism (see Cohen, 1988: 38–40; Shields, 1990; Eade and Sallnow 1991). Like the pilgrim the tourist moves from a familiar place to a far place and then returns to the familiar place. At the far place both the pilgrim and the tourist engage in 'worship' of shrines which are sacred, albeit in different ways, and as a result gain some kind of uplifting experience. In the case of the tourist Turner and Turner talk of 'liminoid' situations (1978). What is being pointed out here is something left under-examined in MacCannell, namely that in much tourism everyday obligations are suspended or inverted. There is licence for permissive and playful 'non-serious' behaviour and the encouragement of a relatively unconstrained 'communitas' or social togetherness. Such arguments call into question the idea that there is simply 'routine' or habitual action, as argued for example by Giddens (1984). What is often involved is semi-routine action or a kind of routinized non-routine.

One analysis of this is Shields' exploration of the 'honeymoon capital of the world', Niagara Falls (1990). Going on honeymoon to Niagara did indeed involve a pilgrimage, stepping out into an experience of liminality in which the codes of normal social experience were reversed. In particular honey-mooners found themselves historically in an ideal liminal zone where the strict social conventions of bourgeois families were relaxed under the exigencies of travel and of relative anonymity and freedom from collective scrutiny. In a novel written in 1808 a character says of Niagara: 'Elsewhere there are cares of business and fashion, there are age, sorrow, and heartbreak; but here only youth, faith, rapture' (quoted Shields, 1990). Shields also discusses how Niagara, just like Gretna Green in Scotland, has become a signifier now emptied of meaning, a thoroughly commercialised cliché.

Some writers in this tradition argue that such playful or 'ludic' behaviour is primarily restitutive or compensatory, revitalising the tourists for their return to the familiar place of home and work (see Lett, 1983 on ludic charter yacht tourism). Other writers, by contrast, adopt a less functionalist interpretation and argue that the general notions of liminality and inversion have to be given a more precise content. It is necessary to investigate the nature of the social and cultural patterns within the tourist's day-to-day existence in order to see just what is inverted and how the liminal experience will work itself out. Gottlieb argues, for example, that what is sought for in a vacation/holiday is inversion of the everyday. The middle-class tourist will seek to be a 'peasant for a day' while the lower middle-class tourist will seek to be 'king/queen for a day' (see Gottlieb, 1982). Although these are hardly very convincing examples they do point to a crucial feature of tourism, namely that there is typically a clear distinction between the familiar and the faraway and that such differences produce distinct kinds of liminal zones.

It therefore seems incorrect to suggest that a search for authenticity is the basis for the organisation of tourism. Rather, one key feature would seem to be that there is difference between one's normal place of residence/work and the object of the tourist gaze. Now it may be that a seeking for what we take to be authentic elements is an important component here but that is only because there is in some sense a contrast with everyday experiences. Furthermore, it has recently been argued that some visitors – what Feifer (1985) terms 'post-tourists' – almost delight in the inauthenticity of the normal tourist experience. 'Post-tourists' find pleasure in the multiplicity of tourist games. They know that there is no authentic tourist experience, that there are merely a series of games or texts that can be played. In later chapters I draw out some important connections between the notion of the post-tourist and the more general cultural development of postmodernism.

For the moment though it is necessary to consider just what it is that produces a distinctive tourist gaze. Minimally there must be certain aspects of the place to be visited which distinguish it from what is conventionally encountered in everyday life. Tourism results from a basic binary division between the ordinary/everyday and the extraordinary. Tourist experiences involve some aspect or element that induces pleasurable experiences which, by comparison with the everyday, are out of the ordinary (see Robinson, 1976: 157). This is not to say that other elements of the production of the tourist experience will not make the typical tourist feel that he or she is 'home from home', not too much 'out of place'. But potential objects of the tourist gaze must be different in some way or other. They must be out of the ordinary. People must experience particularly distinct pleasures which involve different senses or are on a different scale from those typically encountered in everyday life. There are however many different ways in which such a division between the ordinary and the extraordinary is established and sustained.

First, there is seeing a unique object, such as the Eiffel Tower, the Empire State Building, Buckingham Palace, the Grand Canyon, or even the very spot in Dallas where President Kennedy was shot (see Rojek, 1990 on the last). These are absolutely distinct objects to be gazed upon which everyone knows about. They are famous for being famous, although such places may have lost the basis of their fame (such as the Empire State Building, which still attracts two million people a year). Most people living in the 'west' would hope to see some of these objects during their lifetime. They entail a kind of pilgrimage to a sacred centre, which is often a capital city, a major city or the site of a unique mega-event (see Roche, 2000).

Then there is the seeing of particular signs, such as the typical English village, the typical American skyscraper, the typical German beer-garden, the typical French château, and so on. This mode of gazing shows how tourists are in a way semioticians, reading the landscape for signifiers of certain pre-established notions or signs derived from various discourses of travel and tourism (see Culler, 1981: 128).

Third, there is the seeing of unfamiliar aspects of what had previously been thought of as familiar. One example is visiting museums which show representations of the lives of ordinary people, revealing particularly their cultural artefacts. Often these are set out in a 'realistic' setting to demonstrate what their houses, workshops and factories were roughly like. Visitors thus see unfamiliar elements of other people's lives which had been presumed familiar (see Urry, 1996, on reminiscences of the past).

Then there is the seeing of ordinary aspects of social life being undertaken by people in unusual contexts. Some tourism in China has been of this sort. Visitors have found it particularly interesting to gaze upon the carrying out of domestic tasks in a 'communist' country, and hence to see how the routines of life are surprisingly not that unfamiliar.

Also, there is the carrying out of familiar tasks or activities within an unusual visual environment. Swimming and other sports, shopping, eating and drinking all have particular significance if they take place against a distinctive visual backcloth. The visual gaze renders extraordinary, activities that otherwise would be mundane and everyday.

Finally, there is the seeing of particular signs that indicate that a certain other object is indeed extraordinary, even though it does not seem to be so. A good example of such an object is moon rock which appears unremarkable. The attraction is not the object itself but the sign referring to it that marks it out as distinctive. Thus the marker becomes the distinctive sight (Culler, 1981: 139). A similar seeing occurs in art galleries when part of what is gazed at is the name of the artist, 'Rembrandt' say, as much as the painting itself, which may be difficult to distinguish from many others in the same gallery.

I have argued that the character of the gaze is central to tourism. Campbell, however, makes an important point related more generally to the character of consumption as such (1987). He argues that covert day-dreaming and anticipation are processes central to modern consumerism. Individuals do not seek satisfaction from products, from their actual selection, purchase and actual use. Rather satisfaction stems from anticipation, from imaginative pleasure-seeking. People's basic motivation for consumption is not therefore simply materialistic. It is rather that they seek to experience 'in reality' the pleasurable dramas they have already experienced in their imagination. However, since 'reality' rarely provides the perfected pleasures encountered in daydreams, each purchase leads to disillusionment and to the longing for ever-new products. There is a dialectic of novelty and insatiability at the heart of contemporary consumerism.

Campbell seems to view 'imaginative hedonism' as a relatively autonomous characteristic of modern societies and separate from specific institutional arrangements, such as advertising, or from particular modes of social emulation (1987: 88–95). Both claims are dubious in general but particularly so with regard to tourism. It 'is hard to envisage the nature of contemporary tourism without seeing how such activities are literally constructed in our imagination through advertising and the media, and through the conscious competition between different social groups (see Selwyn, 1996, on tourism images). If Campbell is right in arguing that contemporary consumerism involves imaginative pleasure-seeking, then tourism is surely the paradigm case. Tourism necessarily involves daydreaming and anticipation of new or different experiences from those normally encountered in everyday life. But such daydreams are not autonomous; they involve working over advertising and other media-generated sets of signs, many of which relate very clearly to complex processes of social emulation.

One further problem in Campbell's otherwise useful analysis is that he treats modern consumerism as though it is historically fixed. He thus fails to address the changing character of consumption and the possible parallel transformations in the nature of capitalist production (consumption is used here in the sense of 'purchase' and does not imply the absence of production within households). Many writers now argue that a sea change is taking place within contemporary societies, involving a shift from organised to disorganised capitalism (see Lash and Urry, 1987, 1994). Other writers have characterised it as a move from Fordism to post-Fordism, and in particular the claim that there is a shift from mass consumption to more individuated patterns of consumption (see Aglietta, 1987; Hirschhorn, 1984; Piore and Sabel, 1984; Poon, 1993).

But this consumption side of the analysis is undeveloped, indicating the 'productivist' bias in much of the literature. I now set out two ideal types, of Fordist mass consumption and post-Fordist differentiated consumption.

Mass consumption: purchase of commodities produced under conditions of mass production; a high and growing rate of expenditure on consumer products; individual producers tending to dominate particular industrial markets; producer rather than consumer as dominant; commodities little differentiated from each other by fashion, season, and specific market segments; relatively limited choice – what there is tends to reflect producer interests whether private or public.

Post-Fordist consumption: consumption rather than production dominant as consumer expenditure further increases as a proportion of national income; new forms of credit permitting consumer expenditure to rise, so producing high levels of indebtedness; almost all aspects of social life become commodified, even charity; much greater differentiation of purchasing patterns by different market segments; greater volatility of consumer preferences; the growth of a consumers movement and the 'politicising' of consumption; reaction of consumers against being part of a 'mass' and the need for producers to be much more consumer-driven, especially in the case of service industries and those publicly owned; the development of many more products each of which has a shorter life; the emergence of new kinds of commodity which are more specialised and based on raw materials that imply non-mass forms of production ('natural' products for example).

There are obviously many consumption modes which cross-cut this division. However, there is considerable evidence that western societies have been broadly moving from the former to the latter type. If this is so then this shift will also be reflected in the changing character of contemporary tourism (see Poon, 1993; Urry, 1995a). In Britain the holiday camp was the quintessential example of Fordist holiday-making. In the move to post-Fordism such camps have been renamed 'centres' or 'holiday-worlds' and now present themselves as places of 'freedom'. I show in later chapters that there are many other changes occurring in contemporary holiday-making of a broadly 'post-Fordist' sort. These changes have been characterised by Poon (1993) as involving the shift from 'old tourism', which involved packaging and standardisation, to 'new tourism' which is segmented, flexible and customised. The marketing director of British Airways wrote even in the 1980s of 'the *end of mass marketing* in the travel business ... we are going to be much more sophisticated in the way we *segment* our market' (quoted Poon, 1989: 94).

Some such changes are also transforming relations *between* tourism and other cultural practices. In Chapter 5 I shall consider some of the current literature on 'postmodernism', an important feature of which is the importance placed on 'play, pleasure and pastiche', features which have always characterised the tourist gaze. Holiday centres are therefore a kind of prototype for what is now becoming much more widespread, the aestheticisation of consumption. In later chapters I consider how 'globalization' produces further shifts in the production and consumption of tourism sites – especially through the emergence of various global brands.

The next chapter offers a historical sociology of the seaside resort, the quintessential British holiday experience. The rise and fall of such resorts reflects important changes in British society, including the growth of post-Fordist consumption patterns.

2

Mass Tourism and the Rise and Fall of the Seaside Resort

Introduction

The development of the first example of mass tourism, which occurred amongst the industrial working class in Britain, was an exceptionally novel form of social activity. The mass tourist gaze was initiated in the backstreets of the industrial towns and cities in the north of England. Why did this industrial working class come to think that going away for short periods to quite other places was an appropriate form of social activity? Why did the tourist gaze develop amongst the industrial working class in the north of England? What revolution in experience, thinking and perception led to such novel modes of social practice?

The growth of such tourism represents a 'democratisation' of travel. We have seen that travel had always been socially selective. It was available for a relatively limited elite and was a marker of social status. But in the second half of the nineteenth century there was an extensive development of mass travel by train. Status distinctions then came to be drawn between different classes of traveller, but less between those who could and those could not travel. We will consider later how in the twentieth century the car and the aeroplane have even further democratised geographical movement (see Stauth and Turner, 1988; and see Chapter 8). As travel became democratised so extensive distinctions of taste came to be established between different places since where one travelled to became a mark of 'distinction'. The tourist gaze came to have a different importance in one place rather than another. A resort 'hierarchy' developed and certain places were viewed as embodiments of mass tourism, to be despised and ridiculed. Major differences of 'social tone' were established between otherwise similar places. And some such places, the working-class resorts, quickly developed as symbols of 'mass tourism', as places of inferiority which stood for everything that dominant social groups held to be tasteless, common and vulgar.

Explanations of the tourist gaze, of the discourses which established and sustained mass tourism for the industrial working class in the nineteenth century, have tended to be over-general. Such developments have normally been explained in terms of 'nineteenth-century industrialisation' (see Myerscough, 1974; more generally on the history of the beach, see Lencek and Bosner, 1998). In identifying more precisely those aspects of such industrialisation that were especially important, attention will be paid to the growth of seaside resorts, whose development was by no means inevitable. They stemmed from particular features of nineteenth-century industrialisation and the growth of new modes by which pleasure was organised and structured in a society based upon emergent, organised, and large-scale industrial classes (see Walton, 2000).

The Growth of the British Seaside Resort

Throughout Europe a number of spa towns had developed in the eighteenth century. Their original purpose was medicinal: they provided mineral water used for bathing in and drinking. It is not clear exactly how and why people came to believe in these medicinal properties. The first spa in England appears to have been in Scarborough and dates from 1626 when a Mrs Farrow noticed a spring on the beach (see Hern, 1967: 2–3). Within a few decades the medical profession began to advocate the desirable effects of taking the waters, or taking the 'Cure'. Various other spas developed, in Bath, Buxton, Harrogate, Tunbridge Wells and so on. An amazing range of disorders were supposedly improved both by swallowing the waters and by bathing in them. Scarborough, though, was distinctive since it was not only a major spa but was also by the sea. A Dr Wittie began to advocate both drinking the sea water and bathing in the sea. During the eighteenth century there was a considerable increase in sea bathing as the developing merchant and professional classes began to believe in its medicinal properties as a general pick-me-up. At that stage it was advocated for adults and there was little association then between the seaside and children. Indeed since the point of bathing in the sea was to do one good, this was often done in winter and basically involved 'immersion' and not what is now understood as swimming (see Hern, 1967: 21). These dips in the sea were structured and ritualised and were prescribed only to treat serious medical conditions. Bathing was only to be undertaken 'after due preparation and advice' as the historian Gibbon put it (see Shields, 1990), and was also normally carried out naked. The beach was a place of 'medicine' rather than 'pleasure'.

Spa towns could remain relatively socially restrictive. Access was only possible for those who could own or rent accommodation in the particular town. Younger neatly summarises this:

> life in the seventeenth and eighteenth-century watering-places resembled in many ways life on a cruise or in a small winter sports hotel, where the company is small and self-contained, rather than the modern seaside resort, where the individual is submerged in the crowd. (1973: 14–15)

However, as sea bathing became relatively more favoured it was harder for dominant social groups to restrict access. Difficulties were caused in Scarborough because of its dual function as both a spa and as a resort by the seaside. In 1824 the spa property was fenced off and a toll gate opened to exclude the 'improper classes' (Hern, 1967: 16). Pimlott summarises the effects of the widespread development of specialised seaside resorts where this kind of social restriction was not possible:

> The capacity of the seaside resorts, on the other hand, was unbounded. While social life at the spas was necessarily focussed on the pump-room and the baths, and there was no satisfactory alternative to living in public, the sea coast was large enough to absorb all comers and social homogeneity mattered less. (1947: 55)

One precondition then for the rapid growth of seaside resorts in the later eighteenth and especially in the nineteenth centuries was space. Britain possessed an extensive coastline which had few other uses apart from as the location of fishing ports, and which could not be privately controlled since ownership of the shoreline and beach between high and low tide was invested in the Crown (see Thompson, 1981: 14).

The development of such resorts was spectacular. In the first half of the nineteenth century coastal resorts showed a faster rate of population increase than manufacturing towns: 2.56 per cent per annum compared with 2.38 per cent (Lickorish and Kershaw, 1975:12). The population of Brighton increased from 7,000 to 65,000 in half a century, particularly because the Prince Regent had made it fashionable: 'a portion of the West End *maritimized*' (see Shields, 1990). The population of the 48 leading seaside towns increased by nearly 100,000 between 1861 and 1871; their population had more than doubled by the end of the century. By 1911 it was calculated that 55 per cent of people in England and Wales took at least one trip to the seaside and 20 per cent stayed for a longer period each year (Myerscough, 1974: 143).

A complex of conditions produced the rapid growth of this new form of mass leisure activity and hence of these relatively specialised and unique concentrations of services in particular urban centres, concentrations designed to provide novel, and what were at the time utterly amazing, objects of the tourist gaze.

There was a considerable increase in the economic welfare of substantial elements of the industrial population. The real national income per head quadrupled over the nineteenth century (see Deane and Cole, 1962: 282). This enabled sections of the working class to accumulate savings from one holiday to the next, given that at the time few holidays with pay were sought, let alone provided (see Walton, 1981: 252).

In addition there was rapid urbanisation, with many small towns growing incredibly rapidly. In 1801, 20 per cent of the population lived in towns; by 1901 80 per cent did. This produced extremely high levels of poverty and overcrowding. Moreover, these urban areas possessed almost no public spaces, such as parks or squares (see Lash and Urry, 1987: ch. 3). Unlike older towns and cities a fairly marked degree of residential segregation by class developed. This was crucial for the emergence of the typical resort, which relied on attracting particular social groupings from certain parts of these emerging industrial towns and cities. *The Economist* in 1857 summarised the typical pattern of urban development:

> Society is tending more and more to spread into classes – and not merely classes but localised classes, class colonies ... It is the disposition to associate with equals – in some measure with those who have similar practical *interests*, in still

greater measure with those who have similar tastes and culture, most of all with those with whom we judge ourselves on a moral equality, whatever our real standard may be. (20 June 1857: 669; also see Johnson and Pooley, 1982)

One effect therefore of the economic, demographic and spatial transformation of the nineteenth-century town was to produce self-regulating working-class communities, communities which were relatively autonomous of either the old or new institutions of the wider society. Such communities were important in developing forms of working-class leisure which were relatively segregated, specialised and institutionalised (see Clarke and Critcher, 1985).

The growth of a more organised and routinised pattern of work led to attempts to develop a corresponding rationalisation of leisure: 'To a large extent this regularisation of the days of leisure came about because of a change in the daily hours of work and in the nature of work' (Cunningham, 1980: 147).

Particularly in the newly emerging industrial workplaces and cities, work came to be organised as a relatively time-bound and space-bound activity, separated off from play, religion and festivity. Over the course of the eighteenth and nineteenth centuries work was increasingly valued for its own sake and not merely as a remedy for idleness. Some attempts were made to move from an orientation to task towards an orientation to time (see Thompson, 1967; see Lash and Urry 1994: chs 9, 10). Industrialists attempted to impose a rigorous discipline on their newly constructed workforce (Pollard, 1965). Tough and quite unfamiliar rules of attendance and punctuality were introduced, with various fines and punishments. Campaigns were mounted against drinking, idleness, blood sports, bad language, and holidays (see Myerscough, 1974: 4–6; Cunningham, 1980: ch. 3 on 'rational recreation'). Many fairs were abandoned and Saints' Days and closing days at the bank of England were dramatically reduced. From the 1860s onwards the idea of civilising the 'rough' working class through organised recreation became much more widespread amongst employers, middle-class reformers and the state (see Rojek, 1990: ch. 2). The typical forms of preferred recreation were educational instruction, physical exercise, crafts, musical training and excursions. Country holidays for deprived city children, as well as the camps organised by the burgeoning youth movement (the Boys' Brigade, Scouts, Jewish Lads' Brigades and so on), were one element of the social engineering of the working class favoured by the rational recreation movement.

As work became in part rationalised so the hours of working were gradually reduced. Parliament introduced various pieces of protective legislation in the second half of the nineteenth century. Particularly important was the attainment of the half-day holiday, especially on Saturdays (see Cunningham, 1980: ch. 5). Phelps-Brown noted that: 'The achievement of a work-week not exceeding 54 hours and providing a half-holiday was unique in its time and was celebrated as "la semaine anglaise".' (1968, 173; also see Cunningham, 1980: 142–5).

The achievement of longer breaks, of week-long holidays, was pioneered in the north of England and especially in the cotton textile areas of Lancashire (see Walton, 1981; 1997; 2000). Factory owners began to acknowledge 'wakes weeks' as regularised periods of holiday which were in effect traded for much more regular attendance at work during the rest of the year: 'The total closure of a mill at a customary holiday was preferable to constant disruption throughout the summer, and there were advantages in channelling holiday observances into certain agreed periods' (Walton, 1981: 255).

Some employers thus began to view regular holidays as contributing to efficiency. However, the gradual extension of holidays from the mid-nineteenth century onwards mainly resulted from defensive pressure by the workforce itself, particularly the more affluent sections who saw such practices as ways of developing their own autonomous forms of recreation. The factory inspector Leonard Horner ascribed the survival of holidays to custom rather than to 'liberality on the part of the masters' (Walton, 1978: 35). A particularly significant feature of such holiday-making was that it should be enjoyed collectively. As Walton argues, at wakes week 'as at Christmas, Easter and Whitsuntide, custom dictated that holidays should be taken *en masse* and celebrated by the whole community' (1978: 35). From the 1860s onwards wakes weeks came mainly to involve trips to the seaside away from normal places of residence (see Walton and Poole, 1982; Walton, 2000).

In the late eighteenth and early nineteenth centuries there was a shift in values connected with 'the Romantic movement'. Emphasis was placed on the intensity of emotion and sensation, on poetic mystery rather than intellectual clarity, and on individual hedonistic expression (see Feifer, 1985: ch. 5 on the 'romantic' tourist, as well as Newby, 1981). The high priests of Romanticism in Britain were the Shelleys, Lord Byron, Coleridge and the Wordsworths (see Bate, 1991). The effects of Romanticism were to suggest that one could feel emotional about the natural world and scenery. Individual pleasures were to be derived from an appreciation of impressive physical sights. Romanticism implied that the residents of the newly emerging industrial towns and cities could greatly benefit from spending short periods away from them, viewing or experiencing nature. Romanticism not only led to the development of 'scenic tourism' and an appreciation for magnificent stretches of the coastline. It also encouraged sea bathing. Considering the generally inclement weather and the fact that most bathers were naked since no suitable bathing attire had yet been designed by the early nineteenth century, some considerable development of a belief in the health-giving properties of 'nature' must have occurred. Much nineteenth century tourism was based on the natural phenomenon of the sea and its supposedly health-giving properties (see Hern, 1967: ch. 2; Walton, 1983: ch. 2; Sprawson, 1992).

A further precondition for the growth of mass tourism was greatly improved transportation. In the late eighteenth century it took three days to travel from Birmingham to Blackpool. Even the trip from Manchester to Blackpool took a whole day. Only Brighton was reasonably well served by coach. By 1830 forty-eight coaches a day went between London and Brighton and the journey time had been cut to 4½ hours (see Walvin, 1978: 34). But there were two major problems of coach travel. First, many roads were in very poor condition. It was only in the 1830s that the turnpike trusts created a reasonable national network and journey times fell dramatically. Second, coach travel was very expensive, costing something like 2½d. to 3d. a mile. Richard Ayton noted of Blackpool visitors in 1813 that: 'Most of them come hither in carts, but some will walk in a single day from Manchester, distant more than forty miles' (Walvin, 1978: 35).

At first the railway companies in the 1830s did not realise the economic potential of the mass, low-income passenger market. They concentrated instead on goods traffic and on transporting prosperous passengers. But Gladstone's Railway Act of 1844, an important piece of legislation, obliged the railway companies to make provision for the 'labouring classes' (see Walvin, 1978: 37). Even before this the opening of the railway lines between Preston and Fleetwood in 1840 had produced an extraordinary influx of visitors to the port, many of whom then travelled down the coast to Blackpool. By 1848 over 100,000 trippers left Manchester by train for the coast during Whit week; by 1850 it was over 200,000 (Walvin, 1978: 38). The effect on the social tone of Blackpool in the middle of the century was noted at the time:

> Unless immediate steps are taken, Blackpool as a resort for respectable visitors will be ruined ... Unless the cheap trains are discontinued or some effective regulation made for the management of the thousands who visit the place, Blackpool property will be depreciated past recovery. (quoted in Walvin, 1978: 38)

Indeed the 'social tone' of Blackpool appears to have fallen quickly, since fifteen years earlier it was said to have been 'a favourite, salubrious and fashionable resort for "respectable families"' (see Perkin, 1976: 181).

But the role of the railways should not be overemphasised. Generally the railway companies found that the seasonal nature of the holiday trade meant it was not particularly profitable. It was only at the end of the century that they really set about promoting travel to different resorts by outlining the most attractive features of each resort (see Richards and MacKenzie, 1986: 174–9). And only very rarely, as in the case of Silloth in the north-west of England, did they try to construct a wholly new resort which in this case conspicuously failed (see Walton, 1979).

It has also been argued that the pattern of railway development accounted for the difference in 'social tone' between the various rapidly emerging seaside resorts in the mid-nineteenth century. On the face of it a reasonable explanation of these differences would be that those resorts which were more accessible to the great cities and industrial towns were likely to be more popular and this would drive out visitors with higher social status. Thus Brighton and Southend were more popular and had a lower social tone than Bournemouth and Torquay, which were not in day-tripping range from London (Perkin, 1976: 182). But such an explanation does not fully work. Perkin notes that Scarborough and Skegness were practically the same distance from the West Riding, yet they developed very different social tones. Although the railway obviously made a difference to such places its arrival does not completely explain the marked variations that emerged. Nor, Perkin argues, do the actions of local elites. There were in fact strong campaigns in most of the places that became working-class resorts (such as Blackpool or Morecambe) to stop the local railway companies from running Sunday day trips because it was correctly thought that the trippers would drive out the wealthier visitors that all resorts wanted to attract.

Perkin argues instead that the effect of the local elites on the respective 'social tones' of different resorts resulted from the particular ways in which land and buildings were locally owned and controlled. The factor determining each resort's social tone was the competition for domination of the resort between three fractions of capital: local, large capital, especially owners of the main hotels, concert halls, shops etc.; local, small capital, especially boarding-house keepers, owners of amusement arcades, etc.; and large, externally owned, highly capitalised enterprises providing cheap mass entertainment (Perkin, 1976: 185). Particularly important was the prior ownership and control of land in each locality. Perkin shows this in the contrast between Blackpool and Southport, the latter being located nearer to large centres of population and possessing fine wide beaches. Both resorts began with the more or less spontaneous provision of sea-bathing accommodation by local innkeepers, farmers and fishermen. But in Southport land was unenclosed and various squatters who provided sea-bathing facilities soon became tenants of the joint lords of the manor who in turn laid out the spacious and elegant avenue, Lords Street. The landlords also prevented new industrial and much commercial development, with the result that Southport became a resort of large hotels, residential villas, large gardens, and retirement homes for cotton magnates and the like (see Walton, 1981: 251).

Blackpool, by contrast, began as a community of small freeholders. By 1838 there were only twenty-four holdings of land in the town over 25 acres and most of these were well away from the seafront. Even the larger holdings on the front were sold off and divided up into plots for seafront boarding houses. Walton notes that no large resort was so dominated by small lodging houses as Blackpool. This was because:

> There was no room for a planned, high-class estate to grow up on the landowner's own terms, for Blackpool's small freeholders were understandably more concerned with taking the maximum profit from a cramped parcel of land than with improving the amenities of the resort as a whole.
> Land in Blackpool was thus developed at high densities from the first, and few restrictions were placed on developers by landowners, for the fragmented pattern of landownership meant that there was always competition to sell building estates. (Walton, 1978: 63)[ext.]

As a result the whole central area became an ill-planned mass of smaller properties, boarding houses, amusement arcades, small shops and the like, with no space for the grand public buildings, broad avenues and gardens found in Southport. Although local small capital attempted to appeal to the rapidly expanding middle-class tourist market, Blackpool did not possess the scenic attractions necessary to appeal to this market, and simultaneously it was proving immensely popular, partly because of its cheapness, with the industrial working class. This included both trippers and those staying overnight. The numbers of visitors increased greatly during the 1870s and 1880s by which time, the *Morning Post* declared, in Blackpool 'more fun could be found, for less money, than anywhere else in the world' (24 August 1887). Efforts by the Corporation to exclude traders selling cheap goods and services failed, and by the 1890s enough local ratepayers had acquired an interest in catering for the working-class holiday-maker for Blackpool's 'social tone' to be firmly set (Perkin, 1976: 187). The main exception to this pattern was to be found in the area known as the North Shore where the Blackpool Land, Building and Hotel Company acquired control of three-quarters of a mile of seafront and carefully planned a socially select and coherent development (see Walton, 1978: 70–1). It is interesting to note that during the nineteenth century Southport in fact prospered more than Blackpool, with a larger population even in 1901 (Perkin, 1976: 186).

So differences in the social tone of resorts (the 'resort hierarchy') seem to be explicable in terms of the intersection between land ownership patterns and scenic attractiveness. Those places which ended up as working-class resorts, or what might be described as 'manufacturing resorts' linked into a particular industrial city, were those which generally had had highly fragmented land ownership in the mid-nineteenth century and a relatively undesired scenic landscape. Ashworth says of Skegness, or Nottingham-by-the-Sea, that it is situated on 'the most colourless, featureless, negative strip of coastline in England' (the *Guardian*, 21 June 1986). Such resorts developed as fairly cheap places to visit, with the resulting tourist infrastructure to cater for a mass working-class market, but a market normally derived from a specific industrial area. As the market developed, so wealthier holiday-makers went elsewhere looking for superior accommodation, social tone and tourist gaze. Holiday-making is a form of conspicuous consumption in which status attributions are made on the basis of *where* one has stayed and that depends in part upon what the other people are like who also stay there. The attractiveness of a place and hence its location within a resort hierarchy also depends upon *how many* other people are staying in the same place, and especially how many other people there are like oneself.

There were some interesting differences in the nineteenth century between popular holiday-making in the south of Britain and the north (see Walton, 1981). In the south, day excursions were more popular and they tended to be organised by the railway companies, national interest groups like the National Sunday League, or commercial firms like Thomas Cook (see Farrant, 1987, on the development of south coast resorts, of 'London-by-the-Sea'). This last organisation was founded in 1841 when Thomas Cook chartered a train from Leicester to Loughborough for a temperance meeting (Brendon, 1991). His first pleasure excursion was organised in 1844 and the 'package' included a guide to recommended shops and places of historic interest upon which to 'gaze'. Cook wrote eloquently of the desirability of mass tourism and the democratisation of travel:

> But it is too late in this day of progress to talk such exclusive nonsense ... railways and steamboats are the results of the common light of science, and are for the people ... The best of men, and the noblest of minds, rejoice to see the people follow in their foretrod routes of pleasure. (quoted in Feifer, 1985: 168–9; and see ch. 8)

Interestingly, amongst those undertaking Cook's 'packages' to the continent women considerably outnumbered men. In restrictive Victorian Britain Thomas Cook provided a remarkable opportunity for (often single) women to travel unchaperoned around Europe. The immense organisational and sociological significance of Thomas Cook is well summarised by Younger: 'His originality lay in his methods, his almost infinite capacity for taking trouble, his acute sense of the needs of his clients ... He invented the now universal coupon system, and by 1864, more than a million passengers had passed through his hands' (1973: 21).

In the north of England the already existing voluntary associations played a more important organisational and financial role in the evolution of the holiday movement (see Myerscough, 1974: 4–5). Pubs, churches and clubs often hired an excursion or holiday train and provided saving facilities for their members. This also had the advantage that the proximity of friends, neighbours and local leaders provided both security and social control. Large numbers of quite poor people were thereby enabled to go on holiday, spending nights away from home. The pattern was soon established of holiday-makers returning again and again to the same accommodation in the same resort. Blackpool, with its high proportion of Lancashire-born landladies, enjoyed a considerable advantage in this respect. Holiday clubs became very common in many places in industrial Lancashire, although they remained a rarity elsewhere. Walton well summarises late nineteenth-century develop-ments in industrial Lancashire:

> The factory communities, after early prompting by employers and agencies of self-improvement, thus created their own grassroots system of holiday organisa-tion in the later nineteenth century. Each family was enabled to finance its own holiday without assistance from above. The unique Lancashire holiday system was thus based on working-class solidarity in retaining and extending the cus-tomary holidays, and by cooperation and mutual assistance to make the fullest use of them ... Only in Lancashire ... was a balance struck between the survival of traditional holidays and the discipline of industrial labour. Only here did whole towns go on holiday, and find resorts able to look after their needs. (1978: 39)

This pattern was particularly found in the cotton textile industry, partly because of the high employment of women. This meant higher family incomes and a greater interest in forms of leisure that were less male-based and more family/household-based (see Walton, 1981: 253). Elsewhere, Walton maintains, 'too great an attachment to customary holidays and ways of work-ing retarded the development of the working class seaside holiday over much of industrial England' (1981: 263).

Indeed this was a period in which many other leisure events came to be organised – there was a plethora of traditions invented between 1870 and 1914, often promoted and rendered sacred by royal patronage. Examples included the Royal Tournament in 1888, the first Varsity match in 1872, the first Henry Wood Promenade Concert in 1895, the Highland Games (first made royal in 1852), and so on. As Rojek argues, in the late Victorian/ Edwardian period there was a restructured system of moral regulation, which involved not the denial of pleasures but their cultivation. In this national spectacles played a key role, most spectacularly through the 'Trooping the Colour' on Horse Guards Parade (see Rojek 1990: ch. 2). Participating at least once in these leisure events came to be an important part of the emergent sense of Britishness in the late nineteenth century, a sense increasingly derived from people's *leisure* activities.

In the inter-war period the main developments affecting the tourist gaze in Britain were the growth of car ownership to over two million by 1939; the widespread use of coach transport; the considerable growth of air transport, with over 200 million miles flown in 1938; the development of new organi- sations such as the Cyclists' Touring Club, the Cooperative Holidays Association, Sir Henry Lunn's, the Touring Club of France, the International Union of Official Organizations for Tourist Propaganda, the Youth Hostels Association, the Camping Club of Great Britain and so on; the initial develop- ment of the holiday camp, beginning with Joseph Cunningham's Isle of Man camp in 1908 and culminating in this period in Billy Butlin's Skegness camp opened in 1936; and the development of pleasure cruises (see Brunner, 1945; Lickorish and Kershaw, 1975; Ward and Hardy, 1986; Walton, 2000). However, despite all these developments, Brunner maintained that the seaside resort remained the Mecca for the vast majority of British holiday-makers through- out the period. Indeed she claimed that such resorts are 'essentially native to this country, more numerous and more highly specialised in their function as resorts than those of any other land' (1945: 8). Seaside holidays were still the predominant form of holiday in Britain up to the Second World War and had expanded faster than other type of holiday in the inter-war period (see Walvin, 1978: 116–18; Walton, 2000).

To cope with the millions of visitors the resorts had initiated an enormous programme of investment. Private investment in hotels and houses was worth between £200 and £300 million while the municipalities invested very heavily themselves, even though these were often Conservative controlled (see Pickvance, 1990, on the importance of such 'municipal conservatism' in the Thanet resorts). Four resorts, Blackpool, Bournemouth, Brighton and Southend, had become major urban centres by 1931, with populations of over 100,000. Such resorts had unusual demographic characteristics, with much higher proportions than the national average of personal service workers of men and especially of women, and an increasing proportion of retired people.

One final change in the pre-war pattern should be noted. There was a strong growth of the holidays-with-pay movement that culminated in the Holidays Act of 1938 (see Brunner, 1945: ch. 9; and Walvin, 1978: ch. 6). As early as 1920 fifty-eight agreements which guaranteed paid holidays had been signed by the unions; by the mid-1920s about 16–17 per cent of the wage-earning labour force received holidays with pay. Little further progress was made during the depression years especially as it became obvious that legislation would be necessary. Various Private Member's Bills were proposed but they all met stiff opposition. Finally, a Select Committee was set up in 1937 and this culminated in the 1938 legislation, much of which only came into effect after the war had ended. Sir Walter Citrine, giving evidence to the Select Committee for the TUC, declared that going on holiday 'is an increasing factor in working-class life. I think most people now are appreciating the necessity for a complete change of surroundings' (quoted in Brunner, 1945: 9). It was estimated that the number of UK holiday-makers in the post-war period would double from 15 million to about 30 million. So by this time there had grown up an industry which had become particularly 'geared to dealing with people *en masse* and had become highly efficient and organized at attracting and coping with armies of working people from the cities' (Walvin, 1978: 107).

Thus by the Second World War there was widespread acceptance of the view that going on holiday was good for one, that it was the basis of personal replenishment. Holidays had become almost a marker of citizenship, a right to pleasure. And around that right had developed in Britain an extensive infrastructure providing specialist services, particularly in the resorts. Everyone had become entitled to the pleasures of the 'tourist gaze' by the seaside.

The next section details how that gaze came to be organised in one particular 'working-class resort', Morecambe in the top north-west corner of England south of the Lake District. It will be shown just how differentiated is the organisation of that gaze as different resorts came to specialise in the provision of services to distinct social groupings.

'Bradford-by-the-Sea', Beaches and Bungalows

As we have seen, it was in the north of England, and especially in the Lancashire textile towns, that the development of working-class holidays was pioneered in the 1850s and 1860s:

> It was here that the seaside holiday, as opposed to the day excursion, became a mass experience during the last quarter of the nineteenth century. Elsewhere, even in London, the process was slower and patchier. But working-class demand became the most important generator of resort growth in northern England in late Victorian times. (Walton, 1983: 30–1)

Up to the mid-nineteenth century almost all of the largest resorts were located in the south of England, close to the middle-class patrons and sources of finance (see King, 1984: 70–4). Only these resorts could attract visitors from a national market; resorts away from the south coast had to rely on a local or regional market. But by the beginning of the twentieth century this had dramatically changed. A number of major resorts had developed in the north of England. By 1911 Blackpool had become the fifth-largest resort in the country while Lytham, Morecambe, Southport and St Anne's all showed major population increases. This was therefore a period which 'saw the swift and emphatic rise of the specialized working-class resort' (Walton, 1983: 67).

Compared with the previous period the fastest growing resorts were much more widely dispersed throughout the country.

The pattern of growth in Morecambe has been described as follows: 'Morecambe ... tried to become a select resort and commuter terminus for West Riding business men, but became instead the Yorkshireman's Blackpool' (Perkin, 1976: 104; and see Quick, 1962). A condition essential to the growth of the working-class holiday resort was the strong ties of community found in the industrial centres in the north of England (see Walton, 1978: 32). But Morecambe could not hope to compete with Blackpool for the bulk of the holiday trade from Lancashire because Blackpool had established a sizeable tourist infrastructure somewhat earlier. It was also the first local authority in Britain to assume parliamentary power to levy a rate to advertise itself as a holiday destination (*Blackpool in Focus*, 2000). It had better rail links (using the same company throughout the journey) and it was considerably nearer the rapidly expanding towns and cities in south and east Lancashire and could therefore develop a huge day-tripper clientele. Once a resort had established a pull over its 'industrial hinterland' it was unlikely that its position would be challenged, since visits to that resort became part of the 'tradition' or 'path dependency' of holiday-making in those industrial centres. Resorts that developed later, such as Bournemouth or Skegness, generally were able to do so because they had no obvious or similar rivals close by (see Walvin, 1978: 161). In the case of Morecambe it had become clear in the second half of the century that it would be unable to compete with Blackpool for the Lancashire holiday market. Thus the Wigan coal-owner and alderman Ralph Darlington declared to a Commons Committee in 1884 that: 'Morecambe does not stand in estimation with us as a watering place. I should say it is not one at all' (quoted in Grass, 1972: 6). Likewise Thomas Baxter, chairman of the Morecambe Board of Health in 1889, observed that: 'there was no doubt that Blackpool had always had the pull all over Lancashire' *(Observer,* 11 October 1889).

The inability to compete for the Lancashire holiday market combined with the rail link to the Yorkshire woollen towns meant that many visitors to Morecambe came from the West Riding of Yorkshire. This was because the connections with Yorkshire extended not only to the holiday trade but also to patterns of migration. Many people from Yorkshire, both workers and employers, came to live in Morecambe, some of whom commuted to Bradford or Halifax daily (Perkin, 1976: 190). The first mayor of the new Corporation, Alderman E. Barnsbee, was a Bradford man who retired to Morecambe. In addition Morecambe was not the only holiday destination for those living in the West Riding. It had to face considerable competition from the resorts on the east coast, in both Yorkshire and Lincolnshire. Yet it did become increasingly popular. A *Daily Telegraph* correspondent wrote in 1891:

> as Margate is to the average Cockney, so is Morecambe to the stalwart and health-loving Yorkshireman. For it is allowed on all sides that Morecambe is true Yorkshire to the backbone ... Yorkshiremen, Yorkshire lads, and Yorkshire lasses have selected to colonise and to popularise this breezy, rainy, wind-swept, and health-giving watering-place. (quoted in Grass, 1972: 10)

Furthermore in the inter-war period a Lord Mayor of Bradford proclaimed that: 'most of the citizens of Bradford, to say nothing of the children, have enjoyed spending some of their leisure time in this wonderful health resort' (*Visitor*, July 1935, Diamond Jubilee Souvenir).

Morecambe, however, did not attract sufficient numbers of the middle-class visitors that were wanted. Partly this was because the town leaders could not prevent the growth of the day-tripper trade, described by the *Lancaster Guardian* as a 'disorderly and riotous mob' (22 August 1868). And partly this was because the existence of very many relatively small houses (often 'back houses') made it impossible to stop the establishment of new boarding houses and small hotels which provided accommodation for less well-off visitors, especially those from west Yorkshire. There was a considerable debate between the champions of 'respectability', who were organised through the Board of Health until 1894 and the Urban District Council after then, and the providers of 'mass holiday consumption' such as the large entertainment companies. In an editorial in 1901 the *Visitor* supported the latter group on the grounds that in a town with 'no public band, no public parks, no pier supported from the rates', they had 'done their work catering for the visitors admirably this season' (2 October 1901). As early as the late 1890s the advocates of commercial development had won the day and attempts by the Urban District Council to maintain 'respectability' had failed. The *Daily Telegraph* summed up Morecambe in 1891: 'It may be that, to the fastidious, rough honest-hearted Morecambe is a little primitive, and slightly tinged with vulgarity. But it is never dull' (quoted in Perkin, 1976: 191).

In the later parts of the century there were a number of related develop-ments in Morecambe: a rapid rate of population increase (over 10 per cent per annum); a considerable growth of capital expenditure, especially on major facilities including a revolving tower; and an extensive growth of lodging-house and hotel accommodation (see Denison-Edson, 1967).

But its prosperity was dependent upon the level of prosperity, particu-larly in the west Yorkshire area. When Bradford, and especially the woollen industry, was doing well then Morecambe seemed to prosper. As the *Observer* noted in 1883, 'when the Bradford trade has been at a low ebb it has not been at all plain sailing for "Bradford-by-the-Sea"' (25 May). Also Morecambe remained the prisoner of the railway companies and the quality and quantity of the train services they provided.

In the inter-war period Morecambe was successful, partly because there was an extensive growth of paid holidays for those in work, and partly because most holidays were still taken at the seaside and family-households were transported there by rail and to a lesser extent by coach. Spokesmen from Morecambe advocated that all workers should receive a week's holiday with pay (*Visitor*, 22 January 1930). By 1925 there were two holiday camps in Heysham, which was part of the same borough. Morecambe experienced considerable annual growth in population, 3.8 per cent during the 1930s, and its total rateable value rose by 54 per cent between 1930 and 1946 (Denison-Edson, 1967: 28). The 1930s and 1940s were particularly pros-perous, with the town council investing heavily in new objects for the tourist gaze, a clear example of how a Conservative council could engage in 'municipal conservatism'.

I shall now very briefly describe two other resorts by way of comparison: Brighton, on the south coast, and Birchington, in Kent. Each is responsible for having been first to develop new objects of the tourist gaze at the seaside, Brighton with the first beach devoted to 'pleasure', and Birchington with the first bungalows.

I have already noted the early and extensive development of Brighton in the eighteenth century. The beach was viewed as a site for medical treatment and was regulated by the 'dippers', the women responsible for immersion (on the following, see Shields, 1990: Part 2, ch. 2). In the mid-nineteenth century this medicalised beach was replaced by a pleasure beach, which Shields characterises as a liminal zone, a built-in escape from the patterns and rhythms of everyday life. Such a zone had a further characteristic, of carnival, as the beach became noisy and crowded, full of unpredictable social mixing, and involving the inversion of social hierarchies and moral codes. In the classic medieval carnival, the grotesque body was counterposed to the disciplined body of propriety and authority; in the nineteenth century holiday carnival the grotesque body was shamefully uncovered and open to the gaze of others. Literally grotesque bodies became increasingly removed from actual view and were gazed upon through commercialised representations, especially the vulgar picture postcard. Shields summarises the carnival of the beach rendered appropriate for pleasure:

> It is this foolish, impudent, undisciplined body which is the most poignant symbol of the carnivalesque – the unclosed body of convexities and orifices, intruding onto and into others' body-space, [which] threatens to escape, transgress, and transcend the circumscriptions of the body. (1990)

The fact that Brighton was the first resort in which the beach became constructed as a site for pleasure, for social mixing, for status reversals, for carnival, is one reason why in the first few decades of the twentieth century Brighton came to have a reputation for sexual excess and particularly for the 'dirty weekend'. This has become part of the place-image of Brighton, although the beach no longer functions as a site of the carnivalesque.

Whereas Brighton's class associations were with royalty and the aristocracy, the resorts in Kent in the mid-nineteenth century were associated with the relatively new middle class (see King, 1984: 72–8). But as early as 1870 both Margate and Ramsgate were becoming less attractive to this holiday market, especially to the professional middle class, which was increasingly staying in Cliftonville and Westgate. In the latter all the roads were private and only detached houses were allowed. The first bungalows in Britain thus came to be built in 1869–70 in Westgate and more extensively in Birchington in 1870–3, just next door (King, 1984: 74). Until this development there was no specialist house building by the seaside. Indeed in the earlier fishing villages houses were often built with their backs to the sea, as at Ravenglass on the edge of the Lake District. The sea was there for fishing, not for gazing on. Nineteenth-century resorts were public places with some distinctive public buildings, such as assembly rooms, promenades, public gardens, dance halls and so on. Residential provision was similar to that found in inland towns and was not distinctive.

By contrast, the development of the bungalow as a specialised form of housing by the seaside resulted from a number of developments: the heightened attraction of visiting the seaside not for strictly medical reasons but for the bracing air and fine views; the increasing demand from sections of the middle class for accommodation well away from other people, for being able to gaze at the sea in relative solitude; and the rising popularity of swimming as opposed to dipping and hence the perceived need for semi-private access for the whole family and especially for children. Birchington ideally met these conditions; there were no public facilities, there was an attractive coastline for building, the first bungalows were 'rural looking' and offered attractive contrasts with the urban, and tunnels could be built linking each bungalow with the beach. In the twentieth century there has been an extensive 'bungaloid growth' at the seaside so that in some sense in the twentieth century the bungalow *is* the seaside. And as it has become the housing of the lower middle class so its earlier fashionability and bohemianism has disappeared, and indeed it has become an object of considerable status hostility (see King, 1984: ch. 5).

It is worth considering holiday developments in a country much influenced by British culture but where the outcome has been quite different – New Zealand. There are almost no seaside resorts, the closest being Day's Bay, near Wellington, but even here there are few facilities. In addition the bungalow could hardly become associated with the seaside in New Zealand since it is the form of house building found everywhere. There seem to be several main reasons for the lack of resort development in New Zealand: since all the major towns are on the coast it was unlikely that 'going to the seaside' would be seen as in any way special; population growth only occurred after the development of the motor car, so leisure became more privatised and less geographically dependent upon the railway, which was important in Britain, as we have seen; and finally the very strong emphasis on family-organised leisure has been associated with a tendency to self-provisioning rather than purchasing the required services (although see Cloke and Perkins, 1998, on New Zealand's developing 'adventure tourism').

The post-war period saw both the rapid growth of the British seaside resort in the 1950s and its equally rapid decline in many places in the 1970s and 1980s. I deal with these processes fairly briefly here since much of the rest of the book is taken up with a rather broader analysis of how the tourist gaze is being transformed in western societies with the result that the British seaside resort has become a much less favoured object of that gaze.

The End of the Pier?

In this section I chart what has happened to seaside resorts in the post-war period, and try to make sense of the following paradox. In Britain tourism has become a massively important industry, yet the places which were the most developed in terms of their infrastructure to take advantage of this, namely seaside resorts, have not shared in this growth. In the mid-1970s to mid-1980s the proportion of total tourist expenditure spent in the resorts fell from about one-half to one-third and the number of bed nights declined by 25 per cent (Wickers and Charlton, 1988: f6). For example, in Morecambe between 1973 and 1987 the number of small hotels and guesthouses fell from 640 to 267 and the number of bed-spaces from 12,340 to 7,115 (Bagguley et al., 1989: ch. 3). Some hotels were converted into accommodation for those released from psychiatric hospitals, for those on income support, and for the elderly. Resorts have thus become merely one of a large number of potential objects of the tourist gaze. The spending of a week or fortnight's holiday by the seaside in Britain is now a less attractive and significant tourist experience than in the decades around the Second World War (see Walton, 2000, for extensive analysis).

In the immediate post-war period there was no hint of the troubles to come. As Parry says, if the 1920s and 1930s were the heyday of the resorts then the 1950s and early 1960s were a kind of Indian summer: 'rationing ended, "austerity" ceased and business boomed; the holiday abroad was still the preserve of the few and package tours were non-existent' (Parry, 1983: 189). Moreover, the majority of northerners stayed loyal to their own resorts. This traditional or organised pattern continued, with whole towns moving off to the seaside in a given week. A central role in sustaining such patterns was played by the railway. British Railways organised many specials or excursion trains, taking visitors from particular destinations to the resorts which had been traditionally visited. For example, at Easter 1960 at least forty-eight specials arrived at Morecambe, whose stationmaster declared it the busiest Easter in the past eighteen years. Major new investments were planned although most of the visitors still stayed either in traditional hotel or bed-and-breakfast accommodation (which was unlicensed), or in a holiday camp. The latter expanded greatly in the 1950s particularly with the arrival of Pontins (see Ward and Hardy, 1986: ch. 4).

In this period the holiday experience was remarkably regulated. Even where people stayed in apartments this generally involved the provision of set meals for a week. The holiday was based on the time zone of the week (see Colson, 1926). It was almost impossible to book mid-week. Visitors knew when they were to eat, what they would eat, and exactly how long they were to stay. If people were staying in a holiday camp then much else was organised and indeed 'from one camp to the next the mix was identical – the same pattern of entertainment, the same diet, the same type of accommodation, the same weekly routine' (Ward and Hardy, 1986: 161; see Urry 1994, on tourism and time). Although television was appearing the emphasis was still upon the provision of live entertainment. In the 1950s big-name artists were regularly attracted to Morecambe, while Blackpool boasted fourteen live shows (Parry, 1983: 191).

However, much of this began to change dramatically in the 1960s, and the rest of the book charts a series of transformations in the organisation of the tourist gazes away from many of these resorts. We can also note that there is for many people more time away from paid work, because of increased paid holidays for those in paid work, a rising proportion of the population who are full-time students or retired, and a significant proportion of people unemployed, underemployed or in part-time work. Work and non-work are more variable and flexible in comparison with the past, especially for men. Holidays therefore do not offer such dramatic contrasts with paid work as they did previously. They need not only involve two weeks of 'seaside fun' and for many reasonably wealthy retired people life may indeed be akin to a continuous, nomadic existence. I now describe some further changes in what is ordinary and hence what is taken to be extraordinary in what is gazed upon at the seaside.

Seaside resorts in Britain normally possessed at least one pier (Blackpool had three) and often one tower. Both such constructions involved an attempt to conquer nature, to construct a 'man-made' object which at all times and for ever would be there dominating either the sea or the sky. Their domination is what gives them a reason for being there, that is their function. Barthes says of the similar Eiffel Tower that it enables the visitor to participate in a dream (1979). The Tower is no normal spectacle because it gives observers a wholly original view of Paris. Indeed it transforms Paris into nature, 'it constitutes the swarming of men into a landscape ... the city joins up with the great natural themes that are offered to the curiosity of men [sic]: the ocean, the storm, the mountains, the snow, the rivers' (1979: 8). The most famous such building in Britain is the tower at Blackpool, opened in 1894 as an imitation of the Eiffel Tower. It is a unique building in Britain, and effectively signifies the town. Such towers, and to a lesser extent, piers, enable people to see things in their structure, to link human organisation with extraordinary natural phenomena, and to celebrate the participation within, and the victory of, human agency over nature. They are part of that irreducibly extraordinary character of the ideal tourist site. Thompson says of Blackpool Tower:

> It also adds a third dimension to the east/west and north/south axes of movement. Rather like the beach/sea interface, it offers some specific pleasures by transcending the normal and day-to-day. It enables the holidaymaker to enjoy Blackpool from a different perspective. (1983: 126)

In the past two or three decades, the extraordinary character of piers and towers has dramatically declined. Piers have been falling into the sea and do not demonstrate the domination of nature, rather the reverse. In Morecambe for example both piers have now gone. For years Brighton's piers were derelict. Piers and towers now stand for nostalgia, for the 'theme' of the old seaside holiday which is well expressed in the 1988 Isle of Man advertising slogan 'You'll look forward to going back'. At the same time, much more spectacular and modern examples of the mastery of the sea can now be found, in bridges, tunnels, hovercraft, ships, and marinas. Likewise towers connecting the land and the sky are now dwarfed by skyscrapers, hotels, space capsules, and of course by aircraft, all of which are much more obviously 'modern' and extraordinary.

A second major attraction at the seaside resort was the funfair or pleasure park. In Britain Blackpool Pleasure Beach has been since its beginnings in 1906 the leading site for such a regime of pleasure (see Parry, 1983: chs 17, 18; Bennett, 1983). From the 1920s onwards it has always tried to look resolutely modern. 'Its architecture of pleasure has taken on a streamlined, functional appearance' (Bennett, 1983: 145). The employment of the architect Joseph Emberton created a wholly new 'Architecture of Pleasure' in which everything was light, sunny, fresh air and fun (Parry, 1983: 152–4). And it has been periodically updated. The designer of the Festival of Britain, Jack Radcliffe, gave it a new look during the boom period in the 1950s. New rides kept being added, mostly based either on innovations pioneered in world fairs (for example, a ferris wheel based on one exhibited at the Chicago World Fair of 1893), or on futuristic rides found in American amusement parks (such as the *Starship Enterprise* introduced in 1980). Central to the strategy of the management of the Pleasure Beach has been progress, being first (at least in the UK), biggest and best. It even has its own tower using latest technology and which makes *the* Blackpool Tower seem rather quaint (Bennett, 1983: 147). The Park is still owned by a local company and attracts over 7 million visitors a year (Blackpool in Focus, 2000). Most other places at the seaside cannot compete with it and especially with its state-of-the art rides.

The main competition to Blackpool now comes from the new-style amusement and theme parks, such as Alton Towers in the north of England or more spectacularly Disneyland Paris, easily the leading tourist attraction in Europe with 12 million visitors a year. These new parks are not normally located at the seaside, although they generally have a very attractive 'rural' location close to the motorway (rather than the rail) network. Pleasure parks located at the existing seaside resorts will struggle to compete. Such places should exhibit 'modernity', high technology, youth, controlled danger, anticipation and pleasure. But if they are located in 'old-fashioned' resorts (almost anywhere but Blackpool or Brighton) there are many counter-messages, of previous technologies, age, danger through neglect, and regret at not being elsewhere.

Blackpool, by contrast, has more generally tried to construct itself as irreducibly modern, as a cosmopolitan, international leisure centre, the 'Las Vegas of the north', having less now to do with its previous Lancashire/ northern/working-class associations. As Bennett notes: 'At Blackpool, everything is new no matter how old it is' (1986: 146). It is the biggest seaside resort in Europe and in the 1980s had more visitors than the whole of Greece, and more beds than Portugal (Wickers and Charlton, 1988: f6; Waterhouse 1989: 10). It currently sells 14 million bed nights a year as the largest European seaside resort (NWTB 2000; *Blackpool in Focus*, 2000). Keith Waterhouse summarises its over-the-top charms: 'it would have been, in all its gaudy tattiness, the greatest show on earth. It still is, outvulgarised ... only by Las Vegas' (1989: 10). It is currently developing a 'gaming strategy' involving twenty-four-hour casinos that may indeed make it Europe's Las Vegas. By contrast, other seaside resorts appear old-fashioned and cannot offer anything like the same range of facilities. A few have prospered, such as Bridlington, Rhyl, St Ives, Torquay or Southport, and they have the advantage of few modernist buildings to spoil the image of what a typical resort (apart from Blackpool) ought to look like (Walton, 2000: 47–9).

Another feature of most resorts were holiday camps (see Ward and Hardy, 1986). They had begun before the First World War when they literally consisted of a camp of tents. Even at that time their development was said to be a reaction against the relatively poor quality of accommodation and services in the typical seaside boarding house. The most significant development came with the 'luxury' camps started by Billy Butlin, beginning with that in Skegness which opened in 1936. Compared with what was available at the typical hotel or guesthouse, Butlin provided really luxurious facilities, with extensive on-site amusement, good-quality food, high-class entertainments and modern sanitation – what Ray Gosling has termed a 'veritable Beveridge of leisure' (quoted in Ward and Hardy, 1986: 60). Interestingly, when the first camp was opened the visitors appeared bored and Butlin concluded that holiday-makers required some degree of organisation. The famous 'Redcoats' were invented – they 'would lead, advise, explain, comfort, help out, and generally make themselves the closest thing to holiday angels on earth' (quoted in Ward and Hardy, 1986: 63).

The heyday of such camps was in the immediate post-war period up to 1959 when the BBC television series *Hi-de-Hi!* was set. This prosperity resulted from a number of factors including the coming into effect of the 1938 Holidays With Pay Act, the high levels of employment, and the reduced age of marriage and high rate of family formation. In 1948 one in twenty of all British holiday-makers stayed at Butlin's. The holiday camp was a symbol of the post-war society, reflecting the modernist architectural style of the period. Some camps looked little better than scaled-down council estates, such as the former Pontin's at Middleton Sands near Morecambe. Others, such as that at Prestatyn in Wales, captured something of the glamour and fantasy of the ocean liner with its clean, functional styling (Ward and Hardy, 1986: ch. 5).

In the 1950s a considerable effort was made to construct the camps as places for 'family holidays' and to limit the number of single visitors. There was also an attempt to prevent the majority of visitors to the camps being 'working class'. This was unsuccessful as the camps, like their host resorts, became unable to attract large numbers of middle-class visitors, although the camps tried to construct their clientele as classless through treating them all as 'campers'. There was also a shift in the camps towards 'self-catering' especially by Pontin's. They tried to construct this as involving increasing 'freedom' and indeed the term 'camp' has itself been dropped since it implies regimentation. They are now known as 'centres', 'villages' or 'holiday-worlds'. Nevertheless their attraction has undoubtedly diminished, with the number of such camps in England dramatically falling. Ward and Hardy concluded from their study that by the 1970s and 1980s:

holiday camps are something of a period piece ... new concepts of holidaymaking have been developed ... Package holidays to exotic places, coupled with more individualistic off-season breaks, increase the difficulties of the camps ... Much about the holiday camp is now commonplace. (1986: 152)

They are no longer the stuff of which dreams are made. The response of their owners was both to concentrate on larger centres (as at Butlin's), and to segment the market with different centres tailored to different tastes, including adult-only centres, special-interest holidays, and short breaks (see Glancey, 1988).

Such camps are weakly placed to compete with the 'concept' of Center Parcs, or 'villas in the forest'. There are now 13 of these holiday villages across Europe in which an artificial 'seaside' is constructed within a giant double-skinned plastic dome which sustains a constant temperature. In this complex, swimming is entertainment, fun and pleasure with tropical heat, warm water lagoons, palm trees and waterside cafes (similar Japanese parks even boast beaches and breaking waves). Other features include sailing, canoeing and an immense variety of luxuriant vegetation. Such centres do not have to be located near the sea since the technology permits the seaside to be constructed 'anywhere', especially in forest environments that 'hide' the development.

Resorts were believed to be extraordinary because concentrated there were the sea, the sand, sometimes the sun, as well as the absence of the manufacturing industry that was present in almost all other substantial towns and cities. But in recent years a number of transformations have changed all this. As previously mentioned, the 'seaside' can now be constructed and gazed upon anywhere. But the relative attraction of the sea itself has also declined. In the nineteenth century the development of the resorts was based on the presumed health-giving properties of sea bathing. Sunbathing, by contrast, was relatively uncommon partly because of the high value placed upon pale skin which signified delicacy, idleness and seclusion. However, this began to change within the upper classes from the 1920s onwards, particularly with the development of newly fashionable resorts such as Cannes and Biarritz. Amongst such groups a tan was associated with the presumed spontaneity and natural sensuality of black people. Sunbathing was presumed to bring people closer to nature (see Turner and Ash, 1975: 79–83; Ahmed, 2000).

In the post-war period it has been the sun, not the sea, which is presumed to produce health and sexual attractiveness. *The* ideal body has come to be viewed as tanned. This viewpoint has been diffused downwards through the social classes with the result that many package holidays present this as one of the main reasons for going on holiday. The north European resorts have thus come to be seen as less attractive, less fashionable, because they cannot guarantee to produce a tanned body (see Fiske, 1989: Lencek and Bosler, 1998; Ahmed 2000). Although this is changing with the current concern about malignant melanoma and it may become fashionable again to be pale, so far in Europe this concentration on the sun has enormously benefited the development of Mediterranean resorts. This began in France and Spain, then spread to Greece, Italy, Yugoslavia, and then to north Africa and Turkey. Beaches in northern Europe cannot guarantee sunshine. Nor can they necessarily guarantee clean water, if one wishes to swim in the sea, although the European Union has made some strides in 'shaming' a range of countries including Britain over their dirty beaches (see Tidy Britain web site, on the European Blue Flag Campaign). It should be noted that beaches are complex spaces, anomalously located between land and sea, nature and culture. Different stretches of beach are to be read quite differently – with strikingly different forms of activity that are proscribed and prescribed (Lencek and Bosler, 1998).

Seaside resorts have also become less distinctive because of the de-industrialisation of many towns and cities so that there is less need to escape from them to the contrasting seaside. As the everyday has changed, as towns and cities have become de-industrialised and many have themselves become objects for the tourist gaze with the extensive development of city tourism as well as leisure centres with wave machines and other features of the beach, so most seaside resorts are no longer extraordinary.

People used to go to the seaside in order to find concentrations of those services specifically organised for the provision of pleasure. Now, however, many resorts boast poorer services than comparably sized towns.

A number of processes have reduced the distinctiveness of resorts. The growth of television has at a stroke evened out the provision of entertainment so that now one does not need to go to resorts in order to see the big names. As Parry expresses it: 'television paraded the top talent every night of the week' (1983: 192). Further, most resorts are in population terms fairly small and cannot support a high concentration of entertainment services. Often therefore they rely on some level of public provision. However, there is considerable reluctance to pay for such activities through local taxation, and even if they do develop such facilities they are often still less impressive than those to be found in the potential visitor's home town. Many towns and cities away from the coast have built sports and leisure centres, while national entertainment companies and massive shopping complexes have expanded in many places except the seaside. More generally, many towns and cities have developed as centres of consumption, both for their own residents and for potential tourists. Harvey notes that increasingly every town and city 'has to appear as an innovative, exciting, creative and safe place to live, play, and consume. Spectacle and display became the symbols of [a] dynamic community' (1987: 13).

I examine such changes in the following chapters. Just why have 'spectacle and display' become characteristics of almost everywhere? What processes have produced the generalising of the tourist gaze? And what does this mean for the organisation of those industries which have developed to provide services for the tourist gaze?

One important point to consider is the globalisation of contemporary tourism. Every potential object of the tourist gaze now has to compete internationally, and this has led to substantial changes in defining just what is extraordinary and what is internationally ordinary. Parry expresses well how the cheap 'package tour' in the 1960s and 1970s onwards was to have devastating effects upon the seaside resort:

The holidaymaker of the 1930s had no choice and was prepared to take a chance. If he [sic] lived in a mill town at least all his neighbours would have suffered from the same 'poor week'. Not so his counterpart in the 1970s. He wanted sun – and if half the street was to come back from Marbella or Torremolinos with burned backs, peeling noses and queasy stomachs he wasn't going to be left out. (1983: 192–3)

3

The Changing Economics
of the Tourist Industry

Introduction

The relationship between the tourist gaze and those industries that have been developed to meet that gaze is extremely problematic.

Initially, it should be noted that almost all the services provided to tourists have to be delivered at the time and place at which they are produced (see Urry, 1987). As a consequence the quality of the social interaction between the provider of the service, such as the waiter, flight attendant or hotel receptionist, and the consumers, is part of the 'product' being purchased by tourists. If aspects of that social interaction are unsatisfactory (the offhand waiter, the unsmiling flight attendant, or the rude receptionist), then what is purchased is in effect a different service product. The problem results from the fact that the production of such consumer services cannot be entirely carried out backstage, away from the gaze of tourists. They cannot help seeing some aspects of the industry which is attempting to serve them. But furthermore, tourists tend to have high expectations of what they should receive since 'going away' is an event endowed with particular significance. People are looking for the extraordinary and hence will be exceptionally critical of services provided that appear to undermine such a quality.

Other features of tourist industries are likely to produce difficulties for the producers of such services. Such services cannot be provided anywhere: they have to be produced *and consumed* in very particular places. Part of what is consumed is in effect the place in which the service producer is located. If the particular place does not convey appropriate cultural meanings, the quality of the specific service may well be tarnished. There is therefore a crucial 'spatial fixity' about tourist services. In recent years there has been enormously heightened competition to attract tourists. In relationship to Britain there has been a 'Europeanisation' of the tourist market and increasingly a 'globalisation' (see ch. 8). So while the producers are to a significant extent spatially fixed, in that they have to provide particular services in particular places, consumers are increasingly mobile, able to consume tourist services on a global basis. The industry is inevitably competitive since almost every place in the world could well act as an object of the tourist gaze. Such services are inherently labour-intensive and hence employers will seek to minimise labour costs. A variety of strategies are employed to bring this about but some at least will result in tarnishing or wholly undermining the extraordinary character of the consumers' tourist gaze.

The emphasis on the quality of the social interaction between producers and consumers of tourist services means that developments in the industry are not simply explicable in terms of 'economic' determinants. As will be shown later it is also necessary to examine a range of cultural changes which transform people's expectations about what they wish to gaze upon, what significance should be attached to that gaze, and what effects this will have upon the providers of the relevant tourist services. This is an industry that has always necessitated considerable levels of public involvement and investment and in recent years this has increased as all sorts of places attempt to construct or reinforce their position as favoured objects of the tourist gaze. The economics of tourism cannot be understood separately from the analysis of cultural and policy developments to be found later in this book, just as work in tourist industries cannot be understood separately from the cultural expectations that surround the complex delivery of such services. Work relationships in tourist industries are significantly culturally defined.

In this chapter attention will be directed to some of the more obvious recent developments in what can loosely be termed the changing political economy of the tourist industry. The next section gives a brief account of the concept of positional goods, the main economic concept used to account for the economics of tourism, before moving on to the changing UK tourist industry, noting particularly its tendencies to globalisation; and to some of the main changes in the political economy of overseas tourism.

The Social Limits of Tourism

The economist Mishan presents one of the clearest accounts of the thesis that there are fundamental limits to the scale of contemporary tourism (1969; see Urry, 1990, as well as the *Journal of Sustainable Tourism* and the campaigning journal *Tourism in Focus*). These limits derive from the immense costs of congestion and overcrowding. In the 1960s Mishan perceptively wrote of:

'the conflict of interest ... between, on the one hand, the tourists, tourist agencies, traffic industries and ancillary services, to say nothing of governments anxious to augment their reserves of foreign currencies, and all those who care about preserving natural beauty on the other' (1969: 140).

He quoted the example of Lake Tahoe, whose plant and animal life had been destroyed by sewage generated by the hotels built along its banks. A later example would be the way in which the coral around tourist islands like Barbados is dying because of the pumping of raw sewage into the sea from the beachside hotels and because locals remove both plants and fish from the coral to sell to tourists.

Mishan also notes that here is a conflict of interests between present and future generations which stems from the way in which travel and tourism are priced. The cost of the marginal tourist takes no account of the additional congestion costs imposed by the extra tourist. These congestion costs include the generally undesirable effects of overcrowded beaches, a lack of peace and quiet, the destruction of the scenery and the use of fossil fuels contributing to global warming. Moreover, the environmentally sensitive tourist knows that there is nothing to be gained from delaying a visit to the place in question: if anything, the opposite is the case. There is a strong incentive to go as soon as possible – to enjoy the unspoilt view before the crowds get there (as currently with the emerging destination of Havana). Mishan's perspective as someone horrified by the consequences of mass tourism, as opposed to individual travel, can be seen from the following claim: 'the tourist trade, in a competitive scramble to uncover all places of once quiet repose, of wonder, beauty and historic interest to the money-flushed multitude, is in effect literally and irrevocably destroying them' (1969: 141). His middle-class, middle-aged elitism is never far from the surface. For example, he claims that it is the 'young and gullible' that are taken in by the fantasies dreamt up by the tourist industry (one wonders what his views of contemporary Ibiza might be).

His main argument is that the spread of mass tourism does not produce a democratisation of travel. It is an illusion which destroys the very places which are being visited. This is because geographical space is a strictly limited resource. Mishan says: 'what a few may enjoy in freedom the crowd necessarily destroys for itself' (1969: 142). Unless international agreement is reached (he suggested the immensely radical banning of all international air travel!), the next generation will inherit a world almost bereft of places of 'undisturbed natural beauty' (1969: 142). So allowing the market to develop without regulation has the effect of destroying the very places which are the objects of the tourist gaze. Increasing numbers of such places are suffering from the same pattern of self-destruction. One resort that has recently been thought to be so damaged is St Tropez, the place initially made famous by Brigitte Bardot. She claims that it is being swept by a 'black tide of human filth'; that tourists 'are mediocre, dirty, ill-mannered and rude'; and that she intends 'leaving it to the invaders' (see Rocca, 1989; see Mawby, Brunt, Hambly, 2000, on crime and tourism).

This pessimistic kind of argument is criticised by Beckerman, who makes two useful points (1974: 50–2). First, concern for the effects of mass tourism is basically a 'middle-class' anxiety (like much other environmental concern). This is because the really rich 'are quite safe from the masses in the very expensive resorts, or on their private yachts or private islands or secluded estates' (Beckerman, 1974: 50–1). Second, most groups affected by mass tourism do in fact benefit from it, including even some of the pioneer visitors who find available services that were previously unobtainable when the number of visitors was rather small. Hence Beckerman talks of the 'narrow selfishness of the Mishan kind of complaint' (1974: 51).

This disagreement over the effects of mass tourism is given more theoretical weight in Hirsch's thesis on the social limits to growth (1978; also see the collection Ellis and Kumar, 1983). His starting point is similar to Mishan's: he notes that individual liberation through the exercise of consumer choice does not make those choices liberating for all individuals together (1978: 26). In particular he is concerned with the positional economy. This term refers to all aspects of goods, services, work, positions and other social relationships which are either scarce or subject to congestion or crowding. Competition is therefore zero-sum: as any one person consumes more of the good in question, so someone else is forced to consume less. Supply cannot be increased, unlike the case of material goods where the processes of economic growth can easily produce more. People's consumption of positional goods is inherently *relational*. The satisfaction derived by each individual is not infinitely expandable but depends upon the position of one's own consumption to that of others. This can be termed 'coerced competition'. Ellis and Heath define this as competition in which the status quo is not an option (1983: 16–19). It is normally assumed in economics that market exchanges are voluntary; that people freely choose whether or not to enter into the exchange relationship. However, in the case of coerced consumption people do not really have such a choice. One has to participate even though at the end of the consumption process one is not necessarily better off. This can be summarised by the phrase: 'one has to run faster in order to stay still'. Hirsch cites the example of suburbanisation. People move to the suburbs to escape from the congestion of the city and to be nearer the quietness of the countryside. But as economic growth continues, the suburbs get more congested, they expand, and so the original suburbanites are as far away from the countryside as they were originally. Hence they will seek new suburban housing closer to the countryside, and so on. The individually rational actions of others make one worse off and one cannot avoid participation in the leap-frogging process. No one is better off over time as a result of such coerced consumption.

Hirsch maintains that much consumption has similar characteristics to the case of suburbanisation, namely that the satisfaction people derive from it depends on the consumption choices of others. This can be seen most clearly in the case of certain goods which are scarce in an absolute sense. Examples cited here are 'old masters' or the 'natural landscape', where increased consumption by one leads to reduced consumption by another (although see Ellis and Heath, 1983: 6–7). Hirsch also considers the cases where there is 'direct social scarcity': luxury or perhaps snob goods which are enjoyed because they are rare or expensive and possession of them indicates social status or good taste. Examples here would include jewellery, a residence in a particular part of London, or designer clothes. A third type Hirsch considers is that of 'incidental social scarcity': goods whose consumption yields satisfaction which is influenced by the extensiveness of use. Negative examples here would include the purchase of a car and no increase of satisfaction because of increased congestion, as everyone does the same; and the obtaining of educational qualifications and no improved access to leadership positions because everyone else has been acquiring similar credentials (Ellis and Heath, 1983: 10–11).

It is fairly easy to suggest examples of tourism that fit these various forms of scarcity. On the first, the Mediterranean coastline is in the condition of absolute scarcity where one person's consumption is at the expense of someone else. On the second, there are clearly many holiday destinations which are consumed not because they are intrinsically superior but because they convey taste or superior status. For Europeans, the Caribbean or the Far East would be current examples, although these will change as mass tourist patterns themselves alter. And third, there are many tourist sites where people's satisfaction depends upon the degree of congestion. Hirsch quotes a middle-class professional who remarked that the development of cheap charter flights to such a previously 'exotic' country meant that: 'Now that I can afford to come here I know that it will be ruined' (1978: 167).

Although I have set out these different types of positional good identified by Hirsch the distinctions between them are not fully sustainable and they merge into each other. Furthermore, there are a number of major difficulties in Hirsch's argument. It is ambiguous about what is meant by consumption in the case of much tourism. Is it the ability to gaze at a particular object if necessary in the company of many others? Or is it to be able to gaze without others being present? Or is it to be able to rent accommodation for a short period with a view of the object close at hand? Or is it the ability to own property with a view of the object nearby? The problem arises because of the importance of the gaze to tourist activity. A gaze is after all visual, it can literally take a split second, and the other services provided are in a sense peripheral to the fundamental process of consumption, which is the capturing of the gaze. This means that the scarcities involved in tourism are more complex than Hirsch allows for. One strategy pursued by the tourist industry has been to initiate new developments which have permitted greatly increased numbers to gaze upon the same object. Examples include building huge hotel complexes away from the coastline; the development of off-peak holidays so that the same view can be gazed upon throughout the year; devising holidays for different segments of the market so that a wider variety of potential visitors can see the same object; and the development of time-share accommodation so that the facilities can be used all of the year.

Moreover, the notion of scarcity is problematic for other reasons. I begin here by noting the distinction between the physical carrying capacity of a tourist site, and its perceptual capacity (see Walter, 1982). In the former sense it is clear when a mountain path literally cannot take any more walkers since it has been eroded and has effectively disappeared. Nevertheless, even in this case there are still thousands of other mountain paths that could be walked along and so the scarcity only applies to *this* path leading to this particular view, not to all paths along all mountains.

The notion of perceptual capacity changes the situation. Walter is concerned here with the subjective quality of the tourist experience (1982: 296).

Although the path may still be physically passable, it no longer signifies the pristine wilderness upon which the visitor had expected to gaze. Thus its perceptual carrying capacity would have been reached, but not its physical capacity. Walter goes on to note that perceptual capacity is immensely variable and depends upon particular conceptions of nature and on the circumstances in which people expect to gaze upon it. He cites the example of an Alpine mountain. As a material good the mountain can be viewed for its grandeur, beauty and conformity to the idealised Alpine horn. There is almost no limit to this good. No matter how many people are looking at the mountain it still retains these qualities. However, the same mountain can be viewed as a positional good, as a kind of shrine to nature that individuals wish to enjoy without others being present in solitude. Such a solitary 'consumption' demonstrates unambiguous good taste (see Bourdieu, 1984, on such distinctions). There is then a 'romantic' form of the tourist gaze, in which the emphasis is upon solitude, privacy and a personal, semi-spiritual relationship with the object of the gaze. Barthes characterises this viewpoint as found in the *Guide Bleu;* he talks of 'this bourgeois promoting of the mountains, this old Alpine myth ... only mountains, gorges, defiles and torrents ... seem to encourage morality of effort and solitude' (1972: 74).

Walter discusses the example of Stourhead Park in Wiltshire, which illustrates:

> the romantic notion that the self is found not in society but in solitudinous contemplation of nature. Stourhead's garden is the perfect romantic landscape, with narrow paths winding among the trees and rhododendrons, grottoes, temples, a gothic cottage, all this around a much indented lake ... The garden is designed to be walked around in wonderment at Nature and the presence of other people immediately begins to impair this. (1982: 298)

When discussing Mishan I noted his emphasis that 'undisturbed natural beauty' constituted the typical object of the tourist gaze. However, this is in fact only one kind of gaze, what I call the 'romantic'. There is an alternative: the 'collective' tourist gaze, with different characteristics. Here is Walter's description of another Wiltshire house and garden, Longleat:

> a large stately home, set in a Capability Brown park; trees were deliberately thinned ... so that you can see the park from the house, and house from the park. Indeed the house is the focal point of the park ... the brochure lists twenty-eight activities and facilities ... All this activity and the resulting crowds fit sympathetically into the tradition of the stately home: essentially the life of the aristocratic was public rather than private. (1982: 198)

Such places were designed as public places: they would look strange if they were empty. It is other people that make such places. The collective gaze thus necessitates the presence of large numbers of other people, as were found in the seaside resorts discussed in Chapter 2. Other people give atmosphere or a sense of carnival to a place. They indicate that this is *the* place to be and that one should not be elsewhere. And as we saw, one of the problems for the British seaside resort is that there are not enough people to convey this message. As Walter says: 'Brighton or Lyme Regis on a sunny summer's day with the beach to oneself would be an eerie experience' (1982: 298). It is the presence of other *tourists*, people just like oneself that is actually necessary for the success of such places, which depend upon the collective tourist gaze. This is also the case in major cities, whose uniqueness is their cosmopolitan character. It is the presence of people from all over the world (tourists in other words) that gives capital cities their distinct excitement and glamour (see Walter, 1982: 299).

Large numbers of other tourists do not simply generate congestion, as the positional good argument would suggest. The presence of other tourists provides a market for the sorts of service that most tourists are in fact desperate to purchase, such as accommodation, meals, drink, travel and entertainment.

Thus Hirsch's arguments about scarcity and positional competition mainly apply to those types of tourism characterised by the romantic gaze. Where the collective gaze is to be found there is less of problem of crowding and congestion. And indeed Hirsch's argument rests on the notion that there are only a limited number of objects which can be viewed by the tourist. Yet in recent years there has been, as we noted in Chapter 1, an enormous increase in the objects of the tourist gaze, far beyond Mishan's 'undisturbed natural beauty'. Part of the reason for this increase results from the fact that contemporary tourists are collectors of gazes and appear to be less interested in repeat visits to the same auratic site. The initial gaze is what counts in what I call the spectatorial gaze (see ch. 8).

Those who do really value solitude and a romantic tourist gaze do not see this as merely *one* way of regarding nature. Instead they attempt to make everyone sacralise nature in the same sort of way (see Walter, 1982: 300–3). Romanticism, which as we noted in Chapter 2 was involved in the early emergence of mass tourism, has become widespread and generalised, spreading out from the upper middle classes, although the notion of romantic nature is a fundamentally invented and variable pleasure. And the more its adherents attempt to proselytise its virtues to others, the more the conditions of the romantic gaze are undermined: 'the romantic tourist is digging his [sic] own grave if he seeks to evangelize others to his own religion' (Walter, 1982: 301). The romantic gaze is an important mechanism which is helping to spread tourism on a global scale, drawing almost every country into its ambit as the romantic seeks ever-new objects of that gaze, and minimising diversity through the extension of what Turner and Ash term the 'pleasure periphery' (1975).

The contemporary tourist gaze is increasingly signposted. There are markers that identify the things and places worthy of our gaze. Such signposting identifies a relatively small number of tourist nodes. The result is that most tourists are concentrated within a very limited area. As Walter says: 'the sacred node provides a positional good that is destroyed by democratisation' (1982: 302). He by contrast favours the view that there are 'gems to be found everywhere and in everything … there is no limit to what you will find' (Walter, 1982: 302). We should, he says, get away from the tendency to construct the tourist gaze at a few selected sacred sites, and be much more catholic in the objects at which we may gaze. Undoubtedly this has occurred in recent years, particularly with the development of industrial, rural and heritage tourism. However, Walter's analysis of the class character of the romantic gaze is persuasive and I end this section on the economic theory of tourism by noting his thoroughly sociological analysis of the pervasiveness of the romantic as opposed to the collective gaze and the consequential problem of the positional good of many tourist sites:

> professional opinion-formers (brochure writers, teachers, Countryside Commission staff, etc.) are largely middle class and it is within the middle class that the romantic desire for positional goods is largely based. Romantic solitude thus has influential sponsors and gets good advertising. By contrast, the largely working class enjoyment of conviviality, sociability and being part of a crowd is often looked down upon by those concerned to conserve the environment. This is unfortunate, because it ... exalts an activity that is available only to the privileged. (Walter, 1982: 303)

Globalisation and the Economics of Tourism

We have already seen that the English seaside resort went into decline in the mid-1960s, at the moment when mass tourism, at least in Europe, became internationalised. There has continued to be massive growth of international tourist flows (see ch. 1, as well as WTO 2000a, 2000b). This internationalisation of tourism means that we cannot explain tourist patterns in any particular society without analysing developments taking place in most other countries. The internationalisation of tourism especially in Europe means that every tourist site can be compared with those located abroad (especially via the internet). So when people visit somewhere in their own country they are in effect choosing not to visit a site abroad. The internationalisation of tourism means that all potential objects of the tourist gaze can be located on a scale, and can be compared with each other, often now more or less instantaneously via the internet.

The result of such internationalisation is that different countries, or different places within a country, come to specialise in providing particular kinds of objects to be gazed upon. An international division of tourist sites has emerged in the last two decades. Britain has come to specialise in history and heritage and this affects both what overseas visitors expect to gaze upon, and what attracts UK residents to spend time holiday-making within Britain. Moreover, this internationalisation of holiday-making is more developed in the UK than in some other countries. This is partly because of the early and innovative development of the package or inclusive holiday in Britain, and partly because of the availability of many historical sites suitable for attracting large numbers of overseas tourists. Just as the UK economy in general is an open economy so this is specifically true of tourism. I briefly consider the nature of the package holiday industry before considering the main features of the UK domestic holiday industry.

Tour operators based in Britain have sold their inclusive or package holidays at a considerably cheaper price than in comparable European countries.

In the 1980s, in most hotels in Spain, Portugal and Greece, it was the British-based tour operators that offered the lowest price; British-based companies have been particularly effective at reducing unit costs and at generating a huge market for international travel in the UK, and there is still a significant price differential between UK and rest of Europe prices for package holidays (Guardian Unlimited website). There are now about 17 million package holidays sold each year (compared with around 8 million in 1983; BTA, 2000). The main reason why the inclusive holiday has had such an impact in Britain is because of the early emergence of integrated companies, the tour operators, who made spectacularly successful use of the new technologies of jet transport and computerised booking systems (see Reynolds, 1989: 330–3).

A considerable level of concentration has accompanied the development of the package tour industry in Britain. Thus there are four major tour operators, Airtours, First Choice, Thompson, and Thomas Cook. The latter two are both now owned by German companies, Thompson by Preussag and Thomas Cook by C & N Touristic, while First Choice has agreed a strategic alliance with the US company Royal Caribbean (Guardian Unlimited website). And yet there are still many small companies providing inclusive holidays; 640 members of ABTA have a turnover of less than £6m (English Tourism Council, 2000). However, the share taken by the large companies has steadily increased to around 57 per cent (Chandler, 2000: D5–9). It seems that this is partly because they have begun to cater both for more exotic destinations where they can drive down prices through bulk purchase of hotel beds, and for more specialised tastes, for what I term the 'post-tourist'. Thompson, for example, had twenty-four brochures orientated to different market segments even in the 1980s (Williams, 1988; *The Economist*, 27 August 1988).

Since the formation of a single European market, the tour operators in Europe operate in each of the major countries to a far greater extent. This has increased competition and reduced the level of concentration within a single country, as well as increasing cross-border takeovers and mergers. This has also raised the level of vertical integration, with the operators also owning travel agencies, hotels and airlines (see details in Chandler, 2000: D5–9). However, in the latest survey of holiday customers conducted by *Holiday Which?*, these large tour operators were judged to be 'the worst performers in the industry'. The best six companies were all small independent companies. Only Thompson of the large operators managed to avoid being in the category of the 10 worst performers! (Guardian Unlimited website).

This is an industry where new technologies are particularly appropriate because of the immense informational and communication problems involved. Systems now permit customers to 'self-serve' themselves with airline tickets and other standardised products. Indeed it is possible to envisage a 'paperless travel agency'. Consumers are now able to put together much more flexible packages, a kind of holiday 'mix 'n' match' or what the industry terms 'Free and Independent Travel' or FIT, especially via the internet.

Expert systems developments enable the prospective traveller to provide some parameters of intended travel and then allow the computer to generate a number of possible consumer products.

Furthermore, it seems that with increased leisure time people, especially young people, are increasingly moving away from the somewhat standardised package holiday and seeking out a wider variety of forms of leisure activity, including independent travel (Desforges, 1998). The ratio of inclusive holidays taken by UK residents has fallen from 38 per cent of all visits abroad in 1983 to 34 per cent in 1998 (BTA, 2000: 52–3). This is forcing tour operators to develop more flexible kinds of travel arrangements. There has been a marked increase in seats-only flights, partly because of the demand for more flexibility and partly because of the growth in overseas property ownership (see Ryan, 1989). These factors are also likely to force the tour operators to seek greater quality control over all aspects of the holiday, something they have been unsuccessful in achieving so far: it is noteworthy that only 12 per cent of overseas visitors to Britain are on inclusive holidays (Key Note website). Barrett also suggests that some switching to independent travel 'is partly a reaction to the "naffness" of package holidays', that even by the 1980s they were no longer viewed as fashionable or smart (1989b).

So far I have looked at some features of the industry concerned with transporting British and other north European holiday-makers mainly to certain south European countries, within which there is intense spatial concentration (see Goodall, 1988: 25–6). In the next section I shall consider the organisation of the tourist industry in societies that host large numbers of such visitors. But before this I examine some features of the tourist industry concerned with the provision of services *within* Britain.

As far as overseas visitors are concerned there is a huge potential market. In the early 1980s only 7 per cent of US citizens possessed a passport; this figure would merely have to reach 10 per cent for there to be very large increases in the number of potential US visitors (see Cabinet Office, 1983). The preferences of foreign visitors are highly localised, most being attracted to London and to various small inland towns and cities. In fact about 80 per cent begin their visit in London and this is reflected in, for example, the fact that a high proportion of those visiting London West End theatres are foreign visitors (SWET, 1982). The build-up of overseas visitors in London has produced no significant deflection to provincial centres that were not already attracting significant numbers of such visitors. Indeed it may be that if there is no shift in visitor patterns and if hotel space in London remains in short supply, then overseas visitors go to other destinations in Europe rather than to the rest of Britain. In the 1980s it was calculated that there was no increase in the number of *new* visitors to the UK and all of the increase has been in 'repeat' visitors. Such 'repeats' are more common amongst business travellers, West Europeans, visitors aged over 35 and people travelling outside London (BTA/ETB Research Services, 1988).

The six most popular leisure pursuits for overseas visitors are visiting shops or markets (82 per cent), restaurants or cafes (77 per cent), churches, cathedrals and so on (69 per cent), historic sites/buildings (69 per cent), museums and art galleries (64 per cent), and historic cities or towns (62 per cent) (BTA/ETB Research Services, 1988). An astonishing 28 million overseas visits were made to London in 2000 with visitor nights expected to exceed 120 million (Global Hotel Network website). A number of other features of the economic and geographical organisation of British tourism will now be considered.

In 1999 there were 288,000 establishments in the British hospitality industry, generating an annual turnover of £43 billion (Department of Culture, Media and Sport website). In relationship to hotels most accommodation is provided in small units. In the 1980s it was calculated that of the half million hotel bedrooms, 30 per cent were corporately owned while 70 per cent were owned by independents, most with fewer than 50 bedrooms (Slattery and Roper, 1986). Small capital is thus of enduring significance in the provision of tourist accommodation in Britain. Amongst these small capitals four different sectors can be usefully distinguished.

There are the 'self-employed' with no outside labour and reliance upon family labour and trade-based skills. They are economically marginal, formal management skills are weak, and there is no divorce of ownership from control. Many bed-and-breakfast units are of this type. Second, there is the category of 'small employers' who are distinguished from the self-employed by the intermittent employment of outside labour. Many guesthouses and small hotels are of this sort. Third, there are 'owner controllers' who do not use family labour and employ outside labour which may receive a considerable degree of training. Levels of capital investment are higher and there are more formal means of managerial control. These are less economically marginal, although there is no divorce of ownership and control. Many so-called 'country house' hotels where the proprietor is directly involved are like this. Finally, there are 'owner directors', where there is considerable capital investment, formal training, and the separation of ownership and control. This is most common amongst those city centre hotels not part of any chain.

All these different types of small capital in the hotel and catering industry show enormous vulnerability in the market. A quarter of such establishments close within two years, half within four. About one-quarter do survive while the remaining three-quarters are in a continuous state of flux. The rate of turnover is considerably higher in this industry than in most others, which means that there is great job insecurity. The category of 'owner controllers' appears best able to survive. Drew Smith, former editor of *The Good Food Guide*, maintains that: 'it is the personally run restaurant [and hotel] that has bucked the trend, often by the sheer dedication of the owner. At the other end of the market this has usually been because the family has kept the free-hold of the site' (1988: 22). This therefore is an industry of enormous volatility. And although there are some very large operators, as we will see, there are very few restrictions on entry (and exit!). Drew Smith estimates that fifty new restaurants opened each month in London. Indeed there are almost certainly large variations in the propensity to start new restaurants and hotels in different parts of the country. Cornwall, for example, seems to have had relatively weak traditions of local entrepreneurship in all sectors of the economy including tourism, although most tourist-related enterprises are in fact small. In a study of Looe it was found that there was a very high level of geographical mobility amongst entrepreneurs. (Hennessy et al., 1986: 16). Cornwall in general attracts entrepreneurs rather than generating its own.

One major influence on the kinds of tourist-related activities found in different areas (London compared with Looe) is the growth of business tourism and its differential impact. Business tourism is made up of a number of components: meetings held in other parts of the country, conferences, and the provision of travel as a non-taxable perk (see Williams and Shaw, 1988b: 19). There has been a large increase in the number of conferences in particular, with almost one million delegates a year attending them (British Hospitality Association, 2000). The effect of conference and business tourism in particular has generated periodic hotel building booms, for example in London in the late 1960s and early 1970s, the 1980s and the late 1990s. Twenty-three new hotels opened in London in 2000, with an astonishing seventy-eight currently planned (Global Hotel Network website; and see British Hospitality Association, 2000, for details of hotel groups).

A significant development in the past decade or so has been the development of hotel consortia. Such consortia grew up in the 1960s to compensate for the decentralised structure of capital and the problems this created for capital accumulation and systematic cost cutting. Corporate growth is difficult given the low levels of concentration, small unit size and the varying combination of meals, drinks and accommodation for which demand is both seasonal and volatile (see Litteljohn, 1982; Slattery et al., 1985; Bagguley, 1987). Consortia enable hotels to gain economies of scale and hence to be able to compete much more effectively with the economies obtainable by the large chains listed earlier. Consortia fall into a number of types:

marketing consortia: to provide access to a corporate marketing department on the basis of either regional grouping or a specific market segment (such as Prestige)
marketing and purchasing consortia: apart from marketing economies they also negotiate reduced prices for bulk orders
referral consortia: to provide a national or international system of referrals particularly connected with airlines
personnel and training consortia: to provide common training and personnel functions
reservations systems: to provide a system of national or international reservations often linked to various other tourist offices

Internationalisation of leisure provision occurs in many parts of the tourist-related services. This can be seen most obviously in the case of McDonalds with their 23,300 restaurants and their recent move into Golden Arches hotels in Switzerland (see ch. 4). The most significant tourist attraction in

Europe is Disneyland, Paris, which opened in 1992. It attracts 12 million visitors a year with 43 attractions and 14 hours of live shows. It has just opened a huge shopping centre and a second park, Disney Studios, is about to be built on the same site.(Disneyland Paris website).

The tourist-related industries analysed here are thus intensely competitive. Moreover, although the very large operators can move their capital around in response to changing market pressures, most of the industry cannot move, certainly in the short run. This is an industry with great spatial fixity, an exceptional degree of decentralisation, and immense volatility of taste. Since many visitors to hotels and restaurants are only there because of the attractions available in the area so there may well be much support given to enhancing local facilities, to increasing the number or attraction of potential objects of the tourist gaze. Hence, tourist-related capital may well be in favour of large-scale public investment by local authorities to provide new or enhanced objects upon which visitors can gaze.

In the past decades companies involved in the hospitality industry have pursued various cost-reduction strategies:

1   The expansion of self-serviced accommodation.
2   The extensive use of information technology. This results from how slack resources in the industry such as a hotel bed cannot be stored; the immense volatility of demand; and the fact that tourist units are necessarily geographically dispersed. The internet, especially, enables various kinds of network to be established between potential consumers and the many locally specific and decentralised units of supply.
3   Changing the labour input especially via the growth of part-time female employment.
4   Economising on costs through joining a group or consortium.
5   Closing down in slack periods or alternatively trying to generate extra business during the often off-season; developing 'shoulder-seasons'.
6   Generating extra income by improving the quality of the product provided, such as better meals, more trained labour or *en suite* facilities.

The Overseas Impact of Tourism

Tourist development outside the UK has had a broad economic, social and cultural impact. Drawing in part on the concept of the positional good discussed earlier, I consider some Mediterranean countries, and follow this with comments on north America and South-East Asia.

As we saw in Chapter 1, there are complex relationships between tourists and the indigenous populations of the places at which those tourists gaze; the resulting artificiality of many tourist attractions results from the particular character of the social relations that come to be established between 'hosts' and 'guests' in such places (see Smith, 1989, on the following). There are a number of determinants of the particular social relations that are established between 'hosts' and 'guests'.

1 The *number* of tourists visiting a place in relationship to the size of the host population and to the scale of the objects being gazed upon. For example, the geographical size of New Zealand would permit more tourists to visit without either environmental damage or an undesirable social effect. By contrast the physical smallness of Singapore means that extra tourists cannot easily be accommodated except by even more hotel building which would only be possible by demolishing the remaining few Chinese shophouses which in the past have been one of the main objects of the tourist gaze. Similarly the medieval city of Dubrovnik has an absolute physical limit determined both by the city walls and the population of over 4,000 people that live there.

2 The predominant *object* of the tourist gaze, whether it is a landscape (the Lake District), a townscape (Chester), an ethnic group (Maoris in Rotorua, New Zealand), a lifestyle (the 'wild west'), historical artefacts (Canterbury Cathedral or Wigan Pier), bases of recreation (golf courses at St Andrews), or simply sand, sun and sea (Majorca). Those tourist activities that involve observation of physical objects are less intrusive than those that involve observing individuals and groups. Moreover, within the latter category, the observation of the private lives of host groups will produce the greatest social stress. Examples here include the Eskimo, or the Masai who have responded to the gaze by charging a '£ for car' for visits to their mud huts. By contrast, where what is observed is more of a public ritual then social stress will be less pronounced and indeed wider participation may be positively favoured, as in various Balinese rituals (see Smith, 1989: 7).

3 The *character* of the gaze involved and the resulting spatial and temporal 'packing' of visitors. For example, the gaze may be something that can take place more or less instantaneously (seeing/photographing New Zealand's highest mountain, Mount Cook), or it may require prolonged exposure (seeing/experiencing the 'romance' of Paris). In the case of the former, Japanese tourists can be flown in for a visit lasting just a few hours, while the experience of the romance of Paris will necessitate a longer and 'deeper' immersion.

4 The *organisation* of the industry that develops to service the mass gaze: whether it is private or publicly owned and financed; whether it is locally owned or involves significant overseas interests; whether the capital involved is predominantly small- or large-scale; and whether there are conflicts between the local population and the emergent tourist industry. Such conflicts can occur around many issues: conservation as opposed to commercial development, the wages to be paid to locally recruited employees, the effects of development on local customs and family life, what one might call the 'trinketisation' of local crafts, and how to compensate for the essential seasonality of labour (see Smith, 1989).

5   The effects of tourism upon the *pre-existing agricultural and industrial activities*. These may range from the destruction of those activities (much agriculture in Corfu); to their gradual undermining as labour and capital are drawn into tourism (parts of Spain); to their preservation as efforts are made to save pre-existing activities as further objects to be gazed upon (cattle farming and hence grazing in the Norfolk Broads).

6   The economic and social *differences* between the visitors and the majority of the hosts. In northern Europe and north America tourism creates fewer strains since the mass of 'hosts' will themselves be 'guests' on other occasions. It may be that tourism can in a rather inchoate way develop 'international understanding'. The shift in public attitudes in Britain towards a pro-Europeanism in the 1980s is difficult to explain without recognising that some role is played by the European tourism industry and the way in which huge flows of visitors have made Europe familiar and unthreatening. Elsewhere, however, there are usually enormous inequalities between the visitors and the indigenous population, the vast majority of whom could never envisage having either the income or the leisure time to be tourists themselves. These differences are reinforced in many developing countries by the nature of the tourist development, which appears to be exceptionally opulent and highly capitalised, as for example in many hotels in India, China, Singapore, Hong Kong and north Africa, partly because there are so few service facilities otherwise available to either visitors or the host population.

7   The degree to which the mass of visitors demand *particular standards of accommodation and service*, that they should be enclosed in an environmental bubble to provide protection from many of the features of the host society. This demand is most marked amongst inclusive tour visitors, who not only expect western standards of accommodation and food but also bilingual staff and well-orchestrated arrangements. Such tourists rarely leave the security of the western tourist bubble and to some degree are treated as dependent 'children' by the tourist professionals (see Smith, 1989: 10–11). In some cases the indigenous culture actually is dangerous, as in Sicily, parts of New York, and recently in Florence. This demand is less pronounced amongst individual exploring 'travellers', poorer tourists such as students, and those visitors for whom 'roughing it' is part of their expected experience as tourists (see Edensor, 1998: on backpacker tourism).

8   The degree to which the *state* in a given country actively seeks to promote tourist developments or alternatively endeavours to prevent them. Good examples of the former are Spain, Tunisia and Hawaii which are all actively developing a fully-fledged tourist culture where large numbers of tourists have become part of the 'regional scenery' (Smith, 1989). By contrast many of the oil states have for moral/social reasons explicitly decided to restrict tourism by refusing visas (Saudi Arabia is a good example). Likewise during the Cultural Revolution in China the state actively sought to prevent the growth of tourism. When this changed in

the early to mid-1970s western visitors were so unusual that they were often applauded as though they were royalty.

9   The extent to which *tourists can be identified and blamed* for supposedly undesirable economic and social developments. This is obviously more common when such visitors are economically and/or culturally and/or ethnically distinct from the host population. It is also more common when the host population is experiencing rapid economic and social change. However, such change is not necessarily the outcome of 'tourism'. In the case of Tonga, for example, it is not the annual influx of visitors but rather gross overpopulation which accounted for the high inflation rate. And yet of course it is much easier to blame the 'nameless, faceless foreigner' for indigenous problems of economic and social inequality (see Smith, 1989). Moreover, some local objections to tourism are in fact objections to 'modernity' itself: to mobility and change, to new kinds of personal relationships, to a reduced role of family and tradition, and to different cultural configurations (see the 'Global Code of Ethics for Tourism' on the World Tourism Organization website).

The social impact of tourism will thus depend on the intersection of a wide range of factors. For example, great concern has been expressed about the likely consequences of tourism in various Mediterranean countries. The growth of tourism in the Mediterranean is one of the most significant economic and social developments in the post-war period. It is a particularly striking symbol of post-war reconstruction in western Europe.

There is a high income elasticity of demand for tourist services and as incomes have grown in West Germany, France, Scandinavia, the Low Countries and the British Isles, so there has been a more than corresponding increase in demand for overseas travel. Western Europe in fact accounted for 68 per cent of all international tourists (Williams and Shaw, 1988a: 1). In response to such demand the countries of southern Europe developed enormous tourist industries. And those industries have been particularly cost-effective, which in turn has lowered the real cost of overseas travel and hence led to further expansion of demand. Spain was the first and has remained the largest of the Mediterranean destinations. Other major destination countries are France, Italy, Greece, Portugal, and Turkey. In 1984 tourism receipts accounted for over four per cent of the national income of Spain and Portugal, over three per cent of that of Greece, and 2.6 per cent of that of Italy (Williams et al., 1986: 13). Overall, tourism generates a net distribution of wealth from northern to southern Europe, and especially to Spain, Portugal and Italy.

The problematic effects of such tourist developments in at least some of the countries are well known. They result from the huge number of tourists and their seasonal demand for services, the deleterious social effects particularly resulting from the gendered work available, the geographical concentration of visitors, the lack of concerted policy response, the cultural differences between hosts and guests, and the demand by many visitors to be enclosed in expensive 'environmental bubbles'. One place 'overrun' by tourists is Florence, where the resident population of 500,000 accommodated in the 1980s 1.7 million visitors each year. This led to the plan in the 1980s to remove the city's academic, commercial and industrial functions from the centre and to turn Florence over entirely to tourism. It would have meant, according to critics, the 'Disneyfication of Florence' (Vulliamy, 1988: 25).

Robert Graves has written off the similar tourist transformation of Majorca:

> the old Palma has long ceased to exist; its centre eaten away by restaurants, bars, souvenir shops, travel agencies and the like ... Huge new conurbations have sprung up along the neighbouring coast ... The main use of olive trees seems to be their conversion into ... salad bowls and boxes for sale to the tourists. But, as a Majorcan wag remarked, once they are all cut down we will have to erect plastic ones for the tourists to admire from their bus windows. (1965: 51)

It has been suggested that there is a very serious threat to the whole Mediterranean coastline. It is the world's most popular tourist destination. A UN report suggested that the number of visitors could increase from 100 million in the 1980s to 760 million in 2025, thereby placing a huge strain upon food, water and human resources. The growth of existing coastal cities needs to be dramatically slowed down (the *Guardian*, 2 November 1988). But the opposite is occurring with Turkey, a recent country to develop as a major tourist destination. The immediate attraction for local investors in Turkey is that most revenue comes in the form of foreign exchange. Turkish tourism has so far involved the proliferation of some ugly unplanned developments, such as those in Bodrum and Marmara, which may have to be demolished fairly soon. One specialist operator, Simply Turkey, withdrew from selling holidays in Gumbet because it was 'No longer small and pretty, it is a sprawling building site, noisy and dusty, with a beach not large enough to cater for its rapid development' (quoted in Whitaker, 1988: 15). The impact of such rapid tourism growth is felt particularly keenly because south-west Turkey has always attracted considerable numbers of individual 'travellers' due to the exceptional quality of its antiquities. Turkey is hence poised between the conflicting interests of mass tourism and a more socially select tourism, between the collective and romantic tourist gazes.

The second most important area of tourist activity worldwide is north America. Developments here are, interestingly, different from Europe. Central to north American tourism has been the car, the highway, the view through the windscreen and the commercial strip. Jakle talks of how, in the post-war period, cities, towns and rural areas were all remade in what he calls 'universal highway order' (1985: ch. 9 for the following). In 1950 80 per cent of all long-distance trips were made by automobile and by 1963 43 per cent of American families took long vacation trips each year, averaging 600 miles.

There was a rapid improvement of the quality of the road system, to cope with faster travel and higher traffic volume. Unfortunately there was little to see from the new roads except the monotony of the road itself. John Steinbeck wrote that 'it will be possible to drive from New York to California without seeing a single thing' (quoted in Jakle, 1985: 190). Roads came to be built for the convenience of driving, not for the patterns of human life that might be engendered. The ubiquitousness of the radio and to some extent of air conditioning in American cars insulates the passengers from all almost all aspects of the environment except the view through the windscreen (Sheller and Urry, 2000).

And this view reveals almost nothing because even townscapes consist of commercial strips, the casual eradication of distinctive places and the generation of a standardised landscape. Jakle terms this the production of 'commonplaceness'. The commercial strips are common places lacking the ambiguities and complexities that generally make places interesting. They are 'unifunctional landscapes' which became even more uniform in appearance as large corporations operate chains of look-alike and standardised establishments (McDonalds, Howard Johnson, Col. Saunders, Holiday Inn and so on). The automobile journey has become one of the icons of post-war America, reflected in Kerouac's *On the Road* or the film *Easy Rider*. In *Lolita* Humbert Humbert concludes 'We have been everywhere. We have seen nothing' (quoted in Jakle, 1985: 198).

One of the most famous tourist sites in north America is Niagara Falls. Reaction to it has always involved superlatives (see Shields, 1990). Observers reported themselves lost for words. It was an exotic wonder; it had an immense natural aura. However, a series of transformations that have taken place have rendered Niagara as a series of different objects of the tourist gaze. First, in the late nineteenth century the Falls became the most favoured of places for honeymoons and for courtship more generally. Shields links this to the way in which the Falls constituted an admirable liminal zone where strict social conventions of the bourgeoisie were relaxed under the exigencies of travel and relative anonymity. The historic association of waterfalls with passion, whether of love or death, further enhanced the salience of such a zone. Travellers expected the Falls to be exceptional, a place where the limits of ordinary experience were transcended. The trip was analogous to a pilgrimage. Nathaniel Hawthorne wrote of going 'haunted with a vision of foam and fury, and dizzy cliffs, and an ocean tumbling down out of the sky' (quoted in Shields, 1990). More recently however the honeymoon has been emptied of its symbolic liminal status. It has become a meaningless nuptial cliché, referring to nothing but itself. All the emphasis at the Falls is placed on the props, on honeymoon suites and heart-shaped 'luv tubs'. The Falls now stand for kitsch, sex and commercial spectacle. It is as though the Falls are no longer there as such and can only be seen through their images.

Thus the same object in a physical sense has been transformed by a variety of commercial and public interests. The nature of the gaze has undergone immense changes. In the eighteenth century the Falls were an object of intense natural aura; in the nineteenth century they functioned as a liminal zone gazed upon and deeply experienced by courting couples; and in the later twentieth century they have become another 'place' to be collected by the immensely mobile visitor for whom the gaze at the Falls stands for spectacle, sex and commercial development.

A related kind of development has been the growth of so-called 'sex-tourism' in south-east Asia. In South Korea this has been specifically encouraged by the state. Its main form consists of the kisaeng tour specifically geared to Japanese businessmen (see Mitter, 1986: 64–7). Many Japanese companies reward their outstanding male staff with all-expenses tours of kisaeng brothels and parties. South Korean ministers have congratulated the 'girls' for their contribution to their country's economic development. Other countries with a similarly thriving sex industry are the Philippines and Thailand. In the case of the former the state encourages the use of 'hospitality girls' in tourism, and the Ministry of Tourism recommends various brothels (Mitter, 1986: 65). Package tours organised in conjunction with a Manila agent include preselected 'hospitality girls'. Of the money earned only about 7–8 per cent will be retained by the women themselves. In Thailand it is calculated that there are 500,000 women working in the sex industry, with perhaps 200,000 in Bangkok alone (see Lea, 1988: 66–9). Particular processes which have helped to generate such a pattern are: the exceptionally strong set of patriarchal practices which cast women as either 'madonna/virgin' or 'whore'; the belief amongst people from affluent countries that women of colour are more available and submissive; the high rate of incest and domestic violence by fathers/husbands in some such societies; rural depopulation which draws people into the cities looking for any possible work; and the growth of 'specialist' tour companies and websites devoted to facilitating travel by groups of male 'sex-tourists' (see Enloe, 1989: especially on attempts by women to organise groups to protect prostitutes; Clift and Carter, 1999; see Chapter 8).

Similar factors apply elsewhere but such patterns are less obvious. Singapore provides an interesting contrast. In the advertising material for tourists there are no references to sex-tourism. The only clubs listed are various discos and Asian-style shows. Singapore is nevertheless an extremely successful object of the tourist gaze but this has been achieved by playing down its exotic character. Much of the emphasis in the publicity material is on Singapore's attractions as a modern shopping centre, and there is indeed an extraordinary complex of shopping centres along the now wholly misnamed Orchard Road. Singapore has also transformed many of the old areas of Chinese shophouses into modern hotel complexes, including what is claimed to be the tallest hotel in the world, as well as the modernised Raffles Hotel. Singapore is 'in the east' but not really any more 'of the east'. It is almost the ultimate modern city and does not construct itself as 'exotic/erotic' for visitors.

Conclusion

It is clear that the effects of tourism are highly complex and contradictory, depending on the range of considerations outlined earlier. Not surprisingly there has been much discussion about the desirability of tourism as a strategy for economic development in so-called developing societies. This raises many difficult issues.

The growth of tourism in developing countries, such as 'game tourism' in Kenya, 'ethnic tourism' in Mexico, 'sports tourism' in the Gambia and so on, does not simply derive from processes internal to those societies. Such a development possibility results from a number of external conditions: technological changes such as cheap air travel and computerised booking systems; developments in capital including the growth of worldwide hotel groups (Ramada), travel agencies (Thomas Cook), and personal finance organisations (American Express); the widespread pervasion of the 'romantic' gaze so that more and more people wish to isolate themselves from the existing patterns of mass tourism; the increased fascination of the developed world with the cultural practices of less developed societies; the development of the tourist as essentially a 'collector' of places often gazed upon and experienced on the surface; and the emergence of a powerful metropolitan lobby concerned to promote the view that tourism has a major development potential (see Crick, 1988: 47–8).

The economic benefits from tourism are often less than anticipated. Much tourist investment in the developing world has in fact been undertaken by large-scale companies based in north America or western Europe, and the bulk of such tourist expenditure is retained by the transnational companies involved; often only 20–60 per cent of the price remains in the host country (Tourism Concern website). In Mauritius, for example, 90 per cent of foreign exchange earned from tourism is repatriated to companies based elsewhere. This repatriation is particularly likely to happen with the presently high level of vertical integration in the industry (see Crick, 1988: 45).

A further problem, again avoided in Singapore, occurs where tourism accounts for an exceptionally high proportion of the national income of the country. Some Caribbean islands experience this difficulty. It means that if anything serves to undermine tourist demand, an enormous loss of national income results. This is also what happened, for example, in Fiji in 1987 following military coups (see Lea, 1988: 32–6, particularly on the scale of advertising needed to restore consumer confidence especially in Australia).

It must also be asked: development *for whom?* Many of the facilities that result from tourism (airports, golf courses, luxury hotels and so on) will be of little benefit to the mass of the indigenous population. Likewise much indigenous wealth that is generated will be highly unequally distributed and so most of the population of developing countries will gain little benefit. This does of course depend on patterns of local ownership. Finally, much employment generated in tourist-related services is relatively low-skilled and may well reproduce the servile character of the previous colonial regime, what one critic has termed 'flunkey training' (quoted in Crick, 1988: 46).

However, it has to be asked whether many developing countries have much alternative to tourism as a development strategy. Although there are serious economic costs, as well as social costs which I have not even considered here, it is very difficult in the absence of alternatives to see that developing societies have much choice but to develop their attractiveness as objects of the tourist gaze, particularly for visitors from north America, western Europe and increasingly from Japan.

In the next chapter I consider an issue just mentioned: the nature of the jobs that are to be found in tourist-related services, an issue of importance in both developing and developed countries as tourism accounts for an increasing proportion of paid employment throughout the world.

4

Working Under the Tourist Gaze

Introduction

I have so far analysed a number of different aspects of the tourist gaze. In the last chapter it was noted that the gaze can take two forms, the romantic and the collective, and that this distinction relates to the kinds of organisation possible of the tourist-related industries that develop to meet these different gazes. I also noted that in some cases, Niagara Falls for example, the gaze we experience is structured by pre-existing cultural images in which the physical object is barely 'seen' at all. It was also noted that some enormously significant organisational innovations have occurred within the tourist industry, including Thomas Cook's coupon system, the luxury holiday camp, the tour operator, computerised booking systems, fast-food outlets, internet booking and so on.

In this chapter I shall consider in detail the complex relationship between two elements involved in the provision of services to tourists. On the one hand, there are the cultural practices of tourism, which constitute a set of preferred social activities highly structured by distinctions of taste. Such practices lead people to want to be in certain places, gazing at particular objects, in the company of specific other types of people. And on the other hand, a wide variety of services are provided, mainly under conditions of profit maximisation, for such tourists. And as we saw, huge international industries have developed so that the provision of services can be provided at a cost which permits large segmented markets to develop.

Various contradictions may develop between such cultural practices and the particular industries that have emerged. Such industries, particularly of transport, hotels, catering and entertainment, are all concerned with the provision of consumer *services* (sometimes known as the 'hospitality' industry). Such provision is often highly problematic, even to the extent that it is often unclear just what the product is that is being purchased. Furthermore, the tourist gaze is structured by culturally specific notions of what is extraordinary and therefore worth viewing. This means that the services provided, which may of course be incidental to the gaze itself, must take a form which does not contradict or undermine the quality of the gaze, and ideally should enhance it. This in turn poses, as we shall see, immense problems of management of such industries, to ensure that the service provided by the often relatively poorly paid service workers is appropriate to the almost sacred quality of the visitors' gaze on some longed-for and remarkable tourist site.

Two geographical or spatial features should be noted about tourist-related services. First, such services have to be provided in, or at least near to, the objects of the tourist gaze; they cannot be provided just anywhere. Tourist services develop in very particular places and cannot be shifted elsewhere; they have a particular 'spatial fix'. Second, much service production involves close spatial proximity between the producers and the consumers of the service in question. This results from the nature of many service products provided for tourists, such as a meal, a drink, a ride at the funfair, and so on. Such consumer services involve a necessarily close connection between producers and consumers.

Providing a 'Service'

In the case of manufactured products it is normally clear just what the product consists of. In many service industries this is not nearly so straight-forward (see discussion in Bagguley et al., 1990: ch. 3; and in the *Service Industries Journal*). Mars and Nicod describe the problem of specifying the boundary of a given service:

> 'service' as we use it, refers to an action or material thing that is more than one might normally expect. In a transport cafe it can mean no more than passing the sauce bottle with a smile. In the Savoy it might mean making prodigious efforts to supply a rare delicacy or indulging a customer's particular preference or foible.
>
> The more people actually pay for service, the more exacting will be their demand for better *and more individual* service. (1984: 28)

This quotation also demonstrates that the expenditure of labour is central to service work, whether this labour merely consists of passing the sauce or of some much more extensive and discriminating activity. Tourist-related services in particular are labour-intensive and this means that labour costs represent a significant proportion of total costs.

Moreover, since in manufacturing technical change can more radically reduce unit costs, services will over time come to be relatively more expensive. Employers in the various service sectors will seek to monitor and, where possible, to minimise such costs. However, most service enterprises will not be able to lower costs in the manner achieved by McDonald's – to merely 15 per cent of the value of sales (Percy and Lamb, 1987).

As noted, labour is to varying degrees implicated in the delivery of many tourist-related services. This occurs as the intended outcome of a necessar-ily *social* process in which some interaction occurs between one or more producers and one or more consumers. The quality of the social interaction is itself part of the service purchased (see Leidner, 1987). To buy the service is to buy a particular social or sociological experience. Sasser and Arbeit, for example, suggest that: 'Even if the hamburger is succulent, if the employee is surly, the customer will probably not return' (1976: 63). Many services are what are known as high-contact systems in which there is considerable involvement of the customer in the service. As a result it is more difficult to rationalise the system, partly because the customer may provoke a change in the system of operation (see Pine, 1987: 64–5).

Services normally necessitate some social interaction between producers and consumers at the point of production. Unless the service can be more or less entirely materialised, then there has to be some geographical or spatial proximity between one or more of the service producers and consumers. Second, a distinction may be made between two classes of employee: those who have minimal contact with the service consumers and those who have high contact. In the case of the former, employers will seek technical change and the extensive rationalisation of labour; with the latter employees would be recruited and trained on the basis of interpersonal attributes and public relations skills (Pine, 1987: 65). But there are difficulties in such a divisive strategy: there can be resentment between the two groups, such as chefs and waiters; the maintenance of the distinction between the groups may be hard to sustain in complex organisations such as hotels where customers cannot be spatially confined to very restricted areas; and the variability in demand for many services means that a considerable premium is placed on the flexible use of labour, something difficult to organise if there is a strong demarcation between different groups.

Furthermore, the social composition of the producers, at least those who are serving in the front line, may be part of what is in fact 'sold' to the customer. In other words, the 'service' partly consists of a process of production which is infused with particular social characteristics, of gender, age, race, educational background and so on. When the individual buys a given service, what is purchased is a particular social composition of the service producers (see Hochschild, 1983, in the case of flight attendants). In some cases what is also bought is a particular social composition of the other service *consumers*. Examples of this are especially found in tourism/transport where people spend considerable periods of time consuming the service in close proximity to others and hence part of what is being bought is the social composition of these other consumers (hence the apparent appeal of Club Class).

I now examine the significance of 'labour' for the delivery of services. As labour is itself part of the service product, this poses particular difficulties for management. These are particularly significant: the longer the delivery takes, the more intimate the service, and the greater the importance of 'quality' for the consumer. This has the consequence that in some such cases employees' speech, appearance and personality may all be treated as legitimate areas of intervention and control by management.

Mars and Nicod note more generally the significance of the distinction between what is a routine and what is an emergency (1984: 34–5). There is a chronic tension between service receivers who regard all sorts of issues as an emergency (such as an overcooked steak), and service producers who have to learn to deal with such incidents as perfectly routine. This tension is most marked in highly prestigious hotels where customers pay for and expect very high levels of personal service and where such problems cannot be treated as purely matters of routine. By contrast, in less prestigious and cheaper hotels staff develop techniques which suggest that everything is under control even when there may be all sorts of emergencies that routinely develop because of the intensity of work expected.

There are obviously very considerable variations in the expectations held by different customers. Mars and Nicod suggest that in cheaper hotels people expect a fast service but are not particularly bothered about its quality more generally (1984: 37). In top-quality hotels customers expect a wide range of idiosyncratic requests to be met, and indeed that waiters are almost able to anticipate such requests in advance. Mars and Nicod suggest that particular difficulties are caused in middle-ranking establishments where the level and forms of service to be provided are relatively unclear and contestable.

Gabriel provides an interesting and related discussion of the services provided by a gentleman's club (1988: ch. 4). As far as its members are concerned, the club offers them far more than a decent, traditional English meal. The club also offers:

> a whole range of *intangible products*, a place where important contacts can be made, where guests can be offered hospitality, where information can be exchanged, where certain rituals can be preserved and daily re-enacted. The very anachronistic nature of the club is part of this appeal; it is the appeal of the old. (1988: 141)

Gabriel goes on to say that the only way of assessing its success is through its ability to survive 'by providing those "intangible" services which cannot be rationalized and incorporated in the catering machinery' (1988: 141). The members of staff therefore serve more than meals; they are providing an intangible ambience which would be lost if the catering were to be rationalised.

Such services require what can loosely be called 'emotional work'. Amongst other requirements this involves the need to smile in a pleasant, friendly and involved way to consumers (Hochschild, 1983). Marshall notes that in the restaurant he studied: 'Staff were constantly encouraged to "cater for" the customers: to smile, exchange pleasantries, and, if there was time, longer conversations' (1986: 41). Crucial therefore to many consumer services is 'emotional work' of a public and recognisable sort. In the case of flight attendants specific training has brought this about, which results in a commercialisation of human feeling. In other occupations it is not nearly so publicly identifiable. Indeed the emphasis may be more on establishing a more 'genuine' emotional relationship between producers and consumers (as in a hospice) rather than one that is obviously contrived or artificial (see James, 1989). Nevertheless all such emotional work might well be said to be difficult and demanding, under-recognised and relatively under-rewarded. The fact that a great deal of it is provided by women employees is no coincidence.

Hochschild argues that this emotional work has been made more difficult for flight attendants with the intensification of labour on American airlines since deregulation from the mid-1970s onwards: 'The workers respond to the speed-up with a slowdown: they smile less broadly, with a quick release and no sparkle in the eyes, thus dimming the company's message to the people. It is a war of smiles' (1983: 127). Such a decline in quality is exceptionally hard for management to monitor and control, even if they are well aware that the attendants are no longer providing the complete service that passengers expect.

Yet in further research conducted amongst KLM aircrews a more complex picture emerges (see Wouters, 1989). What seems to have happened more recently is that the demands made by the company with regard to sex, age, weight, jewellery, make-up, shoes, smile, behaviour and so on have become rather looser, particularly with the increased diversity of contemporary air travellers. Wouters explains this as follows:

> an aeroplane now has become a melting-pot, not only of nationalities but also of social classes. Behaviour in contacts between flight attendants and passengers correspondingly had to become less uniform or standardized and more varied and flexible ... in each contact there is a need to attune one's behaviour to the style of emotion management of the individual passenger. (1989: 113)

What is also important is that in many services the actual delivery is provided by relatively low-level workers who are badly paid (at least relatively) and who may have little involvement or engagement with the overall enterprise. These relatively low-level workers are normally female and implicit in the work relations are notions of the 'sexual' servicing of customers or indeed of management (see Adkins, 1995). Overlying the interaction, the 'service', are often particular assumptions and notions of gender-specific forms of appropriate behaviour.

For many consumers what is actually consumed as a service *is* the particular moment of delivery by the relatively low-level service deliverers: the smile on the flight attendant's face, the pleasantness of the manner of the waitress, the sympathy in the eyes of the nurse, and so on. The problem for management is how to ensure that these moments do in fact work out appropriately, while minimising the cost of an undesirably intrusive (and hence resented) system of management/supervision, as well as minimising friction with other more highly paid, often male, workers backstage (see Whyte, 1948).

Jan Carlzon, former President of the Scandinavian airline SAS, terms these 'moments of truth' for any organisation (1987). He suggests that in SAS there are something like 50 million moments of truth each year, each of which lasts perhaps 15 seconds when a customer comes into contact with an employee. It is, he says, these moments of truth that determine whether or not SAS will succeed or fail. He argues that the importance of such moments means that organisations have to be completely reorganised, towards service to the customer as the primary objective. As a consequence, the actual service deliverers, the company's 'foot soldiers' who know most about the 'front line' operations, have to be given much more responsibility to respond effectively, quickly and courteously to the particular needs of the customer. This in turn means that the efforts of the front-line employees need to be much more highly valued. Since they are the providers of the 'moments of truth' their motivation is crucial. And, Carlzon argues, in such a service-oriented organisation individual decisions should be made at the point of responsibility and not higher up the hierarchy. The service deliverers have themselves to be the 'managers' and to be much more consumer-orientated.

Another example can be seen in the management literature relating to hotels. Greene asks what is it that makes visitors return again and again to the same hotel (1982). He suggests that this has little to do with a hotel's physical features but rather results from two-way recognition between staff and the hotel's guests. Greene argues that there is nothing more satisfying than walking into a hotel and seeing a familiar face, and then in turn being greeted by name and not by one's room number. He proposes a number of techniques by which hotel staff are reminded of guests' names so that they can be used at each 'moment of truth'. This strategy was carried to considerable lengths by the Porterhouse Restaurant Group, which devised a scheme to motivate its staff to identify as many customers as possible by name. Those who could identify 100 or more became members of the '100 Club', those who could identify 250, members of the '250 Club' and so on. One manageress achieved a UK record of being able to recognise an amazing 2,000 visitors (Lunn, 1989).

Other examples of the 'moments of truth' are provided by Welsh (1989). He sought help and advice for a possible Mediterranean holiday from twelve different travel agents and found the service in many far from satisfactory, and in some conspicuously bad. Welsh summarised how this poses problems for the image of service provided by what were well-known high-street agents: 'an employee who wears the corporate uniform of a large travel agency surely reflects to some degree the attitude of the company as a whole towards its customers' (1989).

Four concluding points should be noted about services. The production of many services is *context* dependent, they depend for their successful production upon aspects of the social and physical setting within which they occur. Examples include the style of furnishings in a travel agent's reflecting an appropriate corporate image, the apparently safe interior of an aeroplane, the antique furniture in the country hotel, the quality of the sound and lighting in an Ibiza club, a historically interesting set of buildings in a resort and so on. In other words, the delivery of many services is interconnected with aspects of the environment and especially with the nature of design and architecture. In certain cases the service cannot be received in an inappropriate physical and social context – part of the 'service', part of what is consumed, is in effect the context. This is particularly the case with tourist-related services.

Further, the quality of many services has become intensely *contested* in contemporary societies. This is for a number of reasons: that services meet an increasingly wide range of people's needs; that their consumption normally involves spending considerable amounts of time since it has to occur serially and not simultaneously (see Gershuny, 1987); that the consumers movement has encouraged people to be much more critical and inquisitive about the quality of services being received; and that consumers are increasingly choosy, eclectic and fickle. Service providers thus have all sorts of difficulties to face when confronted with the essentially contested character of 'service'.

The service product is predominantly *intangible*. So although there are certain tangible elements, such as the food or journey or drink, the crucial elements are intangible. This is shown in a study of small country hotels:

> service is not concerned with the product itself, but with the way in which the product is created and handled, with the manner, knowledge and attitude of the people who deliver it and with the environment in which it is delivered ... in general terms quality is manifestly incapable of measurement. (Callan, 1989: 245)

Finally, there are considerable differences between the perceived quality of service in different societies. In a survey by Mintel, one third of shoppers in Britain considered shop staff incompetent and unhelpful. Standards of service in Britain seem lower than in, say, the USA (but not New York!) or Japan (see *The Sunday Times*, 8 October 1989).

These fairly general points about services will now be applied to the problems involved in providing one particular category of services central to tourism: food and drink.

Catering for the Customer

The development of the catering industry has been long and complex. Catering has now become publicly available. Restaurants, bars and cafes are part of the *public* space of contemporary societies. This is in marked contrast to nineteenth century London, when all the best places to eat were private or semi-private (see on the following Mennell, 1985: ch. 6). There were two particular forms: the private London clubs which grew more numerous from 1820 onwards, and private hotels where meals were served in the private suites of rooms and there was no 'public dining room'. This changed in the 1880s and 1890s with the construction of many grand hotels, stemming from the increased mobility especially brought about by the railway. The new hotels were no longer private. Their public dining rooms were open at least to the wealthy 'public' and rapidly became fashionable. As Mennell notes, their exclusiveness now stemmed not from semi-private association with a particular social circle, but more simply from their expense. Such hotels were no longer solely the preserve of men. They were public, or perhaps semi-public, spaces for wealthy men and women, to see and to be seen in, to enter the public sphere in a particular mannered fashion (see Finkelstein, 1989).

The new hotels entailed innovative forms of organisation, particularly because the new clientele demanded much faster preparation of meals. The key figure in this rationalisation of the kitchen was Escoffier, who brought about a transformation of catering work. Traditionally the kitchen had been divided into a number of distinct sections, each responsible to a chef and for a particular category of dishes, and in which each chef worked independently of the others. Escoffier, by contrast, organised his kitchen into five sections, based not on the type of dish to be prepared but on the kind of operation to be undertaken (such as the *rotisseur* who did roasts, grilled and fried dishes, the *saucier* who made sauces, and so on). These different sections were highly interdependent so that any particular dish resulted from the work carried out by chefs working in a number of different sections. The effect of this reform was to break down traditional craft demarcations and to generate a new division of labour based upon novel forms of specialisation and the interdependence of activities (Mennell, 1985: 155–9).

I now consider some recent evidence and debate surrounding the subsequent division of labour within the kitchen, beginning with the main features of hotel and catering workplaces according to Mars and Nicod (1984). One is that of *ad hoc management*. Because the level of demand for such services is highly volatile and unpredictable, management has to develop *ad hoc* ways of responding to varying demands and unanticipated crises. To cope with this unpredictability, managements largely avoid collective contracts and favour *individual contract-making*. Each employee will negotiate separate arrangements with management. What is of most significance to such employees is the *total reward system*, which includes not only basic pay, but also formalised perks such as accommodation, semi-formalised perks such as tips, and non-formal opportunities for perks and pilferage (Mars and Nicod, 1984:). Finally, there is the distinction between *core* and *peripheral workers* with the former benefiting most from the informal reward system.

These features derive from the key characteristic of restaurants identified in Whyte's classic study, namely, the *combination* of production and service (1948: 17). A restaurant thus differs from a factory which is solely a unit of production; and it differs from a shop which is purely a unit of service:

> The restaurant operator produces a perishable product for immediate sale within his establishment. Success in such a business requires a delicate adjustment of supply to demand and skilful coordination of production and service ... This situation puts a premium upon the skilful handling of personnel ... The restaurant must provide a satisfactory way of life for the people who do the work or else it cannot provide the satisfactions sought by its customers. (Whyte, 1948: 17–18)

There are important implications of the fact that restaurants represent a combination of both production and service. Because employees are dealing with a perishable product, the tempo of work is highly variable; it is difficult to generate a rhythm by which to work and it also means that there are immense problems of co-ordination (Whyte, 1948: 18–19). The restaurant worker has essentially two bosses, the supervisor/employer *and* the customer. The total reward depends upon satisfactory relationships with both. Moreover, low-status employees such as waiters and waitresses, are able to demand prompt action from their status superiors, the chefs and cooks. But this is something that often generates resentment and a slowdown to demonstrate status superiority. Mars and Nicod suggest that these conflicts are likely to be less significant in very high-class hotels and restaurants where there is a common commitment to quality and less pressure on time (1984: 43–7). Whyte discusses various means of overcoming any such problems, that is, to preserve communication between the kitchen and the waiters while limiting face-to-face interaction and hence the possibilities of friction.

Marshall, however, examines a further aspect of the catering industry which Whyte ignores, namely the fact that when staff and customers meet there is a complex intertwining of labour and leisure. Marshall argues that had Whyte 'investigated the staff-customer relationship with similar resolve he would have realised that the proximate culture of restaurant employees is only in part that of the "workplace"' (1986: 34). And it is the mixing of labour and leisure that is the central characteristic of the restaurant he investigates.

Marshall is particularly interested in the contradiction between the poor conditions of work in the restaurant and the lack of resentment about them expressed by the workforce. The pay was bad, the hours worked were exceptionally long, and all the staff had to demonstrate complete job flexibility. And yet there was remarkably little discontent either about the nature of the work or about the obvious wealth of the owner. There was more or less no unionisation, like most of the rest of the industry (see Mars and Nicod, 1984: 109). There was also, rather unusually, little turnover of staff.

It was initially presumed by Marshall that the employer's somewhat idiosyncratic paternalism, combined with the material and symbolic significance of the total reward system, were sufficient to explain the apparent loyalty of the work force. However, through participant observation Marshall came to conclude that these 'employees were convinced that they weren't really "working" for their pay packets at all' (1986: 40). The staff rarely used the language of work. They did not say they were going to work, or were going home from work. The business after all involved the provision of leisure. Many of the customers were friends or relatives of the employees and, at least during slack times, the staff were encouraged to talk to and even participate in the leisure activities going on around them. Little attention was paid to punctuality and the staff were given freedom to organise their own routines of work. Moreover, much of the employee's leisure time was in fact also spent at the restaurant drinking in the bars. Thus many symbolic boundaries between work and leisure did not really operate. The daily round of activities (that is, of what was formally 'work' and what was formally 'leisure') were much more a way of life. Marshall suggests that many other workplaces may have rather similar features, especially where leisure or tourist-related services are provided (fast food outlets almost certainly do not demonstrate such characteristics).

However, at the same time, a range of rather significant transformations occurred in the nature of catering work, particularly with the introduction of new technologies. I begin here with Chivers' extensive survey in the early 1970s (1973; see Bagguley, 1987).

Some features of the work culture and situation of the cook made it unlikely that there will be active trade unionism and class consciousness amongst cooks and chefs. Chefs and cooks, particularly in private hotels and restaurants, typically have an orientation to the idea of service. There is the dedication to task because of the belief that the work they do is skilled, interesting and offers extensive scope for expressing their craft-like abilities. There are status differences between 'chefs' and 'cooks' in that the former view themselves as an elite serving an upper-class clientele in high 'quality' establishments. Such status differences with deep historical roots undermine the perception of a homogeneous 'occupation'. There are many opportunities in the industry to acquire managerial or employer positions. In the early 1970s, for example, there were three times as many 'managerial/employer' positions in hotels and catering than in the UK economy as a whole (see Chivers, 1973). This led to the perception among cooks of a distinct career structure through which they could progress upwards and come to run their own establishment.

But Chivers goes on to argue that extensive technical change occurred amongst such chefs and cooks in the I970s. This was partly because of the introduction of various electrical devices, which replaced many routine hand operations, but mainly because of the widespread development of 'convenience foods':

> where the very nature of the craft was being invaded by technological change in the form of convenience foods (dried, tinned and frozen), opinions revealed doubts and distress. There was recognition of the advantages of such foods in speeding up operations, increasing control over work and reducing wastage, but between a half and three-quarters of chefs and cooks feared a loss of skill and dishes would suffer. Where convenience foods have taken over, they transplant the need for skill from the kitchen to earlier stages of food preparation in factories. The result is that frozen meats, fish, vegetables and desserts enter the kitchen in a condition which requires no more than the semi-skilled operation of reconstitution before service. (Chivers, 1973: 650–1; the microwave oven has further increased these processes of 'reconstitution' even in quite high-class restaurants).

However, further research in the 1980s suggests that the situation may be more complex than this. Gabriel shows that what was more common was the juxtaposition of convenience foods *and* highly skilled craft cooking, depending upon the numbers of staff available and the particular catering requirements on a particular day (1988: 33, 54). The craft skills had certainly not been eliminated and if anything had been partly reintroduced. Nevertheless, in further research in a cook-freeze kitchen Gabriel shows that it is possible to transform a kitchen into a production line. One employee said: 'This is not a kitchen, it is a production line, but we don't get production money' (Gabriel, 1988: 57). But in relationship to cooking it is often difficult to establish just what skilled work really amounts to since it often involves tacit skills not learnt through formal apprenticeships. It involves judgement and intelligence, sensitivity and subjectivity, as now revealed (sometimes in their absence!) on the ubiquitous TV programmes featuring celebrity chefs.

Bagguley argues that there have been two distinct 'phases' of technical change in hotel kitchens, and that these have had rather different gender implications (1987). The first, in the 1950s and 1960s, was the mechanisation of routine manual tasks and resulted in the reduction of women's employment as kitchen hands, chefs and cooks. The second phase – mostly during the 1970s – involved the introduction of pre-prepared foods. During this phase there was a considerable increase in the numbers and proportion of women employed as chefs and cooks.

But it may also be suggested that the 1980s and 1990s represent a third phase, where there has been extensive investment in the fast-food industry and what Levitt terms the 'industrialisation of service' (1981, see Ritzer, 1996, on 'McDonaldization'). Such 'industrialized' food is produced in predictable, calculable, routinised and standardised environments, even where there is franchising. An executive interviewed by Gabriel admitted that fast food is 'not a chef system, but a food management system' (1988: 92). These fast food companies have developed global networks with few 'failings' so that an African McDonalds will be every bit as 'good' as an American McDonalds. Such networks of control depend upon allocating a very large proportion of resources to the system, to branding, advertising, quality control, staff training and the internalisation of the corporate image. An extraordinary 0.5 per cent of the world's population visit a McDonalds *each day* (the *Guardian*, April 6th, 2001).

McDonalds generates new 'food' products such as Big Macs or the simulated Chicken McNuggets which alter people's eating habits and generate new social habits world-wide, such as eating standardised fast food from take-out restaurants (the UK's first such restaurant was opened in 1962). It promotes easy accessibility and flexible consumption at more or less any time ('grazing'). Fast food has broken down the tyranny of fixed mealtimes and the rigid timetabling of the day, especially of course while one is travelling.

McDonaldization produces new kinds of low-skilled standardised jobs, especially for young people who are often themselves travelling the world (McJobs). The employment effect has been to increase the proportion of the catering workforce aged under 21. Even in 1986 in Britain 75 per cent of the 15,000 workers employed by McDonalds were under 21, most worked part-time and annual staff turnover was around 300 per cent. Working in fast food was the most common choice of first-time job in Britain. A fast-food manager explained the recruiting policy: 'We just have to recruit young people because of the pace of work. Older people couldn't stand the pace ... this job, with its clean, dynamic image, appeals to younger people' (quoted in Gabriel, 1988: 97).

In such places the young staff have to learn how to present themselves in particular programmed ways to customers. There are stereotyped forms of address, which are sometimes even printed on the back of the menu. Staff must also learn the company smile. A fast-food worker nevertheless explained: 'It's all artificial. Pretending to offer personal service with a smile when in reality no one means it. We know this, management knows this, even the customers know this, but we keep pretending' (Gabriel, 1988: 93; Ritzer, 1996).

Yet, although almost everything in the fast-food business is rule-bound, these rules are often broken in order to meet the immense demand at particular times of the day and to break the drudgery of the work involved. Management regularly turns a blind eye to the ways in which employees maintain a measure of autonomy and put their mark on work that they would otherwise find immensely monotonous (Gabriel, 1988: 107).

I have so far assumed that the same processes apply in each country. However, Mennell shows that the French and English experiences have been strikingly different. There has been a long-standing dominance in England of the job of 'management', particularly of large hotels, and a corresponding disdain until recently for the occupations of chef and cook (1985: 195). France, by contrast, has seen the development of the chef as a professional. The *chef-patron* enjoyed immensely high status in French society. Mennell suggests that the situation in England has facilitated the more extensive implementation of de-skilling strategies compared with France.

A 'Flexible' Labour Force

Here I show that restructuring through the flexible use of labour is something that has characterised many tourist-related services for decades, and that the understanding of such services necessitates a careful examination of the changing gender relations in such industries, since particular kinds of labour flexibility presuppose a certain gendering of the labour force (see Bagguley, 1991).

T. Atkinson famously identified four forms of flexibility (1984). First, there is *numerical flexibility*, where firms vary the level of labour input in response to changes in the level of output. This may involve the use of part-time, temporary, short-term contract and casual workers. Second, there is *functional flexibility*, which refers to the ability of employers to move employees between different functional tasks according to changes in the work load. Third, there is the strategy of *distancing*, which involves the displacing of internal employment relations by commercial market relations through subcontracting and similar arrangements. Fourth, there is *pay flexibility*, whereby employers attempt to reward individual employees who have for example become 'multiskilled' and functionally flexible employees. These management strategies have the effect of restructuring employment in firms into 'core' and 'peripheral' workers.

The thesis was mostly discussed in the 1980s restructuring of manufacturing industry (see NEDO, 1986; Pollert, 1988). However, service industry has for a much longer period been characterised by these forms of flexibility. In tourist-related services for example we noted the use of pay flexibility, something related to the low levels of unionisation, even in large hotels, and the relative absence of industrial disputes (see Johnson and Mignot, 1982). Furthermore, both functional and numerical flexibility have been clear management goals in hotel and catering from the 1960s onwards. This is demonstrated in research that showed:

> The essential need for full and flexible use of staff has led to a considerable move away from traditional staffing patterns. In many hotels both the occupational structure of the staff and the content of their jobs have changed. The more flexible use of staff was evident in all departments. (Department of Employment, 1971: 31)

A typical day for a functionally flexible 'chamber maid' in the 1960s was described as follows:

> ... make and serve early morning teas; assist in preparation and service of breakfast; make beds and clean bedrooms and bathrooms, and after an afternoon break, assist with the preparation and service of the evening meal; or part-time staff might be engaged for the evening duties. (Department of Employment, 1971: 31)

Similar functional flexibility was noted in the kitchen:

> Few hotels retained the full traditional kitchen brigade. Boulangiers, rotisseurs and sauciers especially were less frequently employed, often being replaced by less specialised sous-chefs. Similarly the employment of separate breakfast cooks was tending to decline, their work being undertaken by assistant cooks, who combined it with other, wider, kitchen duties. The increased use of convenience foods and the consequent reduction in the preparation of vegetables, etc., has enabled the introduction of kitchen assistants with a wider range of duties, previously covered by separate grades. (Department of Employment, 1971: 31)

The report also notes the widespread use of part-time employees to meet fluctuations in demand during the day, of temporary seasonal workers to off-set the well-known seasonality of demand, and of subcontracting certain functions, especially laundering (see Ball, 1988, on seasonality).

Further evidence of the importance of functional flexibility is revealed in research on hotel and catering skills (ETAC, 1983). Six categories of tasks were identified: food preparation and cookery; serving food and drink; handling and storing food and drink before preparation; cleaning activities; administrative and clerical work; supervisory and managerial activities. It was concluded from an extensive survey that:

> Two thirds of the sample worked in three or more of these areas on occasion. About 90 per cent worked in at least two of them. People in managerial or administrative positions had the most diversity in their work, followed by people in kitchen jobs. People working in reception or the front office had the least. Over one third of crafts people said they worked in four or more of these areas ... People in smaller establishments, where one would expect greater flexibility of working, tended to work in more areas than people in larger establishments. (ETAC, 1983: 9)

There is also a distinct gender division in the form and extent of these various flexible working practices (Bagguley, 1991). It seems that it was much more common for men to have jobs which involved functional flexibility. The ETAC report again notes: 'There was a marked tendency for men to be doing a wider variety of tasks than women, which no doubt reflects the high proportion of women in operative positions, which have the least diversity in their work' (1983: 9).

The 'operative positions' – cooks, waiting and bar staff, kitchen hands, domestic staff and cleaners – are overwhelmingly filled by women. Moreover, it is in these positions that such women employees work part-time, that is, demonstrating what Atkinson terms 'numerical flexibility'. In 1984 over 80 per cent of part-time employees in hotels in Britain were women (Dept of Employment, 1987). Such numerically flexible workers are also usually the least functionally flexible. Most part-time employees (mostly women) do not have the opportunity to develop a wide range of skills and experience to become functionally flexible as full-time employees, who are more likely to be male. Thus the gender of the employee determines which form of flexible working is likely to be experienced; and these forms contradict each other.

The development of such flexible forms of employment is affected by various factors. The fact that most tourist-related services have to be provided when the customer demands them and this increases the use of temporary, part-time and functionally flexible workers. In many tourist-related services there is an exceptional variety of functions which have to be met – food production, food service, entertainment, accommodation, bars, etc. – and this provides many opportunities for developing task flexibility. The industrial relations climate in these firms needs to be taken into account. Lack of extensive unionisation and of employees' organisations around occupational groups within the industry means there is little formally organised opposition to new working practices. We have already seen that the managerial style is casual and particularistic depending on informal reward systems (Whyte, 1948; Mars and Nicod, 1984).

Crang pursues some of these issues of informality and style in a study of a 'themed' restaurant in Cambridge (1994; see Crang, 1997, more generally). He notes how service encounters possess a rather complex *performative* character. One can think of this kind of workplace as a stage, involving a mix of mental, manual and emotional labour. Staff are chosen because they possess the right sort of cultural capital, they have to be informal, young, friendly, with the right sort of body and skills to produce appropriate emotional performances during the course of each evening. The self is key here since the performances have to be 'authentically' fun-loving, informal and sociable (see The Industrial Society website).

Staff demonstrate various 'social and emotional' skills as they have to adjust their performances through the cultural readings and interactions with a wide variety of customers. In some ways they have to be amateur social scientists, 'reading' each group of diners and predicting the kind of 'experience' they are expecting. The restaurant is described by the staff as a place of emotions, they talk of 'getting in the mood' at the beginning of the evening, allowing the emotions to flow. The staff, and especially the young female waitressing staff, operate of course under the gaze of customers and are expected to perform in accordance with gender specific notions (see Adkins, 1995).

So far, then, there is plenty of evidence to suggest that flexible working practices have for some time been a key feature of tourist-related industries. However, it does not follow that the workforce can be seen as easily divided up into a core and a peripheral labour force, as the flexibility literature hypothesises (see Atkinson, 1984). Guerrier and Lockwood (1989) suggest that two particular groups in the hotel workforce do not conveniently fit into the core-periphery model. First, there are what they call the 'operative core' – staff, receptionists, kitchen staff, waiting staff and so on – who in large hotels are often relatively functionally inflexible rather than multi-skilled as the model would suggest. Second, there is a peripheral group who carry out more or less identical tasks to the employees just identified. But this peripheral group enjoys much less job security and fewer career prospects. Especially in major 'global' cities, hotels and restaurants make great use of mobile, transient staff often recruited from abroad (who may themselves be travelling the world). With such staff demonstrating very high turnover it may be difficult to sustain adequate skill levels and develop appropriate training programmes. Often companies use 'numerical flexibility' instead of developing the multiple skills of their core staff.

Indeed more generally there appears to be a paucity of career paths in tourist-related services except for those in managerial and chef positions. Metcalf summarises the situation for many workers in the hospitality industry: 'Very few career jobs were identified … Most jobs were characterised by young recruits, no promotion and high turnover. And leavers went into a variety of unskilled jobs …' (1988: 89).

There are relatively few exceptions to this in the industry, an interesting one in the north of England being Bettys and Taylors tearooms found in four north Yorkshire towns (see Burton, 1989). Training is taken very seriously with each trainee allocated to a trainer for a month before working on their own. Also the company has deliberately not expanded beyond the control exercised by the family. There is a customer panel of food samplers to report back on shortcomings and there are good career prospects. This relatively unusual example, ranked in 2000 as the twelfth best employer to work for within the UK, proves by exception the general rule that tourist-related services are amongst the most difficult of 'products' to produce over time (Bettys and Taylors web site). This is particularly so because of the changing cultural expectations about the tourist experience and hence about the delivery of such services.

5

Cultural Changes and the Restructuring of Tourism

Introduction

I have so far conceptualised the tourist gaze as being relatively distinct from other social activities and occurring at particular places for specific periods of time. This viewpoint was reinforced by the analysis in Chapters 3 and 4 of some salient characteristics of the tourist industry. Although it is difficult to demarcate just what is and what is not part of that industry, I presumed a reasonably tight specification. In Chapter 4, for example, I discussed the specific character of service delivery in the so-called hospitality industry.

But changes in the nature of western societies in the past two or three decades have seriously undermined such a precise notion. I argue the following. There has been a reversal of the long-term process of structural differentiation by which relatively distinct social institutions had come to specialise in particular tasks or functions. Part of this reversal is that 'culture' has come to occupy a more central position in the organisation of present-day societies, whose contemporary culture can be at least in part characterised as 'postmodern'. Postmodernism involves a dissolving of the boundaries, not only between high and low cultures, but also between different cultural forms, such as tourism, art, education, photography, television, music, sport, shopping and architecture. In addition, the era of mass communications has transformed the tourist gaze and many of the features of postmodernism have already been partly prefigured in existing tourist practices. What I have termed the 'tourist gaze' is increasingly bound up with, and is partly indistinguishable from, all sorts of other social and cultural practices. This has the effect, as 'tourism' *per se* declines in specificity, of universalising the tourist gaze – people are much of the time 'tourists' whether they like it or not. The tourist gaze is intrinsically part of contemporary experience, of postmodernism, but the tourist practices to which it gives rise are experiencing rapid and significant change. Such change cannot be separated from these more wide-ranging structural and cultural developments within contemporary societies.

In earlier chapters I referred to certain claims that I develop in the latter half of the book. In Chapter 1 it was shown that daydreaming is important in most forms of consumption, and it is obviously central to much holiday-making. But daydreaming is not a purely individual activity; it is socially organised, particularly through television, advertising, literature, cinema, photography and so on.

The idea of the 'post-tourist' was introduced, again pointing out how tourist patterns are not themselves unchanging. In particular, it suggests that tourism might be viewed by some at least as a 'game' and that there really are no simply 'authentic' tourist experiences. In Chapter 2 the development of mass tourism in Britain was analysed, in particular the development of the English seaside resort and the emergent resort hierarchy. Explanations for the demise of such resorts, partly because of the changing powers of different social classes, will be considered later in this chapter.

In Chapter 3 the romantic and the collective tourist gazes were distinguished and some of the social and environmental effects of each were considered. In this chapter it will be suggested that the former has become considerably more significant and is part of the mechanism by which contemporary tourism has been 'globalised' (see Chapter 8). It will also be suggested that objects of the tourist gaze can effectively be classified in terms of three key dichotomies, of which the romantic/collective is one (others are authentic/inauthentic and historical/modern). In Chapter 4 particular attention was directed to the social or sociological character of the delivery of services, that customers increasingly expect and demand a particular social experience. This issue will be explored in a number of ways, particularly through considering the concept of the 'themed' environment (Chapter 7).

The next section begins this complex argument by briefly analysing some salient features of postmodernism.

Postmodernism

In some ways it is difficult to address the topic of postmodernism at all. It seems as though the signifier 'postmodern' is free-floating, having few connections with anything real, no shared meaning of any sort. In this section, however, I shall endeavour to outline a particular set of cultural developments, what one might call a new 'cultural paradigm', and to elaborate some of the sociological conditions that have given rise to it. I suggest that the term 'postmodernism' is appropriately applied to this paradigm.

Thinking of postmodernism in this way makes it clear that it is not a term which refers either to the whole of society (different therefore in scope from, say, 'post-industrial society'); or to one particular sphere of activity (such as architecture). It refers to a system of signs or symbols, which is specific in both time and space. Such a system can be characterised in terms of a specific regime of signification in which particular cultural objects are produced, circulated and received. Such objects involve a particular set of relations between the signifier, the signified and the referent (see Lash, 1990: ch. 1).

Although I maintain that postmodernism refers to the cultural sphere, its relationship to that sphere is somewhat idiosyncratic. As Lash expresses it, postmodernism 'is a regime of signification whose fundamental structuring trait is "de-differentiation"' (1990: 11). This argument can be elucidated in terms similar to those used in much conventional sociology. Modernism involves 'structural differentiation', the separate development of a number of institutional and normative spheres, of the economy, the family, the state, science, morality, and an aesthetic realm. Each of these becomes subject to what Weber called *Eigengesetzlichkeit*, or self-legislation (see Lash, 1990: 8–9). Each sphere develops its own conventions and mode of valuation. Value within the cultural spheres is dependent upon how well a cultural object measures up to the norms appropriate to that sphere. I term this 'horizontal differentiation'.

But a further aspect needs to be considered, what I term 'vertical differentiation'. As each sphere becomes separated off horizontally, so immensely important vertical differentiations develop. Within the cultural sphere this consists of a number of distinctions: between culture and life, between high and low culture, between scholarly or auratic art and popular pleasures, and between elite and mass forms of consumption. Within building design there is the distinction between 'architecture' (which obviously takes many different styles) and various vernacular forms of building. There is also the important distinction between high-level science and the typical layperson's understanding of physical processes (as in the area of medical knowledge).

Modernism, then, is to be understood as a process of differentiation, especially as we have seen here, of the differentiation between the various cultural spheres both horizontally and vertically. Postmodernism, by contrast, involves de-differentiation (Lash, 1990: ch. 1). There are a number of developments.

There is a breakdown in the distinctiveness of each of these spheres of social activities, especially the cultural. Each implodes into the other, and most involve visual spectacle and play. This is seen most clearly in so-called multi-media events but much cultural production, especially via the central role of TV, is difficult to categorise and place within any particular sphere.

Further, such cultural spheres are no longer auratic, in Benjamin's terms (see Benjamin, 1973; Lash and Urry, 1987: ch. 9). To say that a cultural phenomenon had aura was to say that it was radically separated from the social, it proclaimed its own originality, uniqueness and singularity, and that it was based in a discourse of formal organic unity and artistic creativity. Postmodernist culture by contrast is anti-auratic. Such forms do not proclaim their uniqueness but are mechanically and electronically reproduced. There is a denial of the separation of the aesthetic from the social and of the contention that art is of a different order from life. The value placed on the unity of the artistic work is challenged through an emphasis on pastiche, collage, allegory and so on. Postmodern cultural forms are not consumed in a state of contemplation (as at the classical concert) but of distraction. Postmodern culture affects the audience via its immediate impact, through what it does for one, through regimes of pleasure, and not through the formal properties of the aesthetic material. And this serves to undermine any strong distinction between a high culture, enjoyed by an elite knowledgeable about the aesthetics of a given sphere (painting, music, literature), and the popular or low culture of the masses. Postmodernism is anti-hierarchical, opposed to such vertical differentiations.

There is a de-differentiation of the 'cultural economy'. One aspect of this is the breakdown of some at least of the differences between the cultural object and the audience so that there is an active encouragement of audience participation. Examples include the 'living theatre' and TV game shows or confessional TV where anyone can be famous for fifteen minutes. Another aspect is the dissolving of the boundaries between what is artistic production and what is commercial. Developments here include the growth of 'free' artistic pop videos to sell records, of pop songs appearing first within advertisements, of major artistic talents employed within the production of adverts, and the use of 'art' to sell products via sponsorship. Commerce and culture are indissolubly intertwined in the postmodern.

Postmodernism also problematises the distinction between 'representations' and 'reality'. Signification is increasingly figural or visual and so there is a closer, more intimate, relationship between the representation and the reality than where the signification takes place through words or music (without film, TV, video, pop video and so on). Further, an increasing proportion of the referents of signification, the 'reality', are themselves representations. Or as Baudrillard famously argues, what we increasingly consume are signs or representations (1983, 1985). Social identities are constructed through the exchange of sign-values. But these are accepted in a spirit of spectacle. People know that the media, for example, are a simulation, and they in turn simulate the media. This world of sign and spectacle is one in which there is no real originality, only what Eco terms 'travels in hyperreality' (1986). Everything is a copy, or a text upon a text, where what is fake can often seem more real than the real. This is a depthless world or a 'new flimsiness of reality' (Lash, 1990: 15). Lash summarises this argument: *'modernism conceives of representations as being problematic whereas postmodernism problematises reality'* (1990: 13).

Many writers have recently demonstrated that these processes of de-differentiation have begun to characterise many aspects of contemporary culture, although by no means all (see Hebdige, 1986–7, 1988; Foster, 1985b; Lash, 1990; Kroker and Cook, 1986; Harvey 1989). Postmodernism should be thought of as a cultural paradigm or ideal type. To do so is to recognise that there are *other* important cultural elements which will be present in a given society (premodern, realist, modernist, etc.); that many cultural phenomena embody elements of different ideal types; and that different societies are more *or* less postmodern (US more so than Sweden) and indeed that some regions or cities are more postmodern than other places within the same society (Los Angeles more so than New England).

Much of the rest of this book consists of an examination of the relationship between such postmodern developments and a wide variety of contemporary tourist practices. Before this it should be noted that many tourist practices, even in the past, prefigure some of the postmodern characteristics just described (see MacCannell, 1999, on tourism and postmodernism).

Tourism has always involved spectacle. Resorts in England have, for example, competed with each other to provide visitors with the grandest ballroom, the longest pier, the highest tower, the most modern amusement park, the most stylish holiday camp, the most spectacular illuminations, the most beautiful gardens, the most elegant promenade, and so on. Because of the importance of the visual, of the gaze, tourism has always been concerned with spectacle and with cultural practices which partly implode into each other. Much tourist activity has been thoroughly anti-auratic. It has been based on mechanical and electronic reproduction (beginning with 'What the butler saw' machines, through spectacular illuminations, to *son et lumière* and laser shows); it has been thoroughly based on popular pleasures, on an anti-elitism with little separation of art from social life; it has typically involved not contemplation but high levels of audience participation; and there has been much emphasis on pastiche, or what others might call kitsch (as in the famous Hawaiian ballroom at Maplin's holiday camp on the BBC TV programme *Hi-de-Hi!*).

What I have just been describing are some of the characteristics of what, in Chapter 3, I termed the collective tourist gaze. But in that chapter I also discussed the romantic gaze, which is much more obviously auratic, concerned with the more elitist – and solitary – appreciation of magnificent scenery, an appreciation which requires considerable cultural capital especially if particular physical objects signify specific literary texts (as with the England Lakeland poets, for example). However, even within the romantic gaze there have been elements that we now can classify as postmodern. Much of what is appreciated is not directly experienced reality itself but representations, particularly through the medium of photography (see Taylor's exploration of this in *A Dream of England*: 1994). What people 'gaze upon' are ideal representations of the view in question that they internalise from postcards and guidebooks (and TV programmes and the internet). And even when they cannot in fact 'see' the natural wonder in question they can still sense it, see it in their mind. And even when the object fails to live up to its representation it is the latter which will stay in people's minds, as what they have really 'seen' (see Crawshaw and Urry, 1997, for some empirical research on this).

I have suggested that there is a relatively new cultural paradigm, the postmodern; that this is particularly to be understood in terms of the processes of de-differentiation; but that a number of tourist practices have historically prefigured this paradigm. Tourism is prefiguratively postmodern because of its particular combination of the visual, the aesthetic, the commercial and the popular.

Yet there is an important sense in which much tourism has also been minimally modernist. This sense is revealed through the term 'mass tourism' which is how much tourist activity has been structured since the late nineteenth century. We noted in Chapter 2 certain aspects of this attempt to treat people in the same manner and not to set up invidious differentiations between people who were consumers of the same holiday camp or hotel or restaurant.

Central to the modern is the view of the public as a homogeneous mass, that there is a realm of correct values which will serve to unify people. I consider this in more detail later, in the context of some aspects of architectural change. But within tourism, the idea of the modern is reflected in the attempt to treat people *within a socially differentiated site* as similar to each other with common tastes and characteristics, albeit determined by the providers of the service in question. In the next section I consider how one of the key characteristics of postmodernism is people's refusal to accept treatment as part of an undifferentiated mass. Part of postmodernism's hostility to authority is the opposition felt by many people to being seen as part of a mass. Rather, people appear to want to be treated in a much more differentiated manner and this has given rise to so-called lifestyle research on the part of the advertising industry (see Poon, 1993).

the importance of out of work experience

I have so far talked of different cultural paradigms without regard to the social forces that underlie them. But the development of postmodernism should be related to an analysis of the changing powers of different social classes. The weakened collective powers of the working class and the heightened powers of the service and other middle classes have generated a widespread audience for postmodern cultural forms and particularly for what some have termed 'post-tourism'.

My argument here derives from Bourdieu's *Distinction* (1984). A number of features of this are relevant especially to the analysis of the impact of the cultural practices of one class upon another. Bourdieu brings out that the powers of different social classes (and by implication other social agents) are as much symbolic as economic or political. Such symbolic goods are subject to a distinct economy, a 'cultural economy', characterised by competition, monopolisation, inflation, and different forms of capital, including especially cultural capital. Different social classes are engaged in a series of struggles with each other, to increase the volume of capital they possess vis-à-vis other classes, and to increase the valuation placed on the particular forms of capital they happen to possess. Each social class possesses a habitus, the system of classification which operates below the level of individual consciousness and which is inscribed within people's orienting practices, bodily dispositions and tastes and distastes. Classes in competition with each other attempt to impose their own system of classification upon other classes and to exert dominance. In such struggles a central role is played by cultural institutions especially education and intellectuals. The cultural realm has its own logic, currency and rate of convertibility into economic capital. Cultural capital is not just a matter of abstract theoretical knowledge but the symbolic competence necessary to appreciate works of 'art' or 'anti-art' or of 'place'. Differential access to the means of arts consumption is thus crucial to the reproduction of class and hence to the processes of class and broader social conflict. This differential cultural consumption both results from the class system and is a mechanism by which such classes, and other social forces, seek to establish dominance within a society (see Bourdieu, 1984; Lash and Urry, 1987: ch. 9; Featherstone, 1987; Lash, 1990).

inequality

I now relate this thesis to the understanding of the development of post-modernism through the following argument. First, I show that there have been changes in the structuring of contemporary societies which have produced a substantial increase in the size of the service class and more generally in what Bourdieu terms the 'new petty bourgeoisie'. Second, I note that such classes are stronger on cultural than on economic capital and they provide much of the mass audience for ever-new cultural phenomena, counterposed to the taste of more traditional bourgeois and intellectual classes. Third, I show that such classes possess a habitus which is relatively decentred, that is, with a weak classificatory structure and fairly unclear boundaries between it and other social classes (weak on both grid and group). And finally, it is shown that these classes employ their relatively high levels of cultural capital to proclaim the tastelessness of much of both bourgeois and working-class culture. The former is criticised for 'elitism' (that is, insufficiently de-differentiated); the latter for coarseness or lack of subtlety (that is, too close to nature, with insufficient distance or parody). Bourdieu summarises the attitude to the latter:

> The denial of lower, coarse, vulgar, venal, servile – in a word, natural – enjoyment, which constitutes the sacred sphere of culture, implies an affirmation of the superiority of those who can be satisfied with the sublimated, refined, disinterested, gratuitous, distinguished pleasures forever closed to the profane. That is why art and cultural consumption are predisposed, consciously and deliberately or not, to fulfil a social function of legitimating social differences. (1984: 7)

It is clear that in western societies there is both a major service class and, more generally, a substantial white-collar or middle class. In Britain in 1991, for example, 26.3 per cent of men and 12.6 per cent of women in employment were in professional and managerial posts ('socioeconomic groups' 1–4, 13). A further 19.2 per cent of men and a staggering 54.5 per cent of women held lower-level white-collar/clerical posts ('socioeconomic groups' 5, 6; Abercrombie, Warde et al., 2000: 170).

The service class consists of that set of places within the social division of labour whose occupants do not own capital or land to any substantial degree; are located within a set of interlocking social institutions which collectively 'service' capital; enjoy superior work and market situations generally resulting from the existence of well-defined careers, either within or between organisations; and have their entry regulated by the differential possession of educational credentials. These serve to demarcate the service class from more general white-collar workers and generate distinctions of cultural capital and taste (see Butler and Savage, 1995).

Furthermore, Pfeil argues that: 'postmodernism is pre-eminently the "expressive form" of the social and material life-experience of my own generation and class, respectively designated as the "baby boom" and the "professional-managerial class" or PMC' (1985: 264; Ehrenreich, 1989; Savage, Barlow, Dickens, Fielding, 1992).

The service class is discussed by Bourdieu but in somewhat different terms. In talking of 'intellectuals' he contrasts their preference for 'aesthetic-asceticism' with a bourgeois preference for sumptuous interiors. This would be reflected in the liking for, say, Ikea-style interiors amongst 'intellectuals'. Of their leisure patterns Bourdieu writes: 'the most ascetic form of the aesthetic disposition and the culturally most legitimate and economically cheapest practices, e.g., museum-going, or, in sport, mountain-climbing or walking, are likely to occur particularly frequently among the fractions (relatively) poorest in economic capital' (1984: 267). Interestingly, Bourdieu talks of the symbolic subversion by intellectuals of the rituals of the bourgeois order through demonstrating 'ostentatious poverty'. This is reflected in the tendency to dress casually even when at work, to favour bare wood interiors, and activities like mountaineering, hiking and walking, which represent the intellectual's taste for 'natural, wild nature' (1984: 220). It is the intellectuals who best exemplify the 'romantic gaze'. The bourgeois by contrast is said to prefer 'organized, signposted cultivated nature' (Bourdieu 1984: 220; Savage, Barlow, Dickens, Fielding, 1992; see Munt, 1994, on the tourism implications).

What I have referred to as the service class and other white-collar workers would also include two newly emerging groups discussed by Bourdieu who are major consumers of the postmodern: the 'new bourgeoisie', who possess considerable amounts of both cultural and economic capital; and the 'new petit bourgeois' of occupations involving presentation and representation. Much of the work of both categories is symbolic – in the media, advertising, design – acting as cultural intermediaries. Such groups have a very strong commitment to fashion, that is, to the rapid and playful transformations of style (see Featherstone, 1987: 27; Lash and Urry, 1994). Moreover, such groups are often downwardly mobile in terms of social origins and are not necessarily accepted by the intellectuals and the cultural-capital establishment. So there is here a challenge to established culture, to high culture, while at the same time the emergence of celebrity intellectuals has demystified traditional sources of cultural capital. These groups involved in symbolic work construct the conditions for the emergence of the post-modern: 'This interchange, the alertness of intellectuals to new popular styles and the marketability of "the new", creates conditions in which styles travel faster, both from the avant-garde to the popular, the popular to the avant-garde, and the popular to the jet-set' (Featherstone 1987: 27; Savage, Barlow, Dickens, Fielding, 1992).

As a result there comes to be generated a kind of stylistic melting-pot, of the old and the new, of the nostalgic and the futuristic, of the 'natural' and the 'artificial', of the youthful and the mature, of high culture and of low, and of modernism and the postmodern. Martin summarises how the growth of these middle-class groups has upset pre-existing cultural patterns: 'The contemporary culture market muddles together the elite and the vulgar, yesterday's shock and today's joke in one gloriously trivial *bricolage*. Style is everything and anything can become style' (1982: 236–7).

Furthermore, Bourdieu argues, these groups also have a quite different approach to pleasure. The old petit bourgeoisie bases its life on a morality of duty, with 'a fear of pleasure ... a relation to the body made up of "reserve", "modesty" and "restraint", and associates every satisfaction of the

81

forbidden impulses with guilt' (Bourdieu, 1984: 367). By contrast this new middle-class group:

> urges a morality of pleasure as a duty. This doctrine makes it a failure, a threat to self-esteem, not to 'have fun' ... Pleasure is not only permitted but demanded, on ethical as much as on scientific grounds. The fear of not getting enough pleasure ... is combined with the search for self-expression and 'bodily expression' and for communication with others. (1984: 367)

This last argument needs some clarification. Capitalist societies have always been characterised by a strong emphasis upon consumption based upon a romantic ethic. Campbell argues that romanticism has provided that philosophy of 'recreation' necessary for a dynamic consumerism in which the search for pleasure is viewed as desirable in and of itself (1987: 201). Romanticism has produced the widespread taste for novelty which has ensured the ethical support for restless and continuously changing patterns of consumption. But Campbell's argument too does not show how important changes may be taking place in the romantic ethic and modern consumerism, or that these could be linked to the changing power and character of different social forces.

In particular here I suggest that a number of middle-class groupings are indeed in a transformed situation and are having significant effects upon the wider society. These groups demonstrate the following: the central significance of symbolic work; the enormous increase in the importance of the media and of their contemporary role in structuring fashion and taste; the greater freedom and incentive of such groups to devise ever-new cultural patterns; the heightened prestige that accrues for the middle classes not from respectability but from fashionability; the greater significance of cultural capital to such groups and the continuous need to augment it; and a reduced functional need to maintain their economic capital intact (Warde, 1988; Lash and Urry, 1994). The way that the architectural design of gentrified areas reflects the cultural capital of such a class can be seen in Vancouver's 'postmodern landscape of gentrification' (Mills, 1988).

I now analyse the habitus of the service class and see how and in what ways a weak grid and group have provided the basis for postmodernism. The implications for contemporary tourism will be considered in the next section.

The media, and especially TV, have a significant impact here (see Meyrowitz, 1985; Lash and Urry, 1987: ch. 9). The collective identities of different social classes (and other social forces) are structured through 'grid', the basic system of classification, and 'group', the boundaries that distinguish what is internal from what is external. Such collective identities depend upon particular systems of information specific to a given social group. However, the growth of the media has minimised the importance of such separate and distinct systems of information. This is because individuals from all social groupings are exposed to more generally available systems of information, and because each grouping can now see representations of the private spaces of other social groupings. The media have provided an enormously increased circulation of the representations of other people's lives, including those of elite groups and especiallyof the royal family and of other 'celebrities' (see Richards, Wilson, Woodhead, 1999, on 'Saint Diana'). This institutionalised voyeurism in turn enables people to adopt the styles of other groups, to transgress boundaries between different social groupings as supposedly embodying particular values such as high culture, low culture, artistic, tasteful, tasteless. The media have also undermined what is to be thought of as properly backstage, as what should be kept private and what can be made public (especially with the massive growth of confessional TV).

Turning specifically to the middle classes, Bourdieu argues that the new petit bourgeoisie is low on both grid and group. Such people live for the moment 'untrammelled by constraints and brakes imposed by collective memories and expectations' (Bourdieu, 1984: 317). Such people are weak on group in that many feel guilt about being middle class:

> they see themselves as unclassifiable, 'excluded' ... anything rather than categorized, assigned to a class, a determinate place in social space ... freed from the temporal structures imposed by domestic units, with their own life-cycle, their long-term planning, sometimes over several generations, and their collective defences against the impact of the market. (Bourdieu, 1984: 370–1)

Martin provides a similar analysis, describing a destructured habitus amongst middle-class youth, especially developing from the 1960s onwards (1982). This she attributes to an immensely extended liminal zone derived from the decline in parental authority and the extension of the period that one is neither child nor adult. She argues that a particularly extended period of liminality develops in the new middle class in that they have a destructured habitus not only in youth but in many occupations as well, especially the media.

A number of major cultural critics have also developed this argument. Jameson analyses the growth of pastiche rather than parody (1985). While the latter stands in a relationship to real historical time, the former does not. There is the disappearance of the original real historical referent and of an appreciation of how the past has led to the present. Jameson talks of how we seek the past instead through 'our own pop images and stereotypes about the past which remain forever out of reach' (1985: 118). Pastiche, for Jameson, fragments time into a series of 'perpetual presents' (1985: 118). People's lives in what Edgar (1987) terms 'the new era of pastiche and nostalgia' are experienced as a succession of discontinuous events. Although the individual blocks may be calculated and rational, the overall pattern is likely to be irrational. Spreading out from parts of the middle class is a 'calculating hedonism' (see Featherstone, 1987).

Cultural conservatives such as Lasch and Bell have developed a similar argument about time (Lasch, 1980; Bell, 1976). They maintain that our sense of history has been lost. As Frampton argues: 'We live in a paradoxical moment when, while we are perhaps more obsessed with history than ever before, we have, simultaneously, the feeling that a certain historical trajectory, or even for some, history itself, is coming to an end' (1988: 51).

This loss of historical sense has also been associated with a characteristic of the media: that we increasingly live in a three-minute culture. It is *what are the symbols and identities being immediately consumed?*

suggested that TV viewers keep switching from channel to channel unable to concentrate on any topic or theme for longer than a few minutes. Cultural conservatives argue that people no longer live their lives through identities imbued with the consciousness that they are the children of their parents who were in turn children of their parents, and so on. Even within generations the fascination with immediate consumption (purchased through immediate credit rather than saving) means that lifelong projects like marriage become instead a succession of marriages, 'serial monogamy' or affairs. Lawson and Samson (1988), for example, show that there has been a quite marked increase in Britain in the preparedness of younger women in particular to undertake sexual relationships outside marriage (Lawson and Samson, 1988: 432). There has been a similar but not quite so steep a decline in the mean period in the case of men.

Lawson and Samson suggest that two factors have contributed to this: the return of many married women into paid, albeit intermittent, employment outside the home; and the widespread influence of the myth of self-actualisation, or the 'myth of me'. Some support for the significance of the second factor can be found in Ehrenreich's analysis of the flight from commitment of American males to marriage and responsibility (1983). She details a series of transformations which have generated a 'moral climate that endorsed irresponsibility, self-indulgence and an isolationist detachment from the claims of others – and endorsed these as middle class virtues and even as signs of health' (1983: 169). The middle-class components of this revolt against marital commitment which began in the USA in the 1950s were the establishment of *Playboy*, the Beat generation, the medical 'discovery' of stress, the new psychology of growth and self-actualisation, the counter-cultural critique of traditional masculinity, and the growth of a men's movement.

In the next section I return to tourism (after this rather long 'break') and show how these various cultural changes and the development of the service and middle classes have had profound effects on existing centres of tourism, especially the English seaside resort. I shall also demonstrate how postmodernism is ushering in some major new conceptions of what it is to be a contemporary tourist.

Postmodernism and Post-tourism

For a number of reasons the British seaside resort has declined in popularity: in particular we saw that such resorts were no longer 'extraordinary'; their once distinctive features had become commonplace. Some, such as sand and sea, could be found in very many places, especially abroad; some, such as accommodation, had become available in many towns and cities within Britain; and some, such as leisure facilities, had developed almost everywhere and especially away from the seaside. Very many places have generated different kinds of specialist service provision which compete with existing resorts. Almost everywhere has become a centre of 'spectacle and display', and as a result resorts now have relatively little to distinguish themselves from anywhere else (see Zukin, 1991). Indeed to the extent to which their own provision is now often somewhat derelict, the resorts have suffered further difficulties. In Chapter 6 I discuss aspects of the current fascination with 'history and heritage' and show how this also serves to favour certain kinds of towns and cities – but infrequently resorts.

Here I shall link some of the arguments of the previous discussion with current developments in tourism. Indeed the way in which all sorts of places have become centres of spectacle and display and the nostalgic attraction of 'heritage' can both be seen as elements of the postmodern. It is only through the analysis of such wider cultural changes that specific tourist developments can be properly understood. I begin with some comments on the tastes of the service class and the impact of these on seaside resorts.

Such tastes involve the prioritisation of 'culture' over a particular construction of 'nature' or 'natural desires'. Bourdieu expresses this well: 'The nature against which culture is here constructed is nothing other than what is "popular", "low", "vulgar", "common" ... a "social promotion" experienced as an ontological promotion, a process of "civilization" ... a leap from nature to culture, from the animal to the human' (1984: 251).

The typical resort would thus seem the embodiment of a particular construction of nature – as uncivilised, tasteless, animalistic, to be counterposed to the civilisation of culture. Such an attitude can, interestingly, be seen even amongst socialist representatives of the service class. George Orwell imagined a modern design for Coleridge's 'Kubla Khan' as consisting of a holiday camp where air-conditioned caverns were transformed into a series of tea-grottoes in Moorish, Caucasian and Hawaiian styles. The sacred river would be turned into an artificially warmed bathing pool and muzak would be playing in the background 'to prevent the onset of that dreaded thing – thought' (quoted in Hebdige, 1988: 51). Likewise, Richard Hoggart set one of his parodies of cheap romantic fiction in what he called the Kosy Holiday Camp where there was a 'shiny barbarism', a 'spiritual dry-rot' and a 'Candy Floss World' (Hebdige, 1988: 52). Having good taste would involve looking down on such places and only passing through, to view them as a voyeur would (as an Orwell or a Hoggart), never to stay. The only permitted exception might be to appropriate elements from such resorts, such as McGill's postcards, in a postmodern cultural pastiche. The uncivilised resorts are not to be taken seriously, but can perhaps be played at or with.

Such resorts have become increasingly aware that they do not appeal to those elements in Britain who have become influenced by these tastes of the service and middle class. In Morecambe, for example, there was a prolonged debate in the 1980s on whether it should continue to host the Miss Great Britain contest. A particular representation of women as 'cultureless' sex objects (women as 'nature') has increasingly come to be viewed as in bad taste and inappropriate to a civilised resort seeking to appeal to more than the traditional clientele.

At the same time an alternative construction of nature is also part of the service class habitus. There is a pronounced cultural emphasis on certain aspects of the natural. When discussing Bourdieu it was argued that intellectuals subvert the bourgeois order through minimal luxury, functionalism and an ascetic aesthetics (1984: 287). This pattern is reflected in an extraordinary range of contemporary cultural symbols and practices: health foods, real ale, real bread, vegetarianism, nouvelle cuisine, traditional, non-western science and medicine, natural childbirth, wool, lace and cotton rather 'man-made' fibres, antiques rather than 'man-made' reproductions, restored houses/ warehouses, jogging, swimming, cycling, mountaineering, and fell-walking rather than organised, contrived leisure. The middle-class ambivalence to the 'natural' is well captured in Ross' account of a commitment both to natural childbirth and to going to classes to learn how to give birth naturally (1989: 13; Campbell, 1989, on how fishing has been affected by the naturalistic myth of the 'sportsman'; Macnaghten and Urry, 2000b).

A reflection of this attraction of the real or natural in tourism has been the 'Campaign for Real Holidays' conducted in one of the key newspapers of the British service class, the *Independent*. This campaign resulted in the novel travel guide, *The Independent Guide to Real Holidays Abroad*. (Barrett, 1989a). The author states that it is increasingly difficult to have a 'real holiday'. This is because the 'rise and rise of the package holiday has imposed on travel the same problems that mass production has inflicted on beer, bread, ice cream and many other things' (Barrett, 1989a: 1). A real holiday has two main characteristics. First, it involves visiting somewhere well away from where the mass of the population will be visiting; examples include the Maldives, Syria, or Bolivia. Real holidays thus involve the romantic tourist gaze, which has the effect of incorporating almost everywhere in the world as part of the 'pleasure periphery'. Second, the real holiday-maker will use small specialist agents/operators to get to their destination. The *Guide* bemoaned the fact that three-quarters of all foreign holidays taken by Britons are sold by five major companies. The *Guide* favours instead the development of smaller companies who have come to specialise in particular segments of the tourism market, or perhaps one should say the 'traveller market'. It talks of the development of the 'delicatessen' travel agent – these are specialist agencies that promote particular operators to 'a discriminating, independent-minded clientele' (Barrett, 1989a: 4; 1989b).

The existing major companies have not been slow in recognising the importance of this trend to real holidays, involving the culture of 'travel' rather than 'tourism', the romantic rather than the collective gaze, and small niche suppliers rather than mass production/consumption operators. Thomas Cook tells us that this:

> is not a trip for the tourist but a voyage of discovery for the traveller ... there is no packaging ... Thomas Cook treats you not just as an individual but as a VIP ... Thomas Cook provides a service that is both personal and global. This is truly travel à la carte. *(Thomas Cook Escorted Journeys*, Jan. 1989–Dec. 1989)

Accompanying the description of each holiday (travel experience?) is a reading list of useful books on the particular country. A number of emphases should be noted here: on travel rather than tourism, on individual choice, on avoiding the package holiday-maker, on the need to be an educated traveller, and on a global operation that permits individual care and attention – undoubtedly one kind of postmodern experience.

The service class preference for the 'real' or the 'natural' can also be seen in the increasing attraction of both visiting the countryside and protecting it. This is of course not new; Thomas, for example, points out that:

> Whether or not the preoccupation with nature and rural life is in reality pecu-
> liarly English, it is certainly something which the English townsman [sic] has for
> a long time liked to think of as such; and much of the country's literature has
> displayed a profoundly anti-urban bias. (1973: 14; see Williams, 1973, as well as
> Wiener, 1981, on the nineteenth-century antipathy to the urban; Macnaghten
> and Urry, 1998)

It should be noted that this image of the English countryside, 'a bucolic vision of an ordered, comforting, peaceful and, above all, deferential past' is a fundamentally constructed one, comprised of elements that never existed together historically (Thrift, 1989: 26). The countryside today is even less like 'ye Olde English village', even less like Gray's description of Grasmere in the Lake District: 'This little unsuspected paradise, where all is peace, rusticity and happy poverty' (especially given the countryside's regular harbouring of diseased animals).

But at the moment when rural life is being fundamentally transformed particularly because of changes taking place in modern agriculture, the image of the countryside is a very attractive object of the tourist gaze (see Newby, 1982; Shoard, 1987). One reflection of this increased attractiveness is the enormous rise in membership of many organisations concerned with simultaneously protecting the countryside and facilitating access to it. By mid-1996 the membership of the National Trust was 2.4 million, the RSPB 925,000, and Friends of the Earth 250,000 (Macnaghten and Urry, 1998: 29). Connected with this has been the proliferation of new magazines that help to construct ever more redolent signs of the fast-disappearing country-side. At least a dozen 'new traditionalist' magazines appeared in the 1980s, including *Country Homes and Interiors*, *Country Living*, *Country Homes* (Thrift, 1989: 28).

Thrift argues that it is the service class which 'seems to be the social group that has taken the countryside and heritage traditions most to heart' (1989: 31). This class has been leading the push to move into the countryside and indeed historically led the campaigns to open up the countryside against the landlord class (see Urry, 1995b, on this class struggle). Thrift talks of the 'service-class character of places replete with manicured countryside' (1989: 34; Cloke, Phillips, Thrift, 1995; Urry, 1995b). This is having a particular effect upon the market for country houses which has been booming, particu-larly around London. It has also led to the gentrification of run-down rural property as well as the building of new estates in vernacular or rustic style, such estates being usually described as 'villages' (see Cloke, Phillips, Thrift, 1995) This trend will continue as many other people, following the example of the service class, seek to realise the 'village in their mind', to develop place-based consumption (Pahl, 1965; see Urry, 1995b). Furthermore, the service class is more likely to visit the countryside. Those with professional-managerial jobs are twice as likely as those with manual jobs to visit, and they are more likely to be frequent visitors (Urry, 1995b: 211–2). However, differences can be identified between those more likely to work in the public sector who engage in 'natural' pursuits in the countryside such as walking, climbing, camping and so on; as opposed to those private sector managers who engage in country pursuits such as shooting, fishing, sailing, or golf (Urry, 1995b: 212–3; Savage, Barlow, Dickens, Fielding, 1992).

On the face of it this attraction of the countryside seems to have little to do with postmodernism; indeed it looks like its very antithesis. But I suggest here that there is indeed a relationship, albeit complex, between post-modernism and the current obsession with the countryside.

The attractions of the countryside derive in part from the disillusionment with elements of the modern, particularly with the attempt to effect wholesale reconstruction of towns and cities in the post-war period. The countryside is *thought* to embody some or all of the following features: a lack of planning and regimentation, a vernacular quaint architecture, winding lanes and a generally labyrinthine road system, and the virtues of tradition and the lack of social intervention. It hardly needs to be said that rural areas, as in Britain, have in fact been subject to a wide range of modernising processes – especially large-scale agriculture (arguably Britain's *most* rationalised industry), considerable attempts at land-use planning and extensive private sector rural development (see Cloke, 1989).

But only certain sorts of countryside are attractive to the prospective visitor, particularly those consistent with the idea of 'landscape'. Cosgrove summarises this conception in England:

> the landscape idea was active within a process of undermining collective appropri-ation of nature for use. It was locked into an individualist way of seeing ... it is a way of seeing which separates subject and object, giving lordship to the eye of a single observer. In this the landscape idea either denies collective experience ... or mystifies it in an appeal to transcendental qualities of a particular area. (1984: 262; generally here, see Schama, 1995)

Such a 'rural landscape' has erased from it, farm machinery, labourers, trac-tors, telegraph wires, dead animals, concrete farm buildings, motorways, derelict land, polluted water, nuclear power stations and diseased animals. What people see is therefore highly selective, and it is the focused gaze that is central to people's appropriation. The countryside is there to be gazed upon, and ideally one should not be gazing upon other people, whether workers or other tourists. Raymond Williams says that: 'a working country is hardly ever a landscape. The very idea of landscape implies separation and observation' (1973: 120; see Heiman, 1989, on the Hudson valley).

The service class is leading the way in sustaining the romantic gaze of the countryside. But it is a gaze which has become more complex and playful, as rural images have become central to mainstream popular culture, particularly advertising:

> From such a post-modern perspective landscape seems less like a palimpsest whose 'real' or 'authentic' meanings can somehow be recovered with the correct techniques, theories or ideologies, than a flickering text ... whose meaning can be created, extended, altered, elaborated and finally obliterated by the touch of a button. (Daniels and Cosgrove, 1988: 8; see Macnaghten and Urry, 1998: ch. 6)

There is an alternative approach to leisure in the countryside, one in which the term 'landscape' is inappropriate (Cosgrove, 1984: 267–8). The inter-war period in Britain saw attempts, especially by the northern urban working class, to gain access to wild upland countryside for walking, rambling and cycling. Central to these campaigns was an element of class struggle, against the landowners who historically restricted access. The most famous access campaign took place at Kinder Scout in the Peak District in 1932. The aim of the organisers such as Tom Stephenson 'were not to *see* land-scape, so much as to experience it physically – to walk it, climb it or cycle through it' (Cosgrove, 1984: 268). Samuel argues that for the young ramblers of the north: 'the countryside was seen as an energizer: their intention was not so much to see the landscape as to experience it, to touch it with all the senses (1998: 146). These new multi-sensuous practices ignored the existing farming activities of the countryside. Rather than being regarded as visual enticements, villages in the inter-war period were 'rural slums, with rising damp, leaky roofs, tiny windows, and squalid interiors' (Samuel, 1998: 146). Those rambling, climbing, cycling, camping and so on mostly ignored the lives and habitats of those living and working in that countryside.

To the extent to which contemporary appropriations of the countryside involve treating it as a spectacle, even a 'theme', this is a postmodern attitude to the countryside, to be contrasted with an approach which emphasises its 'use' or sense of dwelling (Macnaghten and Urry, 1998). In response to the former attitude many of those living in rural areas have developed packaged, themed environments whereby a relatively sanitised representation of rural life is constructed and presented to visitors:

> We seem to find it far easier to schedule areas for preservation as outstanding landscape for those who would passively view their scenery than to delegate authority for their shaping to those who live, work and actively recreate in them ... Such preserved landscapes have in fact become a national commodity, advertised and sold abroad by the travel industry. (Cosgrove, 1984: 269)

The category of tourist is a relatively privileged one in rural areas. To be able to claim such a status it is normally necessary to be white, and to be wealthy enough to own a car and to be able to organise and purchase certain kinds of accommodation (hotel bed, caravan or recognised camp site). It is also necessary, if people are visiting as a group, to use certain kinds of transport, such as coach or train, and not others, such as a convoy of cars or motorbikes, or a hippie convoy of travellers (see Rojek, 1988, on the 'convoy of pollution'). It is also necessary to engage in certain kinds of behaviour deemed appropriate and not others (in Britain this is known as the 'country code': see Countryside Commission, 1988).

A number of different strands in postmodern architecture will be outlined in the next chapter. One is the partially authentic reconstruction of vernacular buildings from the past as a reaction to elements of both the modern and playful postmodern movements in architecture. There is a similar strand in recent appropriations of the countryside, which one can loosely label 'green tourism' (see Jones, A., 1987). What some people appear increasingly to want is an appropriation of the countryside that will benefit rather than harm the area visited. Research conducted in Wales suggests that what many people like is to be able to visit the 'ordinary' relatively well-preserved countryside rather than specific rural attractions apart from nature reserves (Jones, A., 1987: 355). A vital function of green tourism is to ensure the conservation of areas and their associated wildlife for future generations. The development of such a novel tourism stems from a repudiation of aspects of modern life, especially modern forms of transport, energy and industrial and agricultural production. Particular hostility has been shown to the 'modernised' planting of extensive forests of conifers, particularly by the Forestry Commission but also by private landlords. Such forests are thought to have deleterious environmental and social consequences: the loss of a distinctive wildlife including indigenous birds of prey; reduced levels of employment compared with those that would be supported by tourism; and the elimination of the wild, open and 'romantic' moors that are of such appeal. Indeed a greater influence exercised by tourists would probably preserve the open moorlands against modernised planting of more and more rows of conifers (see Shoard, 1987: 223–5; see Macnaghten and Urry, 2000a, on woodland walking).

Thus some important features of rural tourism stem from the broader development of an environmental politics in the past two to three decades and the resistance to widespread attempts to 'modernise' particular areas or localities. The next chapter will show just how significant is this anti-modern resistance to development in both urban and rural contexts (see Lowe and Goyder, 1983 Macnaghten and Urry, 1998).

One element of the postmodern briefly mentioned above is that of playfulness. Feifer has advanced this argument in relation to tourism through the concept of the 'post-tourist' (1985). She highlights three features. The first is that the post-tourist does not have to leave his or her house in order to *see* many of the typical objects of the tourist gaze, with TV, video and the internet, all sorts of places can be gazed upon, compared, contextualised and gazed upon again. It is possible to imagine oneself 'really' there, seeing the sunset, the mountain range or the turquoise-coloured sea. The typical tourist experience is anyway to see *named* scenes through a *frame*, such as the hotel window, the car windscreen or the window of the coach. But this can now be experienced in one's own living room, at the flick of a switch; and it can be repeated time and time again. There is much less of the sense of the authentic, the once-in-a-lifetime gaze, and much more of the endless availability of gazes through a frame at the flick of a switch. The distinctiveness of the 'tourist gaze' is lost as such gazes are irreducibly part of a postmodern popular culture.

Second, the post-tourist is aware of change and delights in the multitude of choice: 'Now he [sic] wants to behold something sacred; now something informative, to broaden him, now something beautiful, to lift him and make him finer; and now something just different, because he's bored' (Feifer, 1985: 269). The post-tourist is freed from the constraints of 'high culture' on the one hand, and the untrammelled pursuit of the 'pleasure principle' on the other. He or she can move easily from one to the other and indeed can gain pleasure from the contrasts between the two. The world is a stage and the post-tourist can delight in the multitude of games to be played. When the miniature replica of the Eiffel Tower is purchased, it can be simultaneously enjoyed as a piece of kitsch, an exercise in geometric formalism and as a socially revealing artefact (see Feifer, 1985: 270). There is no need to make a fetish out of the correct interpretation since the post-tourist can enjoy playing at it being all three.

Third, and most important, the post-tourist knows that he or she is a tourist and that tourism is a series of games with multiple texts and no single, authentic tourist experience. The post-tourist thus knows that they will have to queue time and time again, that there will be hassles over foreign exchange, that the glossy brochure is a piece of pop culture, that the apparently authentic local entertainment is as socially contrived as the ethnic bar, and that the supposedly quaint and traditional fishing village could not survive without the income from tourism. The post-tourist knows that he [sic] is: 'not a time-traveller when he goes somewhere historic; not an instant noble savage when he stays on a tropical beach; not an invisible observer when he visits a native compound. Resolutely 'realistic', he cannot evade his condition of outsider' (Feifer, 1985: 271; see Crick, 1985, for a critique of the thesis that anthropologists manage to get backstage and overcome the position of outsider).

One interesting game played by the tourist is that of 'child'. This is especially clear in guided coach tours. One is told where to go, how long to go for, when one can eat, how long one has to visit the toilet, and so on. The group (or class) are also asked inane questions and much of the discourse consists of setting up imaginary hostilities between people visiting from different places. And yet such tours seem much appreciated even by those who understand that they are 'playing at being a tourist', and one of the games that has to be embraced is that of 'being a child'.

If post-tourism is of contemporary importance it will clearly have important effects on existing tourist practices. The pleasures of tourism stem from complex processes of both production and consumption. I have emphasised the socially constructed character of the tourist gaze, that both production and consumption are socially organised, and that the gaze must be directed to certain objects or features which are extraordinary, which distinguish that site/sight of the gaze from others. Normally there is something about its physical properties which makes it distinct, although these are often both manufactured and have to be learnt. But sometimes it is merely a place's historical or literary associations which make it extraordinary (such as the building in Dallas from which President Kennedy was supposedly shot, or the vicarage in Haworth, Yorkshire, where the Brontës lived).

The development of post-tourism transforms these processes by which the tourist gaze is produced and consumed. Mercer, for instance, notes that popular pleasures 'require a wholehearted and unselfconscious involvement in a cultural event, form or text' (1983: 84). Particularly important in tourist pleasures are those that involve the energetic breaking of the mild taboos that operate on various forms of consumption, such as eating or drinking to excess, spending money recklessly, wearing outrageous clothes, keeping wildly different time patterns, and so on. As Thompson says: 'People are encouraged to spend by this *disorganisation* of the normal, "acceptable" routines of consumption' (1983: 129). But the post-tourist emphasis on playfulness, variety and self-consciousness makes it harder to find simple pleasures in such mild and socially tolerated rule-breaking. The post-tourist is above all self-conscious, 'cool' and role-distanced. Pleasure hence comes to be anticipated and experienced in different ways from before. A number of changes are occurring here.

The universal availability of the predominantly visual media in advanced western societies has resulted in a massive upward shift in the level of what is 'ordinary' and hence what people view as 'extraordinary'. Moreover, to the extent to which it is true that the media have ushered in a 'three-minute' culture, so this is also likely to encourage people to switch forms and sites of pleasures. It is almost certain that people will gain relatively less satisfaction from continuing to do what they, or more particularly their family, have always done. Thus, holidays have become less to do with the reinforcing of collective memories and experiences and more to do with immediate pleasure. As a result people keep demanding new out-of-the-ordinary experiences. Some examples include the Leprosy Museum in Bergen, 'adventure tourism' in New Zealand, the Japanese Death Railway in Burma, the Gestapo headquarters in Berlin, 'boring tours' in Sydney and the fascination with the possibilities of space tourism (with over 20 websites devoted to this; see George Washington University – Space Tourism Initiative). It is an interesting question whether it is in fact possible to construct a postmodern tourist site around absolutely any object. Mercer, though, argues that to experience pleasure in this more distanced, playful way makes all pleasures less satisfying. And in particular it makes it much harder to enjoy 'simple' pleasures such as those once found in seaside resorts.

Conclusion

Another way of expressing the effects of the postmodern is to consider the dissolving of group and grid and the impact this has on seaside resorts, which were based on strong group and grid. On the former the resort was based on a family-regulated holiday for people of roughly the same class and from similar areas. But with the postmodern dissolving of social identity, many of these forms of group identification within space and over time have vanished, and this has reduced the attractiveness of those resorts which were designed to structure the formation of pleasure in particular class-related patterns. There has been a vast growth in the variety of tourist units, many of which are not family households.

Grid too has changed. Such resorts were based on a specific division of pleasure and pain. Pleasure was associated with being away from the place in which one worked and from the boring and monotonous pain of work, especially of industrial production. Now, however, such a division is much less clear-cut. Pleasures can be enjoyed in very many places, not at all concentrated at the seaside. There has been a proliferation of objects on which to gaze, including what we may term the mediatisation of pleasure. What now is tourism and what is more generally culture is much less clear-cut. Pleasures and pain are everywhere, not spatially concentrated within those particular sites enjoyed for particular periods of time (Urry, 1994).

Resorts will have to change quite dramatically if they are going to survive. Advertising by the Isle of Man indicates one possible way of responding (see Urry, 1988). The advert states that 'You'll look forward to going back', to experiencing a seaside holiday as remembered from one's childhood. Time has supposedly stood still in the Isle of Man and the advert plays on our nostalgia for childhood, when pleasures were supposedly experienced more directly and were less contaminated by an apparent playful sophistication. The next chapter considers this issue of nostalgia and history in more detail.

6

Gazing on History

The Heritage Industry

Tourist sites can be classified in terms of three dichotomies: whether they are an object of the romantic or collective tourist gaze; whether they are historical or modern; and whether they are presented as authentic or inauthentic (see Chapter 8). Characterising sites in such terms is obviously not straightforward and the third dichotomy, authentic/inauthentic, raises many well-known difficulties. Nevertheless it is useful to summarise the differences between sites by employing these dichotomies.

For example, the Lake District in the north-west of England can be characterised as predominantly the object of the romantic gaze, it is historical and it is apparently authentic (Urry, 1995a). By contrast, Alton Towers leisure park, again in the north-west, is the object of the collective gaze, it is mainly modern and it is predominantly inauthentic. These are fairly straightforward characterisations. But more complex are places like the refurbished 'colonial' Havana in Cuba (see Figure 6.1), the Wigan Pier Heritage Centre in Lancashire or the restored mills in Lowell, Massachusetts, the first industrial town in the USA. These are all examples of the heritage industry, a development that has generated much debate. Although they are the objects of the collective gaze, it is controversial whether such sites are as 'historical' and 'authentic', as claimed. There is also much debate as to the causes of this contemporary fascination with gazing upon the historical or heritage (see Lowenthal, 1985, ch. 1 on 'nostalgia' as a physical affliction dating from the late seventeenth century).

Some indicators of this phenomenon in Britain include the 500,000 listed buildings, the 17,000 protected monuments and the 5,500 conservation areas. A new museums is said to open every fortnight, there are 78 museums devoted to railways and 180 water- and windmills are open to the public (Samuel, 1994: Part II). Of the 1,750 museums in 1987, half had been started since 1971. There are also many heritage centres, including Ironbridge Gorge near Telford, the Wigan Pier Heritage Centre, Black Country World near Dudley, the Beamish Open Air Museum near Newcastle, and the Jorvik Viking Centre in York. A former director of the Science Museum has said of this growth in heritage that: 'You can't project that sort of rate of growth much further before the whole country becomes one big open air museum, and you just join it as you get off at Heathrow' (quoted in Hewison, 1987: 24).

Some of the most unlikely places have become centres of a heritage-based tourist development. Bradford, which once sent most of its holiday-makers to Morecambe, has now become a major tourist attraction in its own right,

Figure 6.1   *The restoration of 'Colonial' Havana, Cuba*

with the number of visitors increasing from 1.5 million to 5 million in the
early 1990s (Williams, 1998: 186–9). In the Rhondda valley in South Wales
a museum and heritage park have been established in the former Lewis
Merthyr coalmine (Dicks, 2000). Almost everywhere and everything from
the past may be conserved. In Lancashire environmentalists have sought to
preserve the largest slag heap in Britain, which British Coal had wanted to
remove. The broadcaster Michael Wood writes:

> 'Now that the present seems so full of woe ... the profusion and frankness of our
> nostalgia ... suggest not merely a sense of loss ... but a general abdication, an
> actual desertion from the present' (1974: 346).

The seventeenth-century disease of nostalgia seems to have become a contemporary epidemic.

One feature of recent developments has been the increased privatisation
of the heritage/museum industry, with 56 per cent of museums opening in
the 1980s being in the private sector (Hewison, 1987: 1, ch. 4; Thrift, 1989).
Many of these private initiatives have inspired new ways of representing
history, through commodifying the past in novel forms.

Very large numbers of people visit museums and heritage sites, although
visitors have decreased somewhat in the late 1990s (although the number of
sites opening increased). Around 68 million visits a year are made to such
museums and galleries (Department of Culture, Media and Sport website).

In any year about one-third of the population in the UK visits an historical building, one third a historic park or garden, slightly less than one-third a museum, a quarter a cathedral, slightly less than one-quarter an ancient monument, and one-fifth an art gallery. This compares with less than a fifth who visit a football match or one-quarter who attend opera (English Heritage – Mori Research website).

The proportion of the service class visiting museum and heritage centres in any year is about three times that of manual workers. About two-thirds of the visitors to such places have white-collar occupations (Myerscough, 1986: 303–4). Visits to such sites vary ethnically, with 'white' people somewhat more likely to visit historic buildings or museums than either 'black' or 'Asian' people who wish to learn about various kinds of heritage experience, not just that of 'England' (English Heritage – Mori Research website). However, there is very widespread support for sustaining English heritage sites, with three-quarters of the population believing that their lives are richer for having the opportunity to visit sites of heritage. Nine out of ten people support the use of public funds to preserve heritage. Significant numbers of people who have not recently visited such sites express very positive sentiments towards such heritage work being undertaken (English Heritage – Mori Research website).

Similar developments are taking place in many industrial countries (see Lumley, 1988). Lowenthal says of the USA that 'the trappings of history now festoon the whole country' (1985: xv). The number of properties listed in the US National Register of Historic Places rose from 1,200 in 1968 to 37,000 in 1985 (Frieden and Sagalyn, 1989: 201).

However, various critics of heritage, such as Hewison or Wright, argue that this 'heritage industry' is more extensive in Britain than elsewhere, although the empirical testing of such a hypothesis is fraught with methodological difficulties (Hewison, 1987; Wright, 1985).

Certainly since the late nineteenth century in Britain there has been a tradition of visiting/conserving the countryside, as discussed in the previous chapter. This is reflected in the appreciation both of certain kinds of landscape (including villagescapes) and especially of grand country houses set in attractive rural settings. On the first of these Raban talks of a recent willingness of people to present a particular impression of village England; 'nowhere outside Africa ... were the tribespeople so willing to dress up in "traditional" costumes and cater for the entertainment of their visitors ... The thing had become a national industry. Year by year, England was being made more picturesquely merrie' (1986: 194–5).

Some of these events are now organised as 'costume dramas' by English Heritage, the main body in England concerned with the protection of heritage sites. The tendency to visit grand country houses also remains immensely popular, with 12 million people a year visiting National Trust properties (National Trust website).

There has been a further interest in visiting the countryside, stemming from a widespread interest in the equipment and machinery that was used in farming, and in the patterns of life developed in agriculture. There are over 800 museums containing rural exhibits, some of which have been described as 'pretend farms', with wheelwrights, blacksmiths, horse breeders, farriers and so on (see Vidal, 1988).

There has been a remarkable increase in interest in the real lives of industrial/mining workers. MacCannell points out the irony of these changes: 'Modern Man [sic] is losing his attachments to the work bench, the neighbourhood, the town, the family, which he once called "his own" but, at the same time, he is developing an interest in the "real lives" of others' (1999: 91).

This interest is particularly marked in the north of Britain, where much heavy industry had been located. It is such industries which are of most interest to visitors, particularly because of the apparently heroic quality of the work, as in a coalmine or steel works. However, this should not be over-emphasised, since people also appear to find interesting the backbreaking but unheroic household tasks undertaken by women. This fascination with other people's work is bound up with the postmodern breaking down of boundaries, particularly between the front and the backstage of people's lives. Such a development is also part of a postmodern museum culture in which almost anything can become an object of curiosity for visitors.

The remarkably rapid de-industrialisation of Britain had two important effects. On the one hand, it created a profound sense of loss, both of certain kinds of technology (steam engines, blast furnaces, pit workings) and of the social life that had developed around those technologies. The rapidity of such change was probably greater in Britain than elsewhere and was more geographically concentrated in the north of England, South Wales and central Scotland. On the other hand, much of this industry had historically been based in inner-city Victorian premises, large numbers of which became available for alternative uses. Such buildings were either immensely attractive in their own right (such as the Albert Dock in Liverpool), or could be refurbished in a suitable heritage style for housing, offices, museums or restaurants. Such a style is normally picturesque, with sandblasted walls, replaced windows and attractive street furniture.

This process of de-industrialisation occurred in Britain at a time when many local authorities were developing more of a strategic role with regard to economic development and saw in tourism a way of generating jobs directly and through more general publicity about their place. A good example is Wigan; this is well represented in a publicity booklet called *I've never been to Wigan but I know what it's like* (Economic Development, Wigan, undated). The first five pictures in black and white are of back-to-back terraced housing, mines and elderly residents walking along narrow alleyways. But we are then asked if we are sure this is really what Wigan is now like. The following twelve photos, all in colour, demonstrate the contemporary Wigan, which is revealed as possessing countless tourist sites, Wigan Pier, a colourful market and elegant shops, excellent sports facilities, attractive pubs and restaurants, and delightful canalside walkways. Selling Wigan to tourists is part of the process of selling Wigan to potential investors, who are going to be particularly concerned about the availability of various kinds of services for their employees. Tourism in Wigan is now worth £34 million a year with 170,000 visitors attracted (Guardian Unlimited website).

This was a period in which many smaller enterprises were beginning to grow (see Lash and Urry, 1987: ch. 7). Much emphasis was also placed on small firms in central government policy and in the encouragement provided by local authority economic development programmes. Developing new enterprises in the tourist field, many of which are relatively small, became commonplace in Britain in the 1980s.

With the tendencies to globalisation discussed in Chapters 3 and 8, different countries have come to specialise in different sectors of the holiday market for visitors: Spain for cheaper packaged holidays, Thailand for 'exotic' holidays, Switzerland for skiing and mountaineering holidays, and so on. Britain has come to specialise in holidays for overseas visitors that emphasise the historical and the quaint (north Americans often refer to Britain as that 'quaint country' or that 'old country'). This emphasis can be seen in the way that overseas visitors tend to remain inland in Britain, rarely visiting either the coast or much of the countryside. Such visitors cannot know about more than a handful of sights worth visiting and, apart from London, these will normally include Oxford, Cambridge, Stratford, York, Edinburgh, and some of the sites of industrial tourism. This location within the global division of tourism has further reinforced the particular strength of the heritage phenomenon in Britain.

The preservation of heritage has been particularly marked in Britain because of the unattractive character of its modern architecture (until the 1990s). The characteristic modern buildings of the post-war period have been undistinguished office blocks and public housing towers, many with concrete as the most visible building material. Such buildings have proved to be remarkably disliked by most people, which has seen modern architecture as 'American'. Yet the contrast with the often striking and elegant north American skyscrapers located in the downtown areas is noticeable. In addition Britain had a very large stock of pre-1914 houses and public buildings suitable for conservation, once the fashion for the modern had begun to dissolve in the early 1970s. An interesting example of this can be seen in the changing attitude towards conservation, particularly of the Regency façades in Cheltenham, which is one of the prime townscapes being strenuously preserved even though much of it had once been scheduled for 'redevelopment' (Cowen, 1990).

So heritage is playing a particularly important role in British tourism, and it is more central to the gaze in Britain than in some other countries. But what is meant by heritage, particularly in relationship to notions of history and authenticity (see Uzzell, 1989)? A lively public debate has been raging in Britain concerned with evaluating the causes and consequences of heritage.

This debate was stimulated by Hewison's book on the heritage industry, which was subtitled *Britain in a Climate of Decline* (1987). He begins with the provocative comment that, instead of manufacturing goods, Britain is increasingly manufacturing heritage. This has come about because of the perception that Britain is in some kind of terminal decline. And the development of heritage not only involves the reassertion of values which are anti-democratic, but the heightening of decline through a stifling of the culture of the present. A critical culture based on the understanding of history is what is needed, not a set of heritage fantasies.

Hewison is concerned with analysing the conditions in which nostalgia is generated. He argues that it is felt most strongly at a time of discontent, anxiety or disappointment And yet the times for which we feel most nostalgia were themselves periods of considerable disturbance. Furthermore, nostalgic memory is quite different from total recall; it is a socially organised construction. The question is not whether we should or should not preserve the past, but what kind of past we have chosen to preserve. Roy Strong writes that:

> We are all aware of problems and troubles, of changes within the structure of society, of the dissolution of old values and standards ... The heritage represents some kind of security, a point of reference, a refuge perhaps, something visible and tangible which ... seems stable and unchanged. Our environmental heritage is a deeply stabilising and unifying element within our society. (quoted in Hewison, 1987: 46–7)

(Incidentally both Marx and Nietzsche might be said to have a similarly critical attitude to 'nostalgia': see Lowenthal, 1985: 65.) Hewison notes something distinctive about some contemporary developments. Much contemporary nostalgia is for the *industrial* past. The first major battle in Britain was fought – and lost – in 1962 over the elegant neoclassical arch at the entrance to Euston station. But this gave rise to a survey of industrial monuments by the Council for British Archaeology and a major conference in 1969. Four years later the Association for Industrial Archaeology was founded and by the 1980s industrial museums were developing almost everywhere in the northern half of Britain. Hewison makes much of the contrasts between the development of the industrial museum at Beamish and the devastation brought about by the closure of the steel works at Consett, just ten miles away. The protection of the past conceals the destruction of the present. There is an absolute distinction between authentic history (continuing and therefore dangerous) and heritage (past, dead and safe). The latter, in short, conceals social and spatial inequalities, masks a shallow commercialism and consumerism, and may in part at least destroy elements of the buildings or artefacts supposedly being conserved. Hewison argues that: 'If we really are interested in our history, then we may have to preserve it from the conservationists' (1987: 98). Heritage is bogus history.

Obviously there is much value in many of Hewison's comments. One commentator has suggested that Britain will 'soon be appointing a Curator instead of a Prime Minister' (quoted in Lowenthal, 1985: 4). Similarly Tom Wolfe has recently proposed that the entire British population service a national Disneyland for foreign tourists. And a fantasy of this sort can be seen in Julian Barnes' novel *England, England*, with a proposed theme park covering the whole of the Isle of Wight. The theme park would be known as Englandland and contain scaled down replicas of almost all the well-known historic buildings in England (Barnes, 1999).

However, these criticisms of heritage do bear a remarkable similarity to the critique of the so-called mass society thesis. Indeed social scientists may well be prone to a kind of nostalgia, that is, for a Golden Age when the mass of the population were supposedly not taken in by new and more distorting cultural forms (see Stauth and Turner, 1988). There has, of course, never been such a period.

Hewison also ignores the enormously important popular bases of conservation. For example, he sees the [English] National Trust as a gigantic system of outdoor relief for the old upper classes to maintain their stately homes. But this ignores the widespread support for such conservation. Indeed the National Trust with nearly 2.7 million members is the largest mass organisation in Britain (as in 2000; and see McCone, Kiely, Morris, 1995, on the Scottish equivalent). Moreover, much of the early conservation movement was plebeian in character – for example railway preservation, industrial archaeology, steam traction rallies and the like in the 1960s, well before more obvious indicators of economic decline materialised in Britain. Even Covent Garden, which might be critiqued as the ultimate 'heritage playground', only became transformed into a tourist site because of a major conservation campaign conducted by local residents (see Januszczak, 1987; Samuel, 1994).

Likewise the preservation of some derelict coalmines in Wales has resulted from pressure by local groups of miners and their families who have sought to hold on to aspects of 'their' history; indeed visitors to Big Pit in South Wales, for example, are said to be pleased that it has not been made 'pretty' for visitors (see ch. 8; Urry, 1996). While the only remaining colliery building in the Rhondda valley, a valley iconic of Welshness where there were once 66 deep mines, is now the Rhondda Heritage Park (Dicks, 2000). This is based in what was the Lewis Merthyr mine. The Heritage Park emerged from extensive local campaigning through the discourse of 'memorialism' and it provides the only significant public memorial in the Rhondda to the once totally dominant mining industry (see Dicks, 2000: chaps 6 and 7). Oral history plays a central role in the memories of the mining community. However, it should be noted that this Heritage Park did involve huge disagreements over its scale and form and the degree to which it should be turned from a memorial into a much broader tourism/heritage project which it is said only weakly captures the voices of the local community.

Generally the critics of the heritage industry also fail to link the pressure for conservation with the much broader development of environmental and cultural politics in the 1980s and 1990s. Thus through research on the membership of the National Trust for Scotland, it seems that Scottish heritage is a significant element in the development of cultural nationalism (McCrone, Morris, Kiely, 1995). Heritage is seen by their respondents as involving a strong sense of lineage and inheritance. It has an identity-conferring status. For most of the respondents conserving Scottish heritage is a centrally important enthusiasm. McCrone, Morris, Kiely thus write of the membership of the National Trust of Scotland:

'There is a rich network of local activity groups, travel outings, and active participation in heritage conservation through voluntary labour. What is available to life
members is a coordinated lifestyle achieved through association ... "a timeless
organisation upholding traditional values"' (1995: 155).

Hewison links nostalgia for the industrial past with the growth of postmodernism. But although they are connected some distinctions should be
made. In the 1980s in Chester for example the expansion of a Roman centre
('Diva') would have involved the demolition of a listed Georgian house. Local
conservationists sought to save the house as well as preventing the development of a Roman theme park (with Roman coins, Roman food etc.; see
Stamp, 1987). Hewison conflates these two issues. But mainly he concen-
trates his critique on scholarly conservation, museums and heritage centres.

However, these do often employ academic historians to research the background to the site (see Rose, 1978). Hewison's case could have been made
much more easily against the Camelot theme park or the proposed Roman
theme park in Chester. In the USA there is a similar distinction between the
scholarly representation of Lowell as part of a National Park and the construction of Main Street in various Disneylands. Another distinction that
might be made is between 'crafts' and 'trades'. The former seems part of the
constructed heritage industry, even to the extent that the craftspeople
become part of the exhibit. But this kind of construction can be distinguished
from various 'trades' and the historical reconstruction of the methods and
techniques used, by, say, harness-makers or wheelwrights (see Vidal, 1988).
Hewison's critique is more apposite to the former than the latter.

Hewison moreover presumes a rather simple model by which certain meanings, such as nostalgia for times past, come to be unambiguously transferred to
the visitor by such heritage sites. There is little sense of the complexity by
which different visitors can gaze upon the same set of objects and read and
perform them in a different ways (see Urry, 1996). Indeed sites are not
uniformly read and passively accepted by visitors. Macdonald shows in the case
of an exhibition at the Science Museum that visitors frame and interpret
the visit in ways not expected or planned by its designers (1995: 21). They
connect together exhibits that were not meant to be linked, they read the
exhibits as prescriptive when they are not intended to be, and they mostly do
not describe the exhibition in ways that the designers had intended (see Shaw,
Agarwal, Bull, 2000: 276).

Research at the Albert Dock in Liverpool further showed that people
actively use such sites as bases for reminiscence: 'as the point of departure
for their own memories of a way of life in which economic hardship and
exploited labour were offset by a sense of community, neighbourliness
and mutuality' (Mellor, 1991: 100): 'Reminiscence' may indeed be a major
'practice' at such sites. And reminiscing involves performance – both
by those 'real' performers who are there to stimulate memories, and by
visitors who often have to work co-operatively with others in order to

produce their memories. The performativity of reminiscence is by no means an apparently passive process of visual consumption. In some ways, it is similar to the variety of other spatial practices which take place at tourist sites, such as walking, talking, sitting, photographing and so on (see Edensor, 1998).

There is something condescending about Hewison's view that such a presentation of heritage cannot be interpreted in different ways, or that the fact that the experience may be enjoyable means that it cannot also be educational. This is well-shown in the case of New Salem where tourists are neither monolithic and the meaning of the site is not given and fixed (Bruner, 1994: 410–1). Indeed many tourists play with time frames and experiment with alternative realities. They reconstruct their sense of the past even as such sites possess a strong entertainment and playful character. Bruner concludes that: 'many tourists make associations between what they see at the site and their personal lives' (1994: 410).

The Wigan Pier Centre is, after all, scholarly and educational; it presents a history of intense popular struggle; it identifies the bosses as partly to blame for mining disasters; it celebrates a non-elite popular culture; and was in part organised by a council with the objective of remembering 'heroic labour' (see Figure 6.2). Compared with most people's understanding of history it conveys something of the social processes involved in that history, even if it is hard to see how to build on that history in the future. Indeed, it is not at all clear just what understanding of 'history' most people have anyway. In the absence of the heritage industry just how is the past normally appropriated? It is not through the academic study of 'history' as such (see Lowenthal, 1985: 411). For many people it will be acquired at best through reading biographies and historical novels and seeing historical dramas on TV. It is not obvious that the heritage industry's account is more misleading. Overall Lowenthal's judgement on how to regard various kinds of history seems right: 'We must concede the ancients their place ... But their place is not simply back there, in a separate and foreign country; it is assimilated in ourselves, and resurrected into an ever-changing present' including through the 'heritage industry' (1985: 412).

However, what does need emphasising is that heritage history is problematic because of the emphasis upon visualisation. Visitors see an array of artefacts, including buildings (either 'real' or 'manufactured'), and they then have to imagine the patterns of life that would have emerged around those seen objects (see Bruner, 1994). This is an 'artefactual' history, in which various kinds of *social* experiences are in effect ignored or trivialised, such as the relations of war, exploitation, hunger, disease, the law, and so on (see Jordanova, 1989).

The following three sections explore certain aspects of heritage in more detail: in relation to its use as part of a local strategy for economic regeneration; in its interconnections with recent trends in design and postmodern architecture; and its role is the development of what I term the postmodern museum.

Figure 6.2   *The Wigan Pier Heritage Centre, UK*

Tourism and the Local State

In the previous discussion of the heritage industry it was noted that there is often considerable local support for conservation. I consider more fully here the relationship between local areas and tourism development. In that relationship there are three key elements. First, there are local people who are often concerned to conserve features of the environment which seem in some ways to stand for or signify the locality in which they live. Second, there are a variety of private sector owners and potential owners of tourist-related services. And third, there is the local state, which is comprised of local authorities as well as the local/regional representatives of various national-level bodies, including tourist boards.

An example illustrating this complexity is the Winter Gardens Theatre in Morecambe. This theatre closed in the late 1970s and will cost a great deal to repair. It is widely agreed that the theatre, built in 1897, is architecturally superb. English Heritage describes it as 'outstanding', while John Earl of the Theatres Trust has characterised it as the Albert Hall of the north. It may be conserved, although this is by no means certain. If it is, there is little doubt that amongst other uses will be the staging of old-time music hall (as well as pop and classical concerts), hence conveying nostalgic memories of a somewhat imprecise golden age of pre-TV entertainment.

Clearly such a refurbishment could be subject to criticism as yet another example of the heritage industry. However, it should be noted that without a great deal of local support for conservation the theatre would already have been demolished. There has been an extremely energetic action group convinced that this currently semi-derelict building symbolises Morecambe – that if it is allowed to be demolished, that would be the end of the town itself. It is certain that there is widespread popular support for increasing the attractiveness of Morecambe, to make it more congested and more subject to the tourist gaze. Indeed potential tourists to any site cannot contribute to environmental concern: that has to be expressed by local residents. Although the building is privately owned, it is clear that it will only be refurbished with much support from public bodies. The role of the local state may well be crucial. This example demonstrates two important points about contemporary tourist development: the impact of local conservation groups whose heritage-preserving actions will often increase tourism in an area, sometimes as an unintended consequence; and the significant orchestrating role of the local state.

On the first of these, it is important to note how conservation groups vary very considerably between different places. For example, in 1980 while there were 5.1 members of 'amenity societies' per 1,000 population in the UK as a whole, the ratio was over 20 per 1,000 in Hampshire and over 10 per 1,000 in most of the counties around London, in Devon, North Yorkshire and Cumbria (see Lowe and Goyder, 1983: 28–30 for more detail). Clearly part of the rationale of such groups is to prevent new developments taking place that will harm the supposed 'character' of the locality (in the south-east especially through low-cost housing schemes). The role of the service and middle classes in such groups is crucial – and is a major means by which those possessing positional goods, such as a nice house in a nice village, seek to preserve their advantages. However, conservation movements can often have fairly broad objectives: not merely to prevent development, but to bring about the refurbishment of existing public buildings and more generally to 'museumify' the villagescape or townscape. Moreover, even if the objectives of the movement have nothing to do with tourism, the effect will almost certainly be to increase the attractiveness of the locality to tourists.

An interesting negative example of this can be seen in New Zealand. Close to the largest city in the South Island, Christchurch, is the port of Lyttleton. As this is located within an extinct volcano, there is a superb natural harbour and scenic backdrop to the port. The town consists of mainly unexceptional low-level buildings but with very attractive facades. To the European it looks a typical town of the inter-war period. What is striking about Lyttleton is how undeveloped it was (in the late 1980s), although potentially it is an excellent tourist site. It does not look quaint, merely old (just like a great deal of contemporary Havana). In Hewison's terms it has not been conserved, only preserved. For it to become an object of the tourist gaze, it needs a conservation movement to ensure that these façades are not demolished; an infusion of new capital to transform some of the facades into 'tourist-friendly' shops and cafes; and a strategic plan by the local authority to co-ordinate activities.

One factor that appears to have strengthened conservation movements in the UK is the lower rate of geographical mobility of at least the male members of the service class (see Savage, 1988). As a result such people are likely to develop more of an attachment to place than previously. One can talk therefore of the 'localisation of the service class' and this will have its impact, through the forming of amenity groups, on the level of conservation (Bagguley et al., 1989: 151–2). To the extent that such groups are successful, this will make the place more attractive to tourists. Thus the preservation of the quaint villagescape or townscape in particular, through middle-class collective action, is almost certain to increase the number of tourists and the resulting degree of congestion experienced by residents. One place where this has been particularly marked is Cheltenham. Because of concerted conservation pressure in the late 1960s the formal development policy was dropped in 1974. Since then a conservation policy has been adopted and there has been wholesale rehabilitation of the Regency housing stock for both housing, office and retailing/leisure developments (see Cowen, 1990).

Before considering the various ways in which local states have responded to such pressures, and more generally how they have in recent years attempted to reconstruct the objects of the tourist gaze, I note some reasons why local states have recently become centrally involved in both developing and promoting tourism.

As many local authorities moved into local economic intervention during a period of rapid de-industrialisation, so it seemed that tourism presented one of the only opportunities available for generating employment. It was also noted that many such authorities have found themselves with a particular legacy, of derelict buildings, such as the Albert Dock in Liverpool, and/or derelict land, such as that which now houses the Lowry arts complex on Salford Quays in Manchester (see Figure 6.3). Converting such derelict property into sites which would have a tourism component has often been almost the only alternative available (see Dicks, 2000, on the Rhondda valley).

Earlier I noted how competitive the tourist market has become, particularly as all sorts of places are competing to attract the increasingly selective and discriminating post-tourist. As with many other commodities, the market is much more differentiated and particular places have been forced to develop tourism strategies based upon what I call a 'tourism reflexivity'. Such a reflexivity has involved auditing local facilities, developing a plan of action and targeting appropriate marketing for the identified market niche. In some cases this has involved the local state almost initiating a tourist industry from scratch – as in the case of Bradford (Williams 1998). In some parts of the south-east of the UK there has been a self-conscious 'post-tourist' strategy, especially with large increases in the number of day-trips (Landry et al., 1989).

Local authorities also play an important role because of the structure of ownership in tourist towns. This is often fragmented and it is difficult to get local capital to determine appropriate actions from the viewpoint of the locality as a whole. The council can be often the only agent with the capacity to invest in new infrastructure (such as sea defences, conference centres, harbours), or to provide the sort of facilities which must be found in any such centre (entertainments, museums, swimming pools). This has led in some of the older resorts, such as those on the Isle of Thanet, to the development of 'municipal Conservatism', a combination of small-scale entrepreneurialism and council intervention (see Buck et al., 1989: 188–9). In the last few years in Britain many Labour councils have enthusiastically embraced local tourist initiatives, having once dismissed tourism as providing only 'candy-floss jobs' (Glasgow would be a prime illustration).

Finally, local councils have been willing to engage in promoting tourism because in a period of central government constraint this has been one area where there are sources of funding to initiate projects which may also benefit local residents (especially in the later 1990s through UK lottery funding). Furthermore, such facilities are important since they may attract prospective employees and employers and then keep them satisfied. This seems to have happened in Wigan in the 1980s following the establishment of the Wigan Pier Heritage Centre. The chairman of the North-West Tourist Board argues that:

> The growth of the tourism industry has a great deal to do with the growth of every other industry or business: the opening up of the regions as fine places to visit means they're better places to live in – and thus better places to work ... a higher quality of life benefits employees. (quoted in Reynolds, 1988)

It is problematic to assess the economic impact of any particular tourism initiative. This results from the difficulties of assessing the multiplier. If we consider the question of income generation, the impact of the expansion of tourism cannot be assessed simply in terms of how much income is spent by 'tourists' in hotels, camp sites, restaurants, pubs, and so on. It also depends upon what and where the recipients of that income, such as suppliers to the hotel or bar staff in the pubs, spend it, and in turn where those recipients spend it, and so on. There are some further problems in assessing such multipliers for a local economy: the linkages between firms are particularly complex and opaque partly because of the multitude of small enterprises involved; leakages from the economy are often very difficult to assess; there is no clear and agreed-upon definition of just what is a 'tourist' and hence what is tourist expenditure; the definition of the 'local economy' is in any case contentious so that the larger the geographical unit the higher the *apparent* multiplier. For all these difficulties it does seem that tourist expenditure has a fairly high local multiplier compared with other kinds of expenditure that might occur locally. Most studies in the UK show that something like half of tourism expenditure will remain in the locality, from its direct and indirect effects (see Williams and Shaw, 1988c: 88). However, such income remains highly unequally distributed since tourism areas are notable for their low wage level, even amongst those not employed in the tourism industry as such (see Taylor, 1988, on the wage effects in tourism-rich Blackpool).

Many local states in the UK have undertaken initiatives concerned to reconstruct and re-present whole places as objects of the tourist gaze

(Houston 1986; on the US, see Frieden and Sagalyn, 1989). This has been most marked in the Midlands, the north of England, and Wales; rather less so in Scotland, Northern Ireland and the south-east. A number of local authorities, especially in England, have recently been successful in the tourism field. An interesting example in the north is Hebden Bridge, a small west Yorkshire town (see Waterhouse, R., 1989). Its nadir was in the mid-1960s, when half the native population had left in the previous ten years following the closure of thirty-three clothing works. A strategy came to be formulated to break with the industrial past, to promote Hebden as a place to visit and to convert some of the visitors into new residents. There had been plans for a major development scheme but this was thrown out in 1967. A heritage-led growth strategy was devised instead, a strategy influenced by an early environmental movement in the town and its attraction to artists, designers, musicians and so on. It is now a booming town with a considerable shortage of housing; there are twice as many newcomers as original residents.

Some other places in Britain that have pursued a similar strategy have been assisted by the scheme to establish Tourism Development Action Programmes (TDAPs). These were forms of state-sponsored tourism reflexivity (see chapter 8), involving integrated programmes, lasting between one and three years, which involved research, development and marketing (Davies, 1987). Some places that experienced such a programme were cities, such as Bradford, Tyne and Wear, Lancaster, Gosport and Portsmouth, rural areas such as Exmoor and Kielder Water, and seaside resorts such as Bridlington and Torbay.

The Lancaster TDAP consisted of a partnership between the two relevant local authorities, together with a publicly funded enterprise board and the North-West Tourist Board. The objectives were to develop and implement a marketing strategy, to improve the heritage attractions, to develop links with the countryside and coast, to enhance visitors' experience of Lancaster, and to expand and improve the provision of accommodation. It was clearly recognised that enhancing the tourist potential of Lancaster will simultaneously make the place more attractive to inward investment. In the Position Statement for the programme it was stated that:

> in addition to creating new tourism jobs locally, the development of tourism in Lancaster will help to up-grade the local environment and improve facilities which will assist industrial promotion generally. The City's appearance and the range of facilities it offers are critical to the attraction of new companies to Lancaster. (Special Projects Group, Lancaster City Council, 1987: para. 1.20)

It is interesting that this Position Statement is entitled *Lancaster – Heritage City*. It would seem that three conditions are necessary if Lancaster were to construct itself as a heritage city. First, there would have to be a number of attractive and reasonably well-preserved buildings from a range of historical periods. In Lancaster's case these were medieval (a castle), Georgian (the customs house and many townhouses) and Victorian (old mills).

Second, such buildings would have to be used for activities in some ways consistent with the tourist gaze. An interesting example concerns Lancaster Castle, which has a magnificent Norman gate. Most of the castle is currently closed to the public because it is used as a prison. Now although castles often operated historically as prisons (Lancaster Castle indeed has some famous dungeons), there is thought to be something inappropriate about tourists gazing upon a building which still functions as a prison. Hence the castle has not yet fulfilled its potential as a tourist site.

The third condition is that the buildings should in some sense have been significant historically, that they stand for or signify important historical events, people or processes. Thus in the TDAP Position Statement Lancaster is described as:

> an ancient settlement steeped in history, with Roman origins, an important medieval past ... Through the Duchy of Lancaster it has close associations with the Monarchy ... The city's many attractions, based on its rich history and fine buildings, together with its royal associations, combine for the promotion and marketing of Lancaster's heritage. (Special Projects Group, Lancaster City Council, 1987: paras 4.3, 4.4)

It is worth considering the use of 'history' in the quotation: that because there has been a 'rich' history the old buildings appear not merely old but historically important; and in turn the buildings signify that the place is 'properly old' – that it is indeed steeped in history. There must therefore be a coherent relationship between the built environment and the presumed atmosphere or character of the place being developed for the tourist gaze.

Another way in which a number of cities have been more successful in constructing a relatively coherent tourist image is through so-called cultural tourism (see Craik 1997). For example, in London in the 1980s, 44 per cent of museum attendance was made up of tourists, compared with 21 per cent outside London. Tourists formed 40 per cent of the audience at London's theatres and concerts. It is calculated that 25 per cent of all tourist spending is arts-related (Myerscough, 1988: ch. 5).

But perhaps the best example of cultural tourism in Britain involved the transformation of Glasgow following its designation as the 'European City of Culture for 1990': 'Glasgow's regeneration has been largely arts-led, with the Mayfest and the opening of the Burrell Collection all helping to change the city's image from a decaying industrial backwater to a dynamic growth area [attractive to tourists]' (quoted in McKellar, 1988: 14).

Two-thirds of visitors consider that there is a wide variety of interesting museums and art galleries to visit in the city. And at least one-third think that there are so many cultural activities available that they wish they were able to stay longer. Fewer than one-fifth consider that Glasgow is the rough and depressing place to visit that once would have been the case (Myerscough, 1988: 88–9). Mysteriously but dramatically, Glasgow has become the kind of place that people now want to visit, to see and to be seen in. It has become a preferred object of the gaze of many tourists. One consequence is that the proportion of service jobs has risen from 68 per cent to 84 per cent (The Industrial Society website). This transformation of Glasgow as an object of the gaze is the result of economic restructuring, social change, policy intervention and cultural re-evaluation. And part of that transformation has entailed tourism coming to be of central economic and social significance.

Liverpool is another UK city that has successfully capitalised on its rather particular 'popular' cultural heritage. Strongly featured in the *Discover Merseyside 1988* brochure was the daily 'Beatles Magical History Tour'. The brochure talks of 'Beatleland', which includes the Cavern Walks shopping centre, the John Lennon Memorial Club, the Beatles Shop, Tommy Steele's statue of Eleanor Rigby, and so on. Details are also included of the annual Beatles Convention. Another cultural advantage of Merseyside increasingly featuring in its tourism literature is soccer, something again illustrating how the boundaries between different activities are dissolving through the processes of de-differentiation referred to earlier. Liverpool describes itself as '*The* Football Capital of the World' and there are well-organised 'Soccer City Weekend' packages where important objects of the tourist gaze are Goodison Park and Anfield.

Bradford is also an interesting example, since it had no tourist industry until 1980. It was a prime example of an industrial city of dark satanic mills. The setting up of a tourism initiative was self-consciously undertaken when it was realised that Bradford had a number of ingredients likely to appeal to the holiday-maker. These were, apart from plenty of hotel beds, proximity to internationally renowned attractions such as Haworth and the Dales and Moors; a substantially intact industrial heritage of buildings, railways and canals derived from Bradford's status as 'Worstedopolis'; its location within the high-profile county of Yorkshire; and the existence of a large and vigorous Asian culture that had generated a plethora of small enterprises. The city council, moreover, realised that turning Bradford into a tourist mecca was itself a newsworthy item. They received considerable free publicity in the early 1980s. One crucial element in later campaigns has been to market Asian culture as a major visitor attraction. A separate booklet has been produced entitled *Flavours of Asia*. This details many 'Asian' restaurants, the largest Asian store in Europe, various curry tours, a dozen sari centres as well as a brief history of various Asian religions and of the patterns of immigration to Bradford (see Davies, 1987).

One factor in many tourism-developments within cities has been their location on a waterfront site. The model for such waterfront development is the US, beginning with Baltimore's Harborplace, which attracted 29 million visitors a year even by the 1980s. Other examples worldwide include Boston's Fanueil Hall Marketplace and associated Harborwalk, South Street Seaport in New York, and Sydney's Darling Harbor. The last of these was developed by Sydney property developers, Merlin, who are also involved in Manchester and in the Sheriff's Court Fashion Centre in Glasgow (see Wilsher, 1988). In Britain current waterfront projects include the Albert Dock in Liverpool, Birmingham Canal, Gloucester Docks, and Salford Quays in Manchester,

Figure 6.3   *The Lowry arts complex, Salford Quays, UK*

now housing the Lowry arts complex but once described as the least promising development site in Britain (see Figure 6.3).

The inspiration for development in Britain has arisen from the striking ways in which the downtown areas of American cities have been visually transformed, mainly by private developers but with a fair degree of public coordination. The main features found in the USA are the 'festival marketplace', particularly by the developer James Rouse as in Fanueil Hall in Boston; historical preservation, as in Lowell, Massachusetts; the development of new open spaces or plazas, such as Baltimore; waterfront developments, such as Battery City Park in New York; cultural centres, such as a performing arts centre in Los Angeles; renovation of old hotels, such as the Willard Inter-Continental in Washington DC; refurbished housing, as on Beacon Hill, Boston; and new public transportation systems, even in Los Angeles, the ultimate automobile city (see Fondersmith, 1988; Frieden and Sagalyn, 1989: 210–12; Zukin, 1991).

In the next section I consider in more detail the design and architecture of these various developments. Tourism is about finding certain sorts of place pleasant and interesting to gaze upon, and that necessarily comes up against the design of the buildings and their relationship to 'natural' phenomena. Without the right design no amount of local state involvement will attract tourists. It will be seen that much of the architecture of these developments is in different senses postmodern.

Designing for the Gaze

Given the emphasis on tourist consumption as visual, and the significance of buildings as objects upon which the gaze is directed, it is essential to consider changing patterns and forms that those buildings might take. Moreover, postmodernism cannot be examined without considering the built environment, the sphere which many would say best demonstrates such a cultural paradigm.

I argue, first, that there are a number of postmodern architectures; second, that the impact of these different architectures depends upon whether we are considering private or public buildings; third, that architects and architectural practices are of major importance in shaping the contemporary tourist gaze; fourth, that tourist practices have to be taken much more seriously by commentators on building design; and fifth, that tourists are socially differentiated and hence gaze selectively upon these different architectural styles.

The first point involves considering what is meant by *post* in postmodern. There are three senses: *after* the modern; *return* to the premodern; and *anti* the modern. I briefly summarise the architectural style associated with each of these (see Harris and Lipman, 1986).

After the modern is what one could also term 'consumerist postmodernism'. This takes its cue from Venturi's famous cry to 'learn from Las Vegas' (1972; Jencks, 1977; Frampton, 1988). Caesar's Palace in Las Vegas or Disneyland are the icons of this architecture, which proudly celebrates commercial vulgarity (see Harris and Lipman, 1986: 844–5). Art and life are fused or pastiched in the playful and shameless borrowing of ornamental style (see the massive Trafford Centre, near Manchester, for the 'best' recent British example, including a kind of 'Titanic' food court; see Figure 6.4). Previous elements of high culture are mass-produced, and no longer signify any single style. This is an architecture of surfaces and appearances, of playfulness and pastiche. It is mannerist – as if all the historical styles and conventions of architecture are there to be endlessly drawn on, juxtaposed and drawn on yet again. However, a distinction should be made between the literal consumerism of Las Vegas and the manner in which some postmodern architects have hijacked such styles to construct something of an auratic architecture appealing to the cognoscenti (as in James Stirling's Stuttgart gallery).

Much of the debate about postmodernism has tended to concentrate on significant public buildings, such as Terry Farrell's TV-AM headquarters, Philip Johnson's AT&T building, and James Stirling's Stuttgart gallery. There is less investigation of the impact of such a style on the everyday architecture of particular towns and cities. This is an important issue, since historically most architecture has been partly eclectic, drawing on earlier traditions, such as the Gothic style favoured by the Victorians, or the Egyptian motifs popular with the Art Deco movement (Bagguley, 1990: ch. 5; Lowenthal, 1985: 309–21). The one exception was the modern movement and its perhaps unique rejection of all previous architectural mannerisms. Interestingly, even

Figure 6.4   *'New Orleans' at the Trafford Centre, Manchester, UK*

during the heyday of modernism (say 1930–70 in Britain) two other styles were common: red-brick neo-Georgian shopping parades, and neo-Tudor half-timbered suburban housing.

One set of studies has been conducted on the impact of different architectural styles and on the different social forces which generated them (see Freeman, 1986, on the following; for a related study see Larkham, 1986). The architectural history of two towns was investigated: Aylesbury and Wembley. Modern architecture dominated the centres of both towns in the post-war period. This changed in Aylesbury in the early 1970s and in Wembley in the 1980s. Since then most town centre building has been postmodern. Brick has become the predominant building material during the postmodern period; concrete, glass and brick were all common during the modern period. The earlier break with modernism in Aylesbury rather than Wembley appears to have resulted from the nature of the architectural practices involved:

> In Aylesbury, local firms, perhaps endowed with a rich historical and architectural heritage, were primary adopters of this style [postmodernism] in the early years. The continuing existence of local initiators and architects may, therefore, have been a reason why the dominance of Modernism with its monolithic designs ended so much sooner in Aylesbury than in Wembley. (Freeman, 1986: 75)

But Freeman treats as postmodern a wide range of different styles: what I earlier have termed 'consumerist postmodernism' and what I will go on to discuss as 'patrician postmodernism' and 'vernacular postmodernism'.

Patrician postmodernism involves a *return* to the premodern. Here what is celebrated is the classical form, the architecture of an elite. Leon Krier summarises its attraction: 'People never protested against the tradition of classical architecture ... Architecture has reached its highest possible form in the classical principles and orders ... [which] have the same inexhaustible capacities as the principles which govern nature and the universe itself' (1984: 87, 119).

This reconstructed classicism springs from individuals who believe they have distinct powers of insight, who will be able to return to the aura of the fine building. Architecture here is a self-determining practice, an autonomous discipline able to reproduce the three classical orders. This is linked to the belief that such classicism is really what people want if only their choices were not distorted by modernism. In Britain, Prince Charles in part demonstrates this position, of appearing to speak on behalf of the people who know they do not like modernism and who really want only to gaze on nothing but uninterrupted classical buildings. Roger Scruton's position is somewhat similar (1979). As Wright says: 'While Scruton certainly approaches everyday life, he does so in such a way as to freeze it over. What emerges is an aestheticized, and indeed severely 'classical', definition of *appropriate* everyday life' (1985: 30–1).

It is no accident that it is Krier who was commissioned by the Prince to devise the site plan for the western expansion of Dorchester, a proposal in effect to put Prince Charles' theories into practice. One interesting feature is the rejection of the idea of zoning activities. In Poundbury shops are found in arcades under flats, and workshops are located next to housing.

The British architect best known for the classical tradition is Quinlan Terry who was responsible for the extensive Richmond development, consisting of fifteen separate buildings built in a variety of classical styles. Terry's properties are expensive since they embody large amounts of craft labour on the exteriors, although the interiors are standardly modern. They are to do with 'an elitist and austere *return* to style and a cult of the unique' and yet compared with a modernist towerblock 'Terry's classy and expensive classical buildings may indeed, in a limited ... sense, form a "popular" style of architecture' (Wright, 1985: 31).

Certainly, to the extent to which such contemporary classical buildings mirror in particular the Georgian style, they will be popular objects of the tourist gaze. If there is a single style of house which tourists in Britain want to gaze upon it would appear to be the classical country house (see Hewison, 1987: ch. 3). There is even a handbook instructing people how to furnish and entertain in such Georgian houses, *The Official New Georgians Handbook* (Artley and Robinson, 1985).

Much Georgian building is preserved in many towns and cities in Britain. The most striking Georgian townscape is Bath, where the housing stock is a positional good. One could describe many of the residents as living in a museum and simultaneously surrounded by museums. The city is almost definitive of good taste and a setting in which part of the cultural capital possessed by its residents is the knowledge of such housing and of the skills

113

necessary to improve it while at the same time appearing to conserve it. The contemporary renaissance of Bath is just as important an icon of the postmodern (in the return to the premodern sense) as is the latest jokey theme park or shopping mall.

The third variant of postmodern architecture is not simply after the modern, or involving a return to the premodern – it is *against* the modern. It has much in common with Frampton's concept of 'critical regionalism' (1988) and Foster's notion of a 'critical postmodernism' (1985a; 1985b). The latter defines the critique of modernism as a Eurocentric and phallocentric set of discourses (see Hebdige, 1986–7: 8–9). It is argued that modernism (like of course premodern classicism) privileges the metropolitan centre over provincial towns and cities, the developed world over developing countries, the north Atlantic rim over the Pacific rim, western art forms over those from the 'east' and the 'south', men's art over women's art, the professional over the people, and so on. There is one variant of the postmodern which involves challenging these dominant discourses: in architecture it can be characterised as vernacular postmodernism. Hebdige well characterises the spatial correlates of this shift. He says that there is: 'not so much a lowering of expectations as a shift towards a total transformation in historical time … to the piecemeal habitation of finite space – the space in which we live' (1986–7: 12).

Space in vernacular postmodernism is localised, specific, context-dependent, and particularistic – by contrast with modernist space which is absolute, generalised, and independent of context (see Harvey, 1989, more generally here). Leon Krier talks of the need to create 'localities of human dignity' (1984: 87). In Britain one of the clearest examples of this has been the 'community architecture' movement that Prince Charles has fostered. This movement began with the restoration of Black Road in Macclesfield designed by Rod Hackney. The main principle of such a movement is 'that the environment works better if the people who live, work and play in it are actively involved in its creation and maintenance' (Wates and Krevitt, 1987: 18). This involves much emphasis on the process of design rather than on the end product, on reducing the power of the architecture vis-à-vis clients, on channelling resources to local residents and communities, and on restoration, or where new building is involved, ensuring it is appropriate to local historical context (see Hutchinson, 1989, for a critique).

The locality is central to such an architecture. And there are important resistances in contemporary societies which have made local vernacular architecture particularly popular, at least outside the metropolitan centres. There is the apparent desire of people living in particular places to conserve or to develop buildings, at least in their public spaces, which express the particular locality in which they live. Such old buildings appear to have a number of characteristics: solidity, since they have survived wars, erosions, developers and town planning; continuity, since they provide links between past generations and the present; authority, since they signify that age and tradition are worthy or preservation; and craft, since they were mostly built using otherwise underrated pre-modern techniques and materials (Lowenthal, 1985: 52–63). The best recent example of this in the UK is the

Tate Modern gallery housed in a former power station on the south bank of the Thames – it attracted five million visitors in its first year.

And because of the globalisation of the tourist gaze, all sorts of places (indeed almost everywhere) have come to construct themselves as objects of the tourist gaze; in other words, not as centres of production or symbols of power but as sites of pleasure. Once people visit places outside capital cities and other major centres, what they find pleasurable are buildings which seem appropriate to place and which mark that place off from others. One of the very strong objections to modernism was that it generated uniformity, or placelessness, and was therefore unlikely to generate large numbers of buildings attractive to potential tourists who want to gaze upon the distinct. The only exceptions are found in major cities, such as Richard Rogers' high-tech Pompidou Centre in Paris, which now attracts more visitors than the Louvre, or of course Frank Gehry's Guggenheim in Bilbao, perhaps the single best-known new building across the globe. Outside the major cities the universalisation of the tourist gaze has made most other places enhance difference often through the rediscovery of local vernacular styles that convey particular histories. As Lynch asks, 'what time is this place?' (1973). In other words, places indicate particular times or histories and in that process vernacular postmodernism is centrally important. Wright talks of the 'abstract and artificial aestheticisation of the ordinary and the old', although it can be noted that different places signify very different 'old' times (1985: 230).

Moreover, each such place will be viewed from various perspectives. There will be differences between what visitors and locals 'see' in a place, and between the viewpoints of old and new residents. Wright maintains that: 'People live in different worlds even though they share the same locality: *there is no single community or quarter.* What is pleasantly old for one person is decayed and broken for another' (1985: 237).

So far I have talked about various kinds of architecture and how these do or do not coincide with the likely gazes of both local residents and visitors; earlier I made some comments about the likely role of the state. I have not yet considered the respective influences of architects and developers in the construction of different tourist sites, although in the comparative study of Aylesbury and Wembley the role of locally based architects was important in the former. There is also evidence in the USA that there has been expanding employment of architects in small and medium-sized towns where an expanding middle class has given rise to localities with high incomes, environmental sensitivity and a consciousness of design (see Knox, 1987; Blau, 1988). The same appears to be true of many of the smaller cities in Britain, such as Bath, Chester, Lancaster or York, cities which are or are becoming important tourist sites (see Bagguley et al., 1990).

I conclude with some points about architects, developers and the changing objects of the tourist gaze. Partly influenced by some of these locally based architects, a more participatory and activist-influenced planning developed, 'aimed not only at halting renewal schemes but also at preserving and enhancing the neighborhood lifeworld' (Knox, 1988: 5).

The effectiveness has of course varied enormously and quite often schemes for the desired conservation of an area turn out to have quite different consequences. The renewal of Covent Garden as a result of a planning decision influenced by activists concerned to conserve the buildings has had the consequence of generating an immensely successful tourist site (with resulting congestion, inflated prices and piles of uncollected rubbish). According to Samuel a similar fate will befall Spitalfields in east London. Samuel argues that what is being planned in Spitalfields is an alliance of conservationists and developers working together. One effect of the proposed scheme would turn much of Spitalfields into a tourist site. Samuel writes: 'Conservation here is typically pastiche in which, as in a costume drama, items are treasured for their period effect ... 'Georgianised' Spitalfields, with its immaculate brickwork, restored lintels and tasteful interiors ... What meaning does conservation have ... when a building is frozen in historical limbo?' (1987b; but see Samuel, 1987a; 1994)

A sustained attack was mounted in Britain in the 1980s on the systems of planning control that had been established since the war. A crucial circular 22/80 from the Department of the Environment asserted the superiority of developer 'patronage' over the democratic system of planning control. Design was to be left to developers, except in certain areas, such as National Parks, Areas of Outstanding Natural Beauty, Conservation Areas and so on (see Punter, 1986–7). What came to be established was a two-tier system. Punter summarises the way this met the apparently conflicting objectives of Conservative policy:

> to retain those escapist elements of aesthetic control which protect the interests and property values [and we may add the tourist sites] of their supporters – the gentrified Georgian, Victorian and Edwardian suburbs, the picture postcard villages and 'unspoilt' countryside so sought after by long distance commuters ... In crude terms the remainder of the country is to be left to the mercies of the developers. (1986–7: 10)

In the 1980s new flamboyant developers emerged in most western countries. Some have international interests, such as Donald Trump from New York with his postmodern Trump Tower. In Britain a number of more regionally oriented developers emerged, taking advantage of the increased discretion available to developers. The best known is John Hall, responsible for building the enormous Metrocentre in a deregulated enterprise zone in Gateshead in north-east England (see Hattersley, 1989). Hall sees himself as a representative of the region and has drawn on the local culture to underpin his activities. His vision is based on the centrality of family life and on the need to provide families with a centre that integrates leisure and shops; in such a place people will spend prolifically.

But not all these developments will be financially successful. In the USA there has often been overinvestment in shopping malls in Texas and hotels in Atlanta, while Virginia's waterfront development looks like a financial failure. Harvey provocatively asks: 'How many museums, cultural centres, convention and exhibition halls, hotels, marinas, shopping malls, waterfront developments can we stand? (1988).

The British government know only too well from the experience of the Millennium Dome that planned for visitor numbers often do not materialise (even if it did attract 6.5 million visitors in its one year of operation). Various other millennium opened visitor attractions have failed to attract anything like expected numbers.

Thus I have shown how the universalisation of the tourist gaze is reaping its postmodern harvest in almost every village, town and city in Britain and in many other western countries as well. I now turn to one particular kind of building – the museum.

Postmodern Museums

We have seen a spectacular growth in the number of museums in western countries. This is clearly part of the process by which the past has come to be much more highly valued by comparison with both the present and the future. Also, the past has become particularly valued in the UK because of the way in which international tourism in this country has come to specialise in the construction of historical quaintness. And the attraction of museums increases as people get older – so the 'greying' of the population in the west is also adding to the number and range of museums.

I have strongly argued for the significance of the gaze to tourist activities. This is not to say that all the other senses are insignificant in the tourist experience. But I have tried to establish that there has to be something distinctive to gaze upon, otherwise a particular experience will not function as a tourist experience. There has to be something extraordinary about the gaze.

On the face of it this seems a relatively straightforward thesis. But it is not, because of the complex nature of visual perception. We do not literally 'see' things. Particularly as tourists we see objects constituted as signs. They stand for something else. When we gaze as tourists what we see are various signs or tourist clichés. Some such signs function metaphorically. A pretty English village can be read as representing the continuities and traditions of England from the Middle Ages to the present day. By contrast the use of the term 'fun' in the advertising for a Club-Med holiday is a metaphor for sex. Other signs, such as lovers in Paris, function metonymically. Here what happens is the substitution of some feature or effect or cause of the phenomenon for the phenomenon itself. The ex-miner, now employed at the former coalmine to show tourists around, is a metonym for the structural change in the economy from one based on heavy industry to one based on services. The development of the industrial museum in an old mill is a metonymic sign of the development of a post-industrial society.

There have of course been museums open to the public since the early nineteenth century, beginning with the Louvre in Paris, the Prado in Madrid and the Altes Museum in Berlin. And since the *Michelin Guides* first appeared museums have been central to the tourist experience. Horne describes the contemporary tourist as a modern pilgrim, carrying guidebooks as devotional texts (1984). What matters, he says, is what people are told they are seeing. The fame of the object becomes its meaning. There is thus a ceremonial agenda, in which it is established what we should see and sometimes even the order in which they should be seen.

Such museums were based on a very special sense of aura. Horne summarises the typical tourist experience, in which the museum has functioned as a metaphor for the power of the state, the learning of the scholar and the genius of the artist:

> tourists with little or no knowledge of painting are expected to pay their respects solely to the fame, costliness and authenticity of these sacred objects, remote in their frames. As 'works of art' from which tourists must keep their distance, the value of paintings can depend not on their nature, but on their authenticated scarcity. The gap between 'art' and the tourist's own environment is thereby maintained. (1984: 16)

Museums have thus been premised upon the aura of the authentic historical artefact, and particularly upon those which are immensely scarce because of the supposed genius of their creator. Horne argues that what can be especially problematic about museums is their attribution of reverence to objects simply because of their aura of authenticity (1984: 249). But how we gaze within museums has changed in three central ways. The sense of aura that Horne describes has been undermined through the development of what I call the 'postmodern museum'. This involves different modes of representation and signification. What we 'see' in the museum has been transformed.

First, there has been a marked broadening of the objects deemed worthy of being preserved. This stems from a changed conception of history. There has been a decline in the strength of a given and uncontested national history, which the national museums then exemplify. Instead a proliferation of alternative or vernacular histories has developed – social, economic, populist, feminist, ethnic, industrial and so on. There is a pluralisation and indeed a 'contemporary-isation' of history. The British Tourist Authority calculated in the 1980s that there were up to 12,000 museum-type venues in Britain (see Baxter, 1989). Museums are concerned with 'representations' of history, and what has happened is a remarkable increase in the range of histories worthy of being represented. I have already noted some of these, especially the development of rural and industrial museums. It is now almost as though the worse the previous historical experience, the more authentic and appealing the resulting tourist attraction. No longer are people only interested in seeing either great works of art or artefacts from very distant historical periods. People increasingly seem attracted by representations of the 'ordinary', of modest houses and of mundane forms of work. Glass-blowing, engine driving, shop working, candle-making, cotton spinning, salt-making, cobbling, chemical manufacture, holiday-making, lace-making, domestic chores, coalmining and so on, are all deemed worthy of being represented in contemporary museums, as are the often mundane artefacts associated with each of these activities (see West, 1988, on Ironbridge Gorge; Bennett, 1988, on Beamish; and Hewison, 1987, on Wigan Pier). There has been a quite stunning fascination with the popular and a tendency to treat all kinds of object, whether it is the Mona Lisa or the old cake tin of a Lancashire cotton worker, as almost equally interesting. One could summarise this shift as being 'from aura to nostalgia', and it reflects the anti-elitism of postmodernism (see Edgar, 1987). It should also be noted that all sorts of other phenomena are now preserved in museums, including moving images, radio, television, photographs, cinema, the environment and even the sets of TV soap operas (Lumley, 1988; and see Goodwin, 1989, on the Granada museum).

There has also been a marked change in the nature of museums themselves. No longer are visitors expected to stand in awe of the exhibits. More emphasis is being placed on the participation by visitors in the exhibits themselves. 'Living' museums replace 'dead' museums, open-air museums replace those under cover, sound replaces hushed silence, visitors are not separated from the exhibits by glass, and there is a multi-mediatisation of the exhibit. Overall the musuem and the various media are increasingly de-differentiated. The publicity for the Tyne and Wear museum well expressed this trend towards participation:

> In our museum, the emphasis is on action, participation and fun. Out are the endless old-fashioned glass cases you pored over in hushed silence. In are professionally designed displays, working models to play with, complete period room settings to browse through and sound effects to complete the picture. (quoted in White, 1987: 10)

There are various other changes taking place in museums which are making them much more aware of the diverse publics and of how to 'improve' the experience of visiting museums. In Leicester, for example, some acknowledgement is now made that visitors will come from different ethnic groups and that the museum staff must concern themselves with the various ways in which such visitors may interact with the displays and with the different accounts of histories they present (Hooper-Greenhill, 1988: 228–30). Museum displays are also less auratic. It is now quite common for it to be revealed how a particular exhibit was prepared for exhibition, and in some cases even how it was made to appear 'authentic'. There are various museums where actors play various historical roles and interact with the visitors, even to the extent of participating in various historical sketches. At Beamish, for example, people act out various roles in the different shops, while at Wigan Pier visitors are encouraged to experience a simulated school lesson. Elsewhere ex-miners describe mining work to visitors, and people run machinery which does not actually produce anything but simply demonstrates the machinery – 'the working non-working industry' (White, 1987: 11). Lumley summarises these changes overall by arguing that they involve replacing the notion that the museum is a collection for scholarly use with the idea that it is a means of communication (1988: 15). There is the shift from 'legislator' to 'interpreter', as Bauman expresses it (1987).

In addition there is a changed relationship between what is considered a museum and various other social institutions. Those other institutions have now become more like museums. Some shops, for example, now look like museums with elaborate displays of high-quality goods where people will be attracted into the shop in order to wander and to gaze. In places like the Albert Dock in Liverpool, which contains the Tate Gallery of the North, a maritime museum and many stylish shops, it is difficult to see quite what is distinctive about the shops as such since people seem to regard their contents as 'exhibits'. Stephen Bayley, from the London Museum of Design remarked:

> the old nineteenth century museum was somewhat like a shop ... a place where you go and look at values and ideas, and I think shopping really is becoming one of the great cultural experiences of the late twentieth century ... The two things are merging. So you have museums becoming more commercial, shops becoming more intelligent and more cultural. (quoted in Hewison, 1987: 139)

It has also been suggested that 'factory tourism' should be developed, that factories should in effect be viewed as museum-like. Certainly when factories do organise 'open days' they are very successful. The Sellafield nuclear reprocessing plant in Cumbria has become a major tourist attraction with 178,000 visitors a year. What is happening is that the factory is becoming more like a museum. Likewise, there has been an extensive 'museumification' of English pubs, many of which have become 'mock Imperial Victorian' and undergone 'ye olde-ing' (see Norman, 1988). Small collections of apparently authentic exhibits are now to be found in many pubs and restaurants.

At the same time, museums have become more like commercial businesses:

> the enterprise and flair of the High St is diffusing in the world of museums ... Packaging means establishing a corporate identity ... Shopping is not just making a purchase, it is about the whole experience, including the ambience of the shop, the style of the staff. (Pemberton, quoted in Lumley, 1988: 20)

This poses particular difficulties for museum staff, who should be trying to fashion an identity for museums different from that of commercial enterprises. The problem has arisen because of the growth of tourist and leisure industries (see Morton, 1988). Theme parks, shopping malls and heritage centres have all forced museums to compete, to become much more market-oriented, certainly to run a prominent museum 'shop' and cafe', but also to mount spectacular displays as in the exceptional historical reconstructions in the new Canadian Museum of Civilization. Heritage centres, such as the Jorvik Viking Centre in York or the Pilgrim's Way in Canterbury, are competitors with existing museums and challenge given notions of authenticity. In such centres there is a curious mixing of the museum and the theatre. Everything is meant to be authentic, even down to the smells, but nothing actually dates from the period, as Macdonald describes in the case of a Gaelic heritage centre (1997). These centres are the product of a York-based company Heritage Projects, whose work is particularly challenging to existing museums that are forced to adapt even further (see Davenport, 1987).

The sovereignty of the consumer and trends in popular taste are colluding to transform the museum's social role. It is much less the embodiment of a single unambiguous high culture from which the overwhelming mass of the population is excluded. Museums have become more accessible, especially to the service and middle classes (see Merriman, 1989; Heinich, 1988, on the

Figure 6.5 *Holocaust Museum, Washington DC, USA*

Pompidou Centre). In the leisure of such classes, Merriman (1989) suggests, museum visiting, with its previously high cultural associations, enables the acquisition of a certain cultural capital, an acquisition made possible by the increased degree to which people are now able to 'read' museums. This has helped museums to become important in defining good taste, particularly as we saw earlier, the 'heritage' look. A rural version of this is the 'country decor' look, the parameters of which are partly defined in terms of rural museums and the 'charming' manner in which the various quaint rooms are set out (Thrift, 1989). 'Holocaust' museums, meanwhile involve the prescription of appropriate modes of collective grieving (see Figure 6.5).

Conclusion

Many of these points about gazing on history can be seen at Quarry Bank Mill at Styal in Cheshire (built by Samuel Greg in 1784). Surrounding the mill are the buildings of an entire factory community, two chapels, a school, shop, houses for mill workers, and an apprentice house, all of which have remained physically well preserved. The museum was founded in 1976, described as 'a museum of the factory system', aiming to bring to life the role of the workforce, the Greg family and the circumstances which began the industrial revolution in the textile industry. The museum houses a number of displays on textile finishing and water power. Demonstrators, some dressed in appropriate clothing, show visitors how to spin cotton on a spinning jenny, how to hand-weave, how a carding machine operated, the workings of a weaving mule, and the domestic routines involved in cooking, cleaning and washing for the child workforce. Considerable research by professional historians was undertaken to produce both the displays and the large number of supporting documents, given to or sold to visitors (Rose 1978). Engineers have also been centrally involved in the development of the museum, in order to get the often-derelict machinery reworking.

The mill has produced a range of supporting material for such visitors, including a 'Resource and Document Pack'. Up to 100 guides are employed in explaining aspects of the mill's workings to such visitors. There are also a number of other educational activities undertaken by the museum. Courses run by the mill include weaving, spinning, patchwork and quilting, embroidery and lace, experimental textiles, fashion and clothing, design for textiles, dyeing and printing, and knitting. The mill has made energetic efforts to attract the 'non-museum visiting public' by specifically increasing the entertainment elements of display. This is partly achieved by the use of people to demonstrate many of the processes and to interact in a role-playing way with the visitors. It is also assisted by organising a variety of special events: Mothering Sunday lunches, a tent-making project, St George's Day celebrations, Spooky tours, Apprentices' Christmas and so on. However, there is an obvious danger of both being *seen* as over-commercial and of actually *being* over-commercial.

The mill has had to grapple with the issue of authenticity. Although the building is 'genuine' and has not been particularly cleaned up, the machinery it houses does not stem from the eighteenth century. Some items had been in the mill since the nineteenth or early twentieth centuries, while quite a lot of it, including the immense waterwheel, has been imported from other, often derelict, industrial sites. The work on the machinery has involved using 'traditional' techniques that have had to be specially learnt. The mill tries to make explicit what is authentic, although this is not a straightforward exercise since what is thought to be authentic depends upon which particular period is being considered. Also, of course, existing 'authentic' factories contain machines from a variety of periods. What Quarry Bank Mill ultimately shows is that there is no simple 'authentic' reconstruction of history but that all involve accommodation and reinterpretation.

Finally, the mill does not present an overly romanticised view of working-class life. There is plenty of evidence of the ill-health and squalor of much industrial work. However, the mill literature also draws considerable attention to the views of contemporaries which suggested that conditions in rural factory communities, such as Styal, were considerably better than those in the huge industrial cities, such as neighbouring Manchester and Salford. Thus there seem to have been lower levels of industrial unrest, although this could also be related to forms of surveillance and control available locally. It was also suggested by the curator that visitors would not return for further visits if an overly depressing account of factory life were presented to visitors. However, Quarry Bank Mill is not a shrine to industrial technology – if anything the textile machinery is likely to be regarded by visitors as noisy, dangerous and dirty.

It is worth considering whether it is now possible to construct a museum or heritage centre preserving just any set of objects. It certainly seems possible. Some apparently unlikely museums are the pencil museum in Keswick, a museum of the chemical industry in Widnes, various Holocaust museums, a dental museum in London, and a shoe museum in Street. However, such museums appear to work because some connections between the past and the present are usually provided by 'place'. Occupation, industry, famous person or event may also sometimes provide such connections.

So museums cannot be created about anything anywhere. But a museum on almost any topic can be created somewhere, though whether we should still call them 'museums' is doubtful. The very term 'museum' stems from a period of high art and auratic culture well before 'heritage' and 'multi-media' had been invented and spread across the globe.

7

Seeing and Theming

Introduction

I have shown some of the connections between tourist practices and many other social phenomena. These are complex, partly because of the diverse nature of tourism and partly because other social phenomena increasingly involve elements of the tourist gaze. There is a generalisation of the tourist gaze in postmodern cultures – a generalisation which often takes the form of a vernacular, heritage and themed reshaping of much of the urban and rural landscape.

None of the theories outlined in Chapter 1 are in themselves adequate to grasp the 'essence' of tourism, which is multi-faceted and particularly bound up with many other social and cultural elements. It is inappropriate to think that it is possible to devise '*the* theory of tourist behaviour'. Instead what is required is a range of concepts and arguments which capture both what is specific to tourism and what is common to tourist and certain non-tourist social practices. Central to much tourism is some notion of departure, particularly that there are distinct contrasts between what people routinely see and experience and what is extraordinary, the extraordinary sometimes taking the form of a liminal zone. The following are relevant to understanding the changing sociology of the tourist gaze: the social tone of different places; the globalisation of the tourist gaze; the processes of consuming tourist services; tourist meanings and signs; modernism and postmodernism; history, heritage and the vernacular; and post-tourism and play. Different gazes and hence different tourist practices are authorised in terms of a variety of discourses (see Chapter 8).

In this chapter I consider in more detail two aspects of the tourist gaze notion. First, I examine what is meant by the idea of seeing and in turn being seen, especially via the medium of photography. And I reconsider the simulated character of the contemporary cultural experience, so-called 'hyper-reality' and the construction of 'themed' environments waiting to be viewed by the omnivorous visual consumer.

Seeing and being seen

Mass tourism is a characteristic of modern societies. It could only develop when a variety of economic, urban, infrastructural and attitudinal changes had transformed the social experiences of large sections of the population of European societies during the course of the nineteenth century. The way these changes worked themselves out in Britain were illustrated by analysing the causes and consequences of the growth of a new urban form, the seaside resort.

But there is one aspect of nineteenth-century developments that I have not yet described in any detail. This concerns the emergence of relatively novel modes of visual perception which became part of the modern experience of living and visiting new urban centres, particularly the grand capital cities. Here I shall show the nature of this new mode of visual perception, the connections between it and the growth of the tourist gaze, and the centrality of photography to these processes. The immensely expanding popularity of photography in the later nineteenth century indicates the importance of these new forms of visual perception, and their role in structuring the tourist gaze that was emerging in this period. This new mode of visual experience has been eloquently characterised by Berman, who sees in the rebuilding of Paris during the Second Empire in the mid-nineteenth century the construction of the conditions for the quintessentially modern experience (see Berman, 1983: section 3). It is also one of the most celebrated of tourist gazes.

For Berman what is of central importance to Paris in this period is the reconstruction of urban space which permits new ways of seeing and being seen. This was engendered by the massive rebuilding of Paris by Haussmann, who blasted a vast network of new boulevards through the heart of the old medieval city. The rebuilding of Paris displaced 350,000 people; by 1870 one-fifth of the streets of central Paris were Haussmann's creation; and at the height of the reconstruction one in five of all workers in the capital was employed in construction (see Clark, 1984: 37).

The boulevards were central to this planned reconstruction – they were like arteries in a massive circulatory system, and were planned partly at least to facilitate rapid troop movements. However, they also restructured what could be seen or gazed upon. Haussmann's plan entailed the building of markets, bridges, parks, the Opera and other cultural palaces, with many located at the end of the various boulevards. Such boulevards came to structure the gaze, both of Parisians and later of visitors. For the first time in a major city people could see well into the distance and indeed see where they were going and where they had come from. Great sweeping vistas were designed so that each walk led to a dramatic climax. As Berman says:

> All these qualities helped to make Paris a uniquely enticing spectacle, a visual and sensual feast ... after centuries of life as a cluster of isolated cells, Paris was becoming a unified physical and human space (1983: 151).

Certain of these spectacular views have come to be signifiers of the entity 'Paris' (as opposed to the individual districts).

These boulevards brought enormous numbers of people together in ways that were relatively novel. The street level was lined with many small businesses, shops and especially cafés. The last of these have come to be known all over the world as signs of *la vie Parisienne*, particularly as generations of painters, writers and photographers have represented the patterns of life in and around them, beginning with the Impressionists in the 1860s (see Berman, 1983: 151; Clark, 1984).

In particular Berman talks of the way in which the boulevards and cafés created a new kind of space, especially one where lovers could be 'private in public', intimately together without being physically alone (1983: 152). Lovers caught up in the extraordinary movement of modern Paris in the 1860s and 1870s could experience their emotional commitment particularly intensely. It was the traffic of people and horses that transformed social experience in this modern urban area. Urban life was both exceptionally rich and full of possibilities; and at the same time it was dangerous and frightening. As Baudelaire wrote: 'I was crossing the boulevard, in a great hurry, in the midst of a moving chaos, with death galloping at me from every side' (quoted Berman, 1983: 159).

To be private in the midst of such danger and chaos created the perfect romantic setting of modern times; and millions of visitors have attempted to re-experience that particular quality among the boulevards and cafés of Paris.

This romantic experience could be felt especially intensely in front of the endless parades of strangers moving up and down the boulevards – it was those strangers they gazed upon and who in turn gazed at them. Part then of the gaze in the new modern city of Paris was of the multitude of passers-by, who both enhanced the lovers' vision of themselves and in turn provided an endlessly fascinating source of curiosity.

They could weave veils of fantasy around the multitude of passers-by: who were these people, where did they come from and where were they going, what did they want, whom did they love? The more they saw of others and showed themselves to others – the more they participated in the extended 'family of eyes' – the richer became their vision of themselves. (Berman, 1983: 152)

Haussmann's reconstruction of Paris was not of course without its intense critics (see Clark, 1984: 41–50). It was very forcibly pointed out that demolishing the old *quartiers* meant that much of the working class was forced out of the centre of Paris, particularly because of the exceptionally high rents charged in the lavish apartment blocks that lined the new boulevards. Reconstruction therefore led to rapid residential segregation and to the worst signs of deprivation and squalor being removed from the gaze of richer Parisians and, later in the century, of visitors. Second, Paris was said to be increasingly a city of vice, vulgarity and display – ostentation not luxury, frippery not fashion, consumption not trade (see Clark, 1984: 46–7). It was a city of uncertainty in which there were too many surfaces, too few boundaries. It was the city of the *flâneur* or stroller. The anonymity of the crowd provided an asylum for those on the margins of society who were able to move about unnoticed, observing and being observed, but never really interacting with those encountered. The *flâneur* was the modern hero, able to travel, to arrive, to gaze, to move on, to be anonymous, to be in a liminal zone (see Benjamin, 1973; Wolff, 1985; Tester, 1994).

The *flâneur* was invariably male and this rendered invisible the different ways in which women were both more restricted to the private sphere and at the same time were coming to colonise other emerging public spheres in the late nineteenth century, especially the department store (see Wolff, 1985, 1993). The strolling *flâneur* was a forerunner of the twentieth-century tourist and in particular of the activity which has in a way become emblematic of the tourist: the democratised taking of photographs – of being seen and recorded, and of seeing others and recording them.

Susan Sontag explicitly makes this link between the *flâneur* and photography. The latter:

> first comes into its own as an extension of the eye of the middle-class *flâneur* ... The photographer is an armed version of the solitary walker reconnoitering, stalking, cruising the urban inferno, the voyeuristic stroller who discovers the city as a landscape of voluptuous extremes. Adept of the joys of watching, connoisseur of empathy, the *flâneur* finds the world 'picturesque'. (1979: 55)

While the middle-class *flâneur* was attracted to the city's dark seamy corners, the twentieth-century photographer is attracted everywhere, to every possible object, event and person. And at the same time the photographer is also observed and photographed. One is both see-er and seen. To be a photographer in the twentieth century, and that is so much part of travel and tourism, is also to be viewed and photographed.

There has been an enormous proliferation of photographic images since the invention of photography in 1839. Over that century and a half there has been an utter insatiability of the photographing eye, an insatiability that teaches new ways of looking at the world and new forms of authority for doing so. Photography currently results in the overloading of the visual environment, with apparently sixty billion pictures being taken each year (Crang, 1999; 243). It is moreover a socially constructed way of seeing and recording with a number of key characteristics that I now outline and develop (Sontag, 1979; Berger, 1972; Barthes, 1981; Albers and James, 1988; Osborne, 2000):

1 To photograph is in some way to appropriate the object being photographed. It is a power/knowledge relationship. To have visual knowledge of an object is in part to have power, even if only momentarily, over it. Photography tames the object of the gaze, the most striking examples being of exotic cultures. In the US the railway companies did much to create 'Indian' attractions to be photographed, carefully selecting those tribes with a particularly 'picturesque and ancient' appearance (see Albers and James, 1988: 151).

2 Photography *seems* to be a means of transcribing reality. The images produced appear to be not statements about the world but pieces of it, or even miniature slices of reality. A photograph thus seems to furnish evidence that something did indeed happen – that someone really was there or that the mountain actually was that large. It is thought that the camera does not lie.

3   Yet in fact photographs are the outcome of an active signifying practice in which those taking the photo select, structure and shape what is going to be taken. In particular there is the attempt to construct idealised images which beautify the object being photographed. Sontag summarises: 'the aestheticizing tendency of photography is such that the medium which conveys distress ends by neutralizing it' (1979: 109).

Elsewhere I show how professional photographers actively construct aestheticised images of the Lake District devoid of cars, people, bad weather, litter and so on (Crawshaw and Urry, 1997).

4   The power of the photograph thus stems from its ability to pass itself off as a miniaturisation of the real, without revealing either its constructed nature or its ideological content (but see Martin Parr's photographs in *Small World*, 1995; and see Taylor, 1994).

5   As everyone becomes a photographer so everyone also becomes an amateur semiotician. One learns that a thatched cottage with roses round the door represents 'ye olde England'; or that waves crashing on to rocks signifies 'wild, untamed nature'; or, especially, that a person with a camera draped around his/her neck is clearly a 'tourist'.

6   Photography involves the democratisation of all forms of human experience, both by turning everything into photographic images and by enabling anyone to photograph them, especially with the development of throwaway cameras. Photography is then part of the process of post-modernisation. Each thing or person photographed becomes equivalent to the other, equally interesting or uninteresting. Barthes notes that photography began with photographs of the notable and has ended up making notable whatever is photographed (1981: 34, and see Sontag, 1979: 111). Photography is a promiscuous way of seeing which cannot be limited to an elite, as art. Sontag talks of photography's 'zeal for debunking the high culture of the past ... its conscientious courting of vulgarity ... its skill in reconciling avant-garde ambitions with the rewards of commercialism ... its transformation of art into cultural document' (1979: 131).

7   Photography gives shape to travel. It is the reason for stopping, to take (snap) a photograph, and then to move on. Photography involves obligations. People feel that they must not miss seeing particular scenes since otherwise the photo-opportunities will be missed. Tourist agencies spend much time indicating where photographs should be taken (so-called viewing points). Indeed much tourism becomes in effect a search for the photogenic; travel is a strategy for the accumulation of photographs and hence for the commodification and privatisation of personal and especially of family memories (West, 2000: 9). This seems particularly to appeal to those cultures with a very strong work ethic. Japanese, Americans and Germans all seem to 'have' to take photographs and then to remember through these photographs – it is a kind of leisure equivalent of the distorting obligations of a strong workplace culture (see Sontag, 1979).

8   Involved in much tourism is a hermeneutic circle. What is sought for in a holiday is a set of photographic images, which have already been seen in tour company brochures or on TV programmes (see Selwyn, 1996). While the tourist is away, this then moves on to a tracking down and capturing of those images for oneself. And it ends up with travellers demonstrating that they really have been there by showing their version of the images that they had seen before they set off.

Mass photography has thus been enormously significant in democratising various kinds of mobilities, making notable whatever gets photographed rather than what elites might have specified. And photography gives shape to travel so that journeys consist of one 'good view' to capture on film, to a series of others. The objects and technologies of cameras and films have constituted the very nature of travel, as sites turn into sights, they have con-structed what is worth going to 'sightsee' and what images and memories should be brought back (West, 2000; Osborne, 2000). The camera effects this by turning nature and society into graspable objects (just as photography turns women into materialised objects on a page or video):

> the snapshot transforms the resistant aspect of nature into something familiar and intimate, something we can hold in our hands and memories. In this way, the camera allows us some control over the visual environments of our culture (Wilson, 1992: 122).

Nature, other environments and humans are transformed into objects that are passed from person to person. They are put on walls to decorate a house, they structure reminiscences and they create images of place (Spence and Holland, 1991; Taylor, 1994). Photographs are subjective and objective, both personal *and* apparently accounting for how things really are. Indeed the photographic tourist gaze produces an aesthetics that excludes as much as it includes. It is unusual to see postcards or tourist photographs containing 'landscapes' of waste, disease, dead animals, poverty, sewage and despoila-tion (Crawshaw and Urry, 1997; but see Taylor, 1994; Parr, 1995). West also notes how Kodak's advertising 'purged domestic photography of all traces of sorrow and death' (2000: 1; see Hutnyk, 1996, on 'photogenic Calcutta').

Landscapes and townscapes typically involve the notion of 'mastery'. The photographer, and then the viewer, is seen to be above, and dominating, a static and subordinate landscape lying out inert and inviting inspection. Such photographic practices demonstrate how the environment is to be viewed, dominated by humans and subject to their possessive mastery (Taylor, 1994: 38–9).

Photography has therefore been crucial in the development of tourism; they are not separate processes but each derives from and enhances the other, an 'ensemble' according to Osborne (2000). If photography had not been 'invented' around 1840 and then enormously developed through the cheap Kodak camera then contemporary tourist gazes would have been wholly dif-ferent (see West, 2000). One early example of the impact of the ensemble of photography and tourism is late nineteenth century Egypt. Gregory has described the processes of 'Kodakisation' (1999; and see West, 2000). Egypt became scripted as a place of constructed visibility, with multiple, enframed theatrical scenes set up for the edification, entertainment and visual consumption of 'European' visitors. Cairo became 'no more than a Winter Suburb of London' (Löfgren, 2000: 162). This had the effect of producing what could be described as a 'new Egypt' available for visually consuming visitors.

Such an Egypt consisted of the Suez Canal, of 'Paris-on-the-Nile', of Thomas Cook and Sons, of a cleaned-up 'ancient Egypt', of the exotic oriental 'other' and of convenient vantage-points and viewing platforms for the tourist gaze (see Brendon, 1991: 118, more generally on how Cook's tourists were 'pervading the whole earth'). Analogously West argues that in the US a single corporation (Kodak) had enormous effects; it 'taught modern Americans how to see, to remember, how to love' (2000: xv).

Indeed without photography there would not be the contemporary global tourism industry. Osborne describes: 'the ultimate inseparability of the medium [of photography] from tourism's general culture and economy and from the varieties of modern culture of which they are constitutive' (2000: 70).

Themes and Malls

In this section I discuss one aspect of the gaze, how a variety of environments are produced, marketed, circulated and consumed. I consider aspects of recent theme parks before turning to the themed character of contemporary retailing, noting especially the ubiquitous shopping mall.

First, there is an increasingly pervasive tendency to divide up countries in terms of new spatial divisions with new place names. In the north of England there is 'Last of the Summer Wine Country', 'Emmerdale Farm Country', 'James Herriot Country', 'Robin Hood Country', 'Catherine Cookson Country', 'Brontë Country' and so on. Space is divided up in terms of signs that signify particular themes – but not themes that necessarily relate to actual historical or geographical processes. A similar process can be seen in Canada where the theme of 'Maritimicity' developed since the 1920s as a result of the provincial state and private capital seeking to develop modern tourism in Nova Scotia. McKay describes it as 'a peculiar petit-bourgeois rhetoric of lobster pots, grizzled fishermen, wharves and schooners ... a Golden Age mythology in a region that has become economically dependent on tourism' (1988: 30). In particular Peggy's Cove has over the years become a purer and purer simulacrum, a copy of a prosperous and tranquil fishing village that never existed.

Even stranger is the case of the Granada Studios in Manchester. Part of the display consists of a mock-up of certain sets from the soap opera *Coronation Street*, including the Rover's Return public house. This is very popular with visitors, who are keen to photograph it. But as one commentator noted: 'when we develop our photos of that Rover's Return scenario we will consume a representation of a representation of a representation' (Goodwin, 1989). This set is part of the 'Coronation Street Experience' in which the Rover's Return pub is given a fictional history, starting in 1902.

Other themed attractions in Britain include the Jorvik Centre in York, the Camelot theme park in Lancashire, the American Adventure in the Peak District, the Oxford Story, the Crusades experience in Winchester ('history brought to life'), and the Pilgrim's Way in Canterbury. The last is described in the advertising material as 'a pilgrimage to the past'. However, the sense of history is bizarre since:

> a man on children's television is the model for a dummy who is the adjunct to a non-existent scene in a mediaeval religious poem, none of whose words you hear (Faulks, 1988).

Another distinctive example is to be found in Llandrindod Wells in Wales. Once a year most of the population dress up in Edwardian costume, but it has recently been suggested that the population could be dressed that way *for the entire year*. Thus the whole town and its population would be turned into a permanent Edwardian themed town. Already Visby in Sweden, an island in the Baltic, experiences a 'medieval week' when everyone dresses up in medieval costume, bringing the medieval 'theme' to life.

Themes are, in Debord's terms, elements of the 'society of the spectacle' (1983) or what Eco describes as 'travels in hyper-reality' (1986). In such themed areas the objects observed must seem real and absolutely authentic. Those responsible for Jorvik or the Oxford Story have attempted to make the experience authentic, through the use of smells as well as visual and aural simulation. The scenes are in a sense more real than the original, hyper-real. Or at least the surfaces, as grasped through the immediate senses, are more real. Lowenthal notes that 'habituation to replicas tends to persuade us that antiquities should look complete and "new"' (1985: 293). The representations thus approximate more closely to our expectations of reality, of the signs that we carry around waiting to be instantiated: 'Disneyland tells us that faked nature corresponds much more to our daydream demands ... Disneyland tells us that technology can give us more reality than nature can' (Eco, 1986: 44).

This theming was taken to the extreme in New Zealand. A popular nineteenth-century tourist attraction was a set of pink and white terraces rising up above Lake Rotomahana. These were destroyed by volcanic eruptions in 1886 although photographs of them have remained popular ever since. They are a well-known attraction even if they have not existed for a century. Now, however, the physical attraction has been recreated by running geothermal water over artificially built terraces in a different location, but one close to existing tourist facilities. This set of what might be called 'themed' terraces will look more authentic than the original which is only known about because of the hundred-year-old photographic images.

This technological ability to create new themes which appear more real than the original has now spread from tourist attractions *per se*, beginning with Disneyland, to shopping centres or malls. Many malls are now extraordinary tourist attractions in their own right and represent an exceptional degree of cultural de-differentiation, as discussed in Chapter 5. Consider the following publicity material for the West Edmonton Mall (see Figure 7.1):

> Imagine visiting Disneyland, Malibu Beach, Bourbon Street, the San Diego Zoo, Rodeo Drive in Beverly Hills and Australia's Great Barrier Reef ... in one weekend – and under one roof ... Billed as the world's largest shopping complex of its kind, the Mall covers 110 acres and features 828 stores, 110 restaurants, 19 theatres ... a five-acre water park with a glass dome that is over 19 storeys high ... Contemplate the Mall's indoor lake complete with four submarines from which you can view sharks, octopi, tropical marine life, and a replica of the Great Barrier Reef ... Fantasyland Hotel has given its rooms a variety of themes: one floor holds Classical Roman rooms, another *1001 Nights* Arabian rooms, another, Polynesian rooms ... (Travel Alberta, undated)

The mall has been very successful: as early as 1987 attracting over nine million visitors, making it the third most popular tourist attraction in north America after two Disney parks. The Mall represents a symbolic rejection of the normally understood world geography in which there are distant centres with Edmonton on the periphery. What is being asserted is a new collective sense of place based on transcending the geographical barrier of distance and of place. The real-space relations of the globe are thus replaced by imaginary-space relations (Shields, 1989: 153).

This has only been possible because of the pervasiveness of tourist signs, of the rapid circulation of photographic images. It is this exchange of signs which makes possible the construction of a pastiche of themes, each of which seems more real than the original, particularly because of the way that shopping malls in general emphasise newness and cleanliness: 'It is a world where Spanish galleons sail up Main Street past Marks and Spencer to put in at 'New Orleans', where everything is tame and happy shoppers mingle with smiling dolphins' (Shields, 1989: 154).

The closest to this in Britain are the Trafford Centre near Manchester and the Metrocentre in the north east. The latter was located in a place normally considered peripheral to British and European life. It was constructed on derelict land and contains three miles of shopping malls with 300 shops, 40 restaurants, a 10-screen cinema, a bowling alley, an enormous fantasy kingdom of fairground rides and entertainments, a crèche, and three themed areas. These themes are 'Antique Village', with a phoney waterwheel and plastic ducks on the village pond; a 'Roman Forum', with areas on which to recline Roman-style; and a 'Mediterranean Village', with Italian, Greek and Lebanese restaurants lining a windingly quaint Mediterranean street. Shopping is clearly here only part of the appeal of the mall, which is as much concerned with leisure and tourism. Within a few minutes' walk one can consume a range of tourist themes, can stroll gazing and being gazed upon as though 'on holiday', and can experience an enormous range of entertainment services.

Figure 7.1   *West Edmonton Shopping Mall, Canada*

Malls represent membership of a community of consumers. To be in attendance at the 'court of commodities' is to assert one's existence and to be recognised as a citizen in contemporary society, that is, as a consumer. However, the recent marketing philosophy has been to develop spectacles of 'diversity and market segmentation', although this is less clear in the case of mass middle-class malls such as the Metrocentre. The development of such differentiation in particular centres is because the display of difference will increase a centre's tourist appeal to many others within the same market 'segment' from elsewhere. For example, Trump Tower in New York was the ultimate 1980s upper-middle-class white shopping mall (see Figure 7.2 for the Russian equivalent).

Figure 7.2   *Gum Shopping Arcades, Moscow, Russian Federation*

Developments of this sort also represent the changing nature of public space in contemporary societies. An increasingly central role is being played by privately owned and controlled consumption spaces. These involve high levels of surveillance where certain types of behaviour, clothing and comportment are expected, such as not sitting on the floor. The entrance and pathways of malls are 'policed' and 'undesirable' categories of the population, such as the homeless, can be excluded. The Metrocentre boasts that it is safest place in Britain to shop. There are some analogies between Bentham's panopticon prison and the visual and electronic surveillance found in these malls. They are also conspicuous for cleanliness and newness, with no space for untidy litter, the old, the shabby or the worn. Malls have to exude up-to-dateness and fashionability which is why they have to be regularly refurbished (see Fiske, 1989: 39–42).

Malls attract their share of 'post-shoppers', people who play at being consumers in complex, self-conscious mockery. Users should not be seen simply as victims of consumerism, as 'credit card junkies', but also as being able to assert their independence from the mall developers. This is achieved by a kind of tourist *flânerie*, by continuing to stroll, to gaze, and to be gazed upon: 'Their wandering footsteps, the modes of their crowd practice constitute that certain urban ambiance: a continuous reassertion of the rights and freedoms of the marketplace, the *communitas* of the carnival' (Shields, 1989: 161).

In an Australian study Pressdee showed that in spite of the control mechanisms in such malls 80 per cent of unemployed young people visited them at least once a week, and that more or less 100 per cent of young unemployed women were regular visitors (1986). Late-night shopping on Thursday was when young people with little intention to buy invaded the mall. The youths consumed images and space instead of commodities. Fiske talks of:

> a kind of sensuous consumption that did not create profits. The positive pleasure of parading up and down, of offending 'real' consumers and the gents of law and order, of asserting their difference within, and different use of, the cathedral of consumerism became an oppositional cultural practice. (1989: 17)

Fiske also points out the central importance of shops as public, or at least semi-public, spaces particularly attractive to women (1989). I noted earlier the importance of the nineteenth-century development of the department store in this respect, that it was both respectable and safe for unattached women. Zola described the department store as 'a temple to women, making a legion of shop assistants burn incense before her' (quoted in Pevsner, 1970: 269). The mall is somewhat similar, and indeed shopping is a sphere of social activity in which women are empowered. It links together the public and the domestic and involves activity in which women are permitted to demonstrate competence.

Finally, one should note a further setting for themed environments which have become particularly popular in the last decades, world fairs, which have developed into enormous international tourist attractions. For example, over 500,000 visitors a day attended the 1992 Expo in Seville (Harvey, P., 1996: 155). The development and popularity of these world fairs represent the growing intrusion of leisure, tourism and the aesthetic into the urban landscape. They provide further examples of the de-differentiation of leisure, tourism, shopping, culture, education, eating, and so on.

Expo's are organised around different national displays (Harvey, P., 1996: Chapter 3). There are many themed environments based on different national stereotypes, such as the British pub, American achievement in sport, the German beer garden and South Sea Islands exotic dancing. Such themes are designed to demonstrate national pride in the cultural activities presumed specific to that country. Generally this pride was demonstrated either in repackaging aspects of that country's traditions and heritage or in demonstrating the high level of modern technology achieved.

As with the Vancouver Expo, no single hegemonic set of messages was conveyed by the fair. Indeed they are such postmodern phenomena that this would be difficult to achieve. Such fairs are, if anything, a kind of micro-version of international tourism. Rather than tourists having to travel world-wide to experience and gaze upon these different signs, they are conveniently brought together in one location, simply on a larger scale than the West Edmonton mall. Harvey says more generally: 'it is now possible to experience the world's geography vicariously, as a simulacrum' (1989: 300). This can be seen from the entertainment provided at such world fairs. At Vancouver there were 43,000 free on-site performances given by an incredible 80,000 performers (Ley and Olds, 1988: 203). Although there was high culture, including a presentation from *La Scala* to an audience of 40,000, most entertainment consisted of folk or popular forms, all in all a postmodern cultural pastiche, rather like the availability of cuisines from around the world available in most major American cities (Pillsbury, 1990). Most performances were recognisably from a specific country and consisted of the sort of ethnic entertainment that is provided for tourists in each country that they visit. The difference here was that the visitors only had to walk from one tent or display to the next in order to gaze upon another cultural event signifying yet another nation.

The Universal Exhibition at Seville in 1992 offers a further prism into these processes. Such exhibitions operate as a technology of nationhood, providing narrative possibilities for the imagining of national cultures and indeed the national 'brand' (Harvey, P., 1996: ch. 3). Through powerful images, symbols and icons, nation-states are represented as repositories of stability, continuity, uniqueness and harmony. However, Seville was also a place of international capital, funding various national displays, the Expo as a whole and their own exhibition spaces, especially with communicational and informational advances that transcend national borders. In these displays the emphasis is placed upon consumer desire, individual choice, cosmopolitanism and the freedom of the market to cross national borders (the tourist crossing of borders is also to be found in collecting stamps in the Exhibition Passport). Universal Exhibitions are places to celebrate global scapes and flows and of the companies that mobilise such mobilities; while nations are principally there as spectacle and sign in the branding processes that such Expos construct and celebrate (see McCrone, Morris, Kelly, 1995, on Scotland the brand).

Many of the displays in Expos purport to be educational, and indeed groups of school-age children constitute a major category of visitors. And this is a further feature of the de-differentiation of the cultural spheres. Education and entertainment are becoming merged, a process very much assisted by the increasingly central role of the visual and electronic media in both. Indeed theme parks are involved in providing 'edu-tainment', something most clearly seen at London's Millennium Dome.

Holidays are thus not so straightforwardly contrasted with education and learning as in the past. In many ways much tourism is more closely interwoven with learning, returning in a way to the Grand Tour. I have already noted the increasing popularity of museums, the fascination with the lives of industrial workers in particular, and the popularity of hyper-real historical re-creations. Some developments are the increased desire to learn a new sport on holiday (skiing, bunjee jumping, watersports, hang-gliding); the development of arts and cultural tourism; the heightened attraction of unusual industrial sites, such as Sellafield nuclear reprocessing plant and the substantial increase in educational holidays (in schools, universities and hotels). Many hotel groups now offer a wide range of educational breaks at various themed hotels. Amongst the subjects studied on various themed weekends are arts and antiques, bridge, watercolour painting, archery, clay pigeon shooting, fly fishing, golf and pony-trekking.

Conclusion

In this chapter I have elaborated two aspects of the gaze, its connection with the practices of photography and its themed nature. Both these aspects propel contemporary tourism into a more general economy of signs.

In conclusion I note some ways in which tourism experiences are divided by class, gender and ethnicity. In earlier discussions I emphasised the importance of social class divisions in structuring how tourist developments occurred in different ways in different places. These effects include the respective social tone of different resorts and the patterns of landholding; the importance of the aristocratic connection in constructing the fashionability of certain places; the growth of the middle-class family holiday and the development of the bungalow as a specialised building form by the seaside; the importance of the 'romantic gaze' and its role in constructing nature as an absolutely central positional good; the character of the 'collective' gaze and the role of others like oneself in constituting the attraction of certain places; and the enhanced cultural capital of the service class and its impact in heightening the appeal of rural and industrial heritage, and of postmodernism.

But seeing and theming are also inflected by divisions of gender and ethnicity. These interconnections are important in forming the preferences that different social groupings develop about where to visit and in structuring the effects of such visits upon host populations and the fashionability of different sites. There are two key issues here: the social composition of fellow tourists and the social composition of those living in the places visited. These are important because most tourist practices involve movement into and through various sorts of public space – such as theme parks, shopping malls, beaches, restaurants, hotels, pump rooms, promenades, airports, swimming pools and squares. In such spaces people both gaze at and are gazed upon by others (and are photographed and photograph others). Complex preferences have come to develop for the range of appropriate others that different social groups expect to look at and photograph in different places; and in turn different expectations are held by different social groups about who are appropriate others to gaze at oneself. Part of what is involved in tourism is the purchase of a particular themed experience, and this depends upon a specifiable composition of the others with whom that experience is being shared.

I noted in Chapter 3 the development of sex-tourism in certain south-east Asian societies as well as in major cities throughout the world and in various Caribbean and African societies. In south-east Asia the combination of gender and ethnic subordination had colluded to construct young Asian women as objects of a tourist/sexual gaze for male visitors from other societies – visitors who are ethnically dominant. The resulting tourist patterns cannot be analysed separately from relations of gender and racial subordination (see Hall, 1994; Kinnaird and Hall, 1994). The importance of gender inequalities can be seen in another way. In almost all societies men have enjoyed a higher standard of living than women. In Britain this has resulted from a privileged treatment in the household's distribution of food, heat and other material resources; and from the ability to escape the home to spend large amounts of leisure time in the 'masculine republic' of the pub (see Hart, 1989). To the extent to which contemporary leisure patterns are more 'privatised' and shared within the household, this may involve a reduced inequality of both household income and leisure time.

This relates in an important way to the development of holidays. Until the nineteenth century access to travel was largely the preserve of men. But this changed with the development of 'Victorian lady travellers', some of whom visited countries that were at the time considered 'uncivilised' and 'uncharted' especially for women (see Enloe, 1989: ch. 2). Other women took advantage of Cook's tours. As one woman wrote: 'We would venture anywhere with such a guide and guardian as Mr Cook' (quoted in Enloe, 1989: 29). From then onwards access to holidays has not been so unequally distributed as has access to some other forms of leisure. Couples normally undertook working-class holidays to English seaside resorts. Moreover, the fact that such holidays developed first in industrial Lancashire was partly the result of high levels of female employment in the cotton textile industry, especially in weaving. This meant that household earnings were higher than in other areas and women had more say over its distribution.

The early forms of mass tourism were based around the heterosexual couple; during the course of the nineteenth century the holiday unit had increasingly come to be made up of such a couple plus their children (and as recorded in innumerable photographs). And by the inter-war period the family holiday had become child-centred. This was given a significant boost by the development of the holiday camp in the 1930s in which child-based activities were central. Their development was of benefit to women since it meant that much childcare was undertaken by paid workers. The more recent growth of self-catering has moved in the opposite direction with only a minority of holidays in Britain now in serviced accommodation.

It is important to note how holiday-making discourses are predominantly heterosexual, involving pictures of actual couples, with or without children, or potential couples. In brochures produced by tour operators there are three predominant images. These are the 'family holiday', that is a couple with two or three healthy school-age children; the 'romantic holiday', that is a heterosexual couple on their own gazing at the sunset (indeed the sunset is a signifier for romance); and the 'fun holiday', that is same-sex groups each looking for other-sex partners for 'fun'. There is also, as we have noted, the 'sex holiday' for men. It is well known that social groups that do not fall into any of these particular visual categories are poorly served by the tourist industry. Many criticisms have been made of how difficult holiday-making is for single people, single-parent families, homosexual couples or groups, and those who are disabled (although the growth of gay tourism, to Amsterdam or San Francisco, has been a marked feature of the 1990s, with gay themed bars for example).

Another social category often excluded from conventional holiday-making are black Britons. The advertising material produced by holiday companies shows that tourists are white; there are few black faces amongst the holiday-makers. Indeed if there are any non-white faces in the photographs it would be presumed that they are the 'exotic natives' being gazed upon. The same process would seem to occur in those areas in Britain that attract large numbers of foreign tourists. If black or Asian people are seen there it would be presumed that they were visitors from overseas, or perhaps service workers, but not British residents themselves on holiday. The countryside is particularly constructed as 'white', as Taylor shows with regard to typically dominant photographic images (1994).

An interesting question is the degree to which members of ethnic minorities do undertake western-type holidays. Aspects of the western holiday, in which one travels elsewhere because of the sun, hotel or scenery, form a cultural practice that will seem rather idiosyncratic at least to some recent migrants to Britain (see Ahmed, 2000, on the ambiguities of the sun tan). Some migrants at least would consider that travel should have a more serious purpose than this: to look for work, to join the rest of one's family, to visit relatives, or to participate in diasporic travel.

Many tourist developments are likely to exclude many ethnic groups, such as the heritage industry discussed in the previous chapter. It was noted that white faces overwhelmingly populate such a heritage. Ethnic groups are important in the British tourist industry, though, and in some respects play a key role. They are employed in those enterprises concerned with servicing visitors, especially in the major cities (10 per cent of the restaurant workforce is non-white compared with five per cent in the workforce as a whole: Department of Culture, Media and Sport website).

Furthermore, in recent years certain ethnic groups have come to be constructed as part of the 'attraction' or 'theme' of some places. This is most common in the case of Asian groups. In Manchester this has occurred around its collection of Chinese restaurants in a small area, and resulted from the internationalisation of British culinary taste in the post-war period (see Frieden and Sagalyn, 1989: 199–201). By the 1980s city planners were committed to a new vision of 'Chinatown', reconstructed and conserved as a now desirable object of the tourist gaze (see Anderson, 1988, on Vancouver).

Further analysis of this would need to explore the social effects for those of Asian origin of becoming constructed as an exotic object and whether this distorts patterns of economic and political development. It would also be interesting to consider the effects on the white population of coming to view those of Asian origin as not so much threatening or even inferior but as exotic, as curiously different and possessing a rich and in part attractive culture. Such debates are developing in the context of many cultures taken to be exotically different, as such cultures become 'themed', 'photographed' and displayed around the world.

8

Globalising the Gaze

Tourism and the Global

In 1990 when *The Tourist Gaze* was first published it was unclear how significant the processes we now call 'globalisation' were to become. Indeed the internet had only just been invented and there was no indication how it would transform countless aspects of social life, being taken up more rapidly than any previous technology. And no sooner than the internet had begun to impact, than another 'mobile technology', the mobile phone, transformed communications practices on the move. Overall the 1990s have seen remarkable 'time-space compression' as people across the globe have been brought closer through various technologically-assisted developments. There is increasingly for some social groups what Cairncross terms the 'death of distance' (1997), while Bauman describes the shift from a solid, fixed modernity to a much more fluid and speeded-up 'liquid modernity' (2000).

And part of this sense of compression of space has stemmed from the rapid flows of travellers and tourists physically moving from place to place, and especially from hub airport to hub airport. Elsewhere I distinguish between virtual travel through the internet, imaginative travel through phone, radio and TV, and corporeal travel along the infrastructures of the global travel industry (Urry, 2000: ch. 3). The amount of 'traffic' along all these has magnified over this last decade and there is no evidence that virtual and imaginative travel is replacing corporeal travel, but there are complex intersections between these different modes of travel that are increasingly de-differentiated from one another. As Microsoft ask: 'where do you want to go today?'; and there are diverse and interdependent ways of getting 'there'.

What I thus call corporeal travel has thus taken on immense dimensions and comprises the largest ever movement of people across national borders (see Chapter 1). Because of these liquidities the relations between almost all societies across the globe are mediated by flows of tourists, as place after place is reconfigured as a recipient of such flows. There is an omnivorous producing and 'consuming [of] places' around the globe (see Urry 1995). Core components of contemporary global culture now include the hotel buffet, the pool, the cocktail, the beach (Lencek and Bosker, 1998), the airport lounge (Gottdiener, 2001) and the bronzed tan (Ahmed, 2000).

This omnivorousness presupposes the growth of 'tourism reflexivity', the set of disciplines, procedures and criteria that enable each (and every?) place to monitor, evaluate and develop its tourism potential within the emerging patterns of global tourism. This reflexivity is concerned with identifying a particular place's location within the contours of geography, history and culture that swirl the globe, and in particular identifying that place's actual and potential material and semiotic resources. One element in this 'tourism reflexivity' is the institutionalisation of tourism studies, of new monographs, textbooks, exotic conferences, departments and journals (including in the 1990s, *International Journal of Tourism Research, Tourism Studies, Journal of Sustainable Tourism, Journeys, Tourism Geographies*). There are also many consultancy firms interlinked with local, national and international states, companies, voluntary associations and NGOs. The emergence of this 'tourism industry' is well-captured in the appalling figure of Rupert Sheldrake, an anthropologist of tourism, in David Lodge's *Paradise News* (1991).

This reflexivity is not simply a matter of individuals and their life-possibilities but of sets of systematic, regularised and evaluative procedures that enable each place to monitor, modify and maximise their location within the turbulent global order. Such procedures 'invent', produce, market and circulate, especially through global TV and the internet, new or different or repackaged or niche-dependent places and their corresponding visual images. And the circulating of such images develops further the very idea of the globe itself seen as it were from afar (see Franklin, Lury, Stacey, 2000).

Of course not all members of the world community are equal participants within global tourism. Side by side with global tourists and travellers within many of those 'empty meeting places' or 'non-places' of modernity such as the airport lounge, the coach station, the railway terminus, the motorway service stations, docks and so on are countless global exiles (MacCannell, 1992; Augé, 1995). Such exiles are fleeing from famine, war, torture, perse-cution and genocide, as economic and social inequalities and consequential displacements of population have magnified in recent years and have forced mobility upon many. The recent growth of 'people smuggling' has generated a multi-billion pound industry with some millions in transit across the world at any time.

But significantly for the 'tourist gaze' an array of developments are taking 'tourism' from the margins of the global order, and indeed of the academy, to almost the centre of this emergent world of 'liquid modernity'. First, tourism infrastructures have been constructed in what would have been thought of as the unlikeliest of places. While clearly most people across the world are not global tourists *qua* visitors, this does not mean that the places that they live in and the associated images of nature, nation, colonialism, sacrifice, community, heritage and so on, are not powerful constituents of a rapacious global tourism. Some destinations now significantly included in the patterns of global tourism include Alaska, Auschwitz-Birkenau, Antarctica especially in the Millennium year, Changi Jail in Singapore, Nazi occupation sites in the Channel Islands, Dachau, extinct coal mines, Cuba and especially its 'colonial' and 'American' heritages, Iceland, Mongolia, Mount Everest, Northern Ireland, Northern Cyprus under Turkish 'occupation', Pearl Harbour, post-communist Russia, Robben Island in South Africa, Sarajevo's

Figure 8.1   *1950s American cars are reforming the place-image of Cuba*

'massacre trail', outer space, Titanic, Vietnam and so on (see Lennon and Foley 2000, on 'dark tourism'; O'Rourke 1988, on 'holidays in hell'). In certain cases becoming a tourist destination is part of a reflexive process by which societies and places come to enter the global order (or 're-enter' as in the case of Cuba during the 1990s, in part using pre-communist American cars in their place-marketing; see Figure 8.1).

Further, there are large increases in the growth of tourists emanating from many very different countries, especially those of the Orient, that once were places visited and consumed by those from the west. Now rising incomes for an Asian middle class (as well as the student study tour and 'backpacker tourism') have generated a strong desire to see those places of the west that appear to have defined global culture. The development of a huge middle-class tourist trade from mainland China will be the next major development. Hendry however describes how various theme parks full of exotic features of 'westernness' are now being established *within* various Asian countries (2000). She describes this as *The Orient Strikes Back*, the putting on display of many features of western culture for Asians to wonder at and to exoticise, without having to leave their home country.

Moreover, many types of work are now found within these circuits of global tourism and so it is difficult not to be implicated within, or affected by, one or more of these circuits that increasingly overlap with a more general 'economy of signs' spreading across multiple spaces of consumption (Lash and

Urry, 1994). Such forms of work include transportation, hospitality, travel, design and consultancy; the producing of 'images' of global tourist sites, of global icons (the Eiffel Tower), iconic types (the global beach), and vernacular icons (Balinese dances); the mediatising and circulating of images through print, TV, news, internet and so on; and the organising through politics and protest campaigns for or against the construction or development of tourist infrastructures. And it involves the almost ubiquitous sex tourism industries; Crick describing prostitution as a 'common by-product of mass tourism' involving up to a million prostitutes in some south Asian countries (1989: 323; Craik 1997, 131–3; Clift and Carter, 1999).

Also, increasingly roaming the globe are enormously powerful and ubiquitous global brands or logos (see Klein, 2000). Their fluid-like power stems from how the most successful corporations over the last two decades have shifted from the actual manufacture of products to become brand producers, with enormous marketing, design, sponsorship, public relations and advertising expenditures. Such brand companies include many that are involved in travel and leisure: Nike, Gap, Easyjet, Body Shop, Virgin, Club Med, Starbucks and so on produce 'concepts' or 'life-styles'. They are 'liberated from the real-world burdens of stores and product manufacturing, these brands are free to soar, less as the dissemination of goods and services than as collective hallucinations' (Klein, 2000: 22). Klein brings out the importance in this of the 'global teen market', with about one billion young people disproportionately consuming similar consumer brands across the globe (Klein, 2000: 118–21).

There are thus countless ways in which huge numbers of people and places get caught up within the swirling vortex of global tourism. There are not two separate entities, the 'global' and 'tourism' bearing some external connections with each other. Rather they are part and parcel of the same set of complex and interconnected processes. Moreover, such assembled infrastructures, flows of images and of people, and the emerging practices of 'tourist reflexivity' should be conceptualised as a 'global hybrid' (Urry, 2000: ch. 2). It is hybrid because if is made up of an assemblage of technologies, texts, images, social practices and so on, that *together* enable it to expand and to reproduce itself across the globe. This is analogous to the mobilities of other global hybrids, such as the internet, automobility, global finance and so on, that spread across the globe and reshape and re-perform what is the 'global'.

In this chapter I make various interventions into these emerging patterns of global tourism, highlighting some transformations in 'thinking-travel' that have appeared in the last decade or so. I begin with some observations about visuality and note that, not only do we need to recognise the variety of senses involved in contemporary tourism but also to consider what happens in a global world of omnipotent vision. Second, I consider some issues of performance, the body and the pleasures of corporeal travel, noting especially that much tourism involves kinaesthetic movement. And finally, I consider some metaphors and features of a 'mobile culture' and reflect upon whether such a culture means that there can be no effective study of 'tourism' *per se*, as the tourist gaze is simply everywhere and in a kind of way nowhere in particular.

Developing the Gaze

I have argued for the fundamentally visual nature of tourism experiences. Gazes organise the encounters of visitors with the 'other', providing some sense of competence, pleasure and structure to those experiences. The gaze demarcates an array of pleasurable qualities to be generated within particular times and spaces. It is the gaze that orders and regulates the relationships between the various sensuous experiences while away, identifying what is visually out-of-ordinary, what are the relevant differences and what is 'other'.

Various authors have criticised this concept of the 'tourist gaze'. It is said to be insufficiently developed in relationship to its Foucauldian legacy and especially to the associated notion of the medical gaze (Hollingshead, 2000; but see Urry, 1992; 2000: ch. 2). The concept, it is said, does not connect to the immense literature on the history of visuality (see Jay, 1993). Also most holiday experiences are said to be physical or corporeal and are not merely visual (Veijola and Jokinnen, 1994). Relatedly, it is argued that the notion of the gaze is too static and passive and ignores performance and adventure (Perkins and Thorns, 1998). MacCannell argues that the idea of the tourist gaze, although illuminating in some respects, fails to identify a kind of 'second gaze', that knows that looks deceive, that there are things unseen and unsaid, and that each gaze generates its own 'beyond' (2001). And also it is said that the idea of the gaze does not capture the moving, mobile, fleeting character of seeing or 'glancing' the other – it focuses upon the tourist while stationary, at 'rest', not actively moving in and through the physical and social world (Larsen, 2001). In this section I clarify some elements of what the idea of the 'gaze' is meant to achieve, while in the following section I respond to some of these points by *embodying* and *mobilising* the tourist gaze.

First, the notion of the tourist gaze is not meant to account for the individual motivations for travel. Rather I emphasise the systematic and regularised nature of various gazes, each of which depends upon a variety of social discourses and practices as well as on aspects of building, design and restoration that foster the necessary 'look' of a place or an environment. Such gazes implicate both the gazer and the gazee in an ongoing and systematic set of social and physical relations. These relations are discursively organised by many professionals: photographers, writers of travel books and guides, local councils, experts in the 'heritage industry', travel agents, hotel owners, designers, tour operators, TV travel programmes, tourism development officers, architects, planners, tourism academics and so on. In contemporary tourism these technical, semiotic and organisational discourses are combined to 'construct' visitor *attractions* (see Dicks, 2000, on the Rhondha Heritage Park located within a former coal mine).

There is also no simple relationship between what is directly seen and what is signified. As discussed in Chapter 1, MacCannell describes the complex relations involved in developing and reproducing such an 'attraction'; these relations occur between a 'marker', the 'sight' and the 'tourist' (1999: 41). MacCannell also examines how an attraction develops over time. He describes the processes of sight sacralisation, by which an object may get turned into a sacred site of the tourism industry through a series of stages, one of which is the 'mechanical reproduction' of the sight in question through miniature souvenirs and, especially, endless photographic reproduction (MacCannell, 1999).

Moreover, in almost all situations different senses are inter-connected with each other to produce a sensed environment of people and objects distributed across time and space. There are not only landscapes (and visual townscapes), but also associated soundscapes (as in contemporary Cuban tourism, especially following the film *Buena Vista Social Club*), 'smellscapes' (as experienced in walking through particular woods: see Macnaghten and Urry, 2000a), 'tastescapes' (especially following the late eighteenth century invention of the restaurant; see Spang, 2000), and geographies of touch (as with the hand of the climber, see Lewis, 2001).

Focussing though on the gaze brings out how within tourism the organising sense within the typical tourist experience is visual. And this mirrors the general privileging of the eye within the long history of Western societies. Sight is viewed as the noblest of the senses, the most discriminating and reliable of the sensuous mediators between humans and their physical environment. This emphasis on sight is present within western epistemology, within religious and other symbolisms and within notions of how society should be visible, made transparent, to government (Urry, 2000: ch. 4).

However, there is nothing inevitable or natural about this organising power of vision. Indeed there was a centuries-long struggle for visuality to break free from the other senses with which it had been entangled. The very idea of a tourist gaze stems from such contestations within intellectual, governmental and religious thinking over the past few centuries. Febvre argues that in sixteenth century Europe: 'Like their acute hearing and sharp sense of smell, the men of that time doubtless had keen sight. But that was just it. They had not yet set it apart from the other senses' (1982: 437; Cooper, 1997). As a result people were said to live within a fluid world where entities rapidly changed shape and size, boundaries quickly altered and where there was little systematic stabilisation of the social or physical worlds. 'Interaction' describes the fluid, changing forms of perception that characterised sixteenth century life (Cooper, 1997).

Between then and 1800 there were many changes. Visual observation rather than the *a priori* knowledge of mediaeval cosmology came to be viewed as the basis of scientific legitimacy. This subsequently developed into the very foundation of the scientific method of the west, based upon sense-data principally produced and guaranteed by sight. Foucault shows in

The Order of Things how natural history involves the observable structure of the visible world and not functions and relationships invisible to the senses (1970). A number of such sciences of 'visible nature' developed organised around visual taxonomies, including especially that of Linnaeus (Gregory, 1994: 20). Such classifications were based upon the modern *epistème* of the individual subject, the seeing eye, and the observations, distinctions and classifications that the eye is able to make (Foucault, 1970).

Treatises on travel consequently shifted from a scholastic emphasis on touring as an opportunity for discourse via the ear, to travel as *eyewitness* observation. And with the development of scientific expeditions (the first recorded in 1735: Pratt, 1992: 1), travellers could no longer expect that their observations would become part of science itself. Travel was thus justified not through science but through the idea of connoisseurship – 'the well trained eye' (Adler, 1989: 22). A connoisseurship of buildings, works of art and of landscapes developed especially in the late eighteenth century with the growth of 'scenic tourism' in Britain and then across Europe. '[S]ightseeing became simultaneously a more effusive passionate activity and a more private one' (Adler, 1989: 22). Such connoisseurship came to involve new ways of seeing: a 'prolonged, contemplative [look] regarding the field of vision with a certain aloofness and disengagement, across a tranquil interval' (Bryson, 1983: 94; Taylor, J., 1994: 13). During the eighteenth century a more specialised visual sense developed based upon the *camera obscura*, the claude glass, the use of guidebooks, the widespread knowledge of routes, the art of sketching and the availability of sketchbooks, the balcony and so on (Ousby, 1990). This can be well seen in the case of Sweden, between Linnaeus's scientific expeditions in the 1730s to collect flowers and minerals, to Linnerhielm's travels in the 1780s to collect views and moods. The latter expresses this shift in the nature of travel: 'I travel to see, not to study' (Löfgren, 2000: 17; Pratt, 1992).

This visual sense enables people to take possession of objects and environments, often at a distance (as Simmel argues; see Frisby and Featherstone, 1997: 116). It facilitates the world of the 'other' to be controlled from afar, combining detachment and mastery. It is by seeking distance that a proper 'view' is gained, abstracted from the hustle and bustle of everyday experience (see Pratt's account of 'imperial eyes': 1992). Areas of wild, barren nature, which were once sources of sublime terror and fear, were transformed into what Raymond Williams terms 'scenery, landscape, image, fresh air', places waiting at a distance for visual consumption by those visiting from towns and cities full of 'dark satanic mills' (1972: 160; Macnaghten and Urry, 1998: 114–5). Elsewhere I describe the complex multi-layered making of the English Lake District by which inhospitable terror got changed into beauty and desire (Urry, 1995a). Similarly, before the end of the eighteenth century the Alps had been regarded as mountains of immense inhospitality, ugliness and terror. But Ring describes how they became 'civilised': they 'are not simply the Alps. They are a unique visual, cultural, geological and natural phenomenon, indissolubly wed to European history' (2000: 9). And also by the end of the

[handwritten margin note: How is it romantically spectacularly accumulated?]

eighteenth century 'tropical nature' too had been romanticised by travellers who began to see the scenery as though it were a 'painting' (Sheller, 2002).

Over the next century nature of all sorts came to be widely regarded as scenery, views, and perceptual sensation. Partly because of the Romantics: 'Nature has largely to do with leisure and pleasure – tourism, spectacular entertainment, visual refreshment' (Green, 1990: 6, on mid-nineteenth century France). By 1844 Wordsworth was noting that the development of the idea of landscape had recently developed; and of course he promoted both the Alps and the Lake District as landscapes of attraction. He notes that previously barns and outbuildings had been placed in front of houses 'however beautiful the landscape which their windows might otherwise have commanded' (Wordsworth, 1984: 188). By the mid-nineteenth century houses were built with regard to their 'prospects' as though they were a kind of 'camera' (Abercrombie and Longhurst, 1998: 79). The language of views thus prescribed a particular visual structure to the very experience of nature (Green, 1990: 88). And the building of piers, promenades and domesticated beaches enabled the visual consumption of the otherwise wild, untamed and 'natural' sea (Corbin, 1992).

The visual sense of possession developed across nineteenth century western Europe although this depended on viewing 'tropical nature' as well as on that of a 'civilised nature' (see Sheller, 2002). There was a growing separation of the senses, especially of vision from touch, smell and hearing. This was especially reflected in the emergence of the role of the *flâneur* who looked but did not touch according to Baudelaire (see Tester, 1994). New technologies of the gaze began to be produced and circulated, including postcards, guidebooks, photographs, commodities, arcades, cafés, dioramas, mirrors, plate-glass windows, as well as places of incarceration based upon the 'unimpeded empire of the gaze' (Foucault, 1976: 39; Urry, 1992).

As I showed in Chapter 7, photography is central within the modern tourist gaze. And strikingly tourism and photography could be said to commence in the west in their modern form around the seminal year of 1840. Louis Daguerre and Fox Talbot announced their separate and some-what different 'inventions' of the camera, in 1839 and 1840 respectively. In 1841, Thomas Cook organised what is now regarded as the first packaged 'tour', the first railway hotel was opened in York just before the 1840s railway mania, the first national railway timetable, Bradshaws, appeared, Cunard started the first ever Ocean steamship service, and Wells Fargo, the forerunner of American Express, began stagecoach services across the American west (Lash and Urry, 1994: 261). Also in 1840 Dr Arnold, the famous Headmaster of Rugby School, declared that 'Switzerland is to England ... the general summer touring place' (cited Ring, 2000: 25). 1840 then is one of those remarkable moments when the world seems to shift and a new patterning of relationships becomes irreversibly established. This is the moment when the 'tourist gaze', that peculiar combining together of the means of collective travel, the desire for travel and the techniques of photo-graphic reproduction, becomes a core component of western modernity.

So far I have talked of the awesome dominance of the visual for the character of tourist development. In many senses we do live in a society of spectacle (see Debord, 1994). Almost all environments across the globe have been transformed, or are being transformed, into diverse and collectable spectacles, spectacles often now involving 'gates' in order that paying visitors can enter, be charged and can consume them. Fainstein and Judd have examined the production of a variety of such 'places to play' (and pay) that are now being enormously extended across the globe (1999).

At the very same time there is this visual proliferation, so the visual gaze is commonly denigrated within many discourses of travel (as Buzard, 1993, shows historically). The person who only lets the sense of sight have free rein is ridiculed. Such sightseers, especially with a camera draped around their neck, are conventionally taken to be superficial in their appreciation of environments, peoples and places. Martin Parr's photographic collection *Small Worlds* reveals and exposes such a denigration of the (normally male) camera-wearing tourist (1995; see Osborne, 2000: ch. 7).

There can be an embarrassment about mere sightseeing. Sight may be viewed as the most superficial of the senses getting in the way of real experiences that should involve the other senses and necessitate long periods of time in order for proper immersion (see Lewis, 2001). Famously, Wordsworth argued that the Lake District demands a different eye, one that is not threatened or frightened by the relatively wild and untamed nature. It requires 'a slow and gradual process of culture' (Wordsworth, 1984: 193). This criticism of the mere sightseeing tourist is taken to the extreme with the critique of the 'hyper-real', simulated designed places that have the appearance of being more 'real' than the original (Baudrillard, 1983, 1988). With hyper-reality the sense of vision is said to be reduced to a limited array of visible features, it is then exaggerated and dominates the other senses. Hyper-real places are characterised by surface appearances that do not respond to or welcome the viewer. The sense of sight is condensed to the most immediate and visible aspects of the scene, such as the seductive façades of Main Street in Disneyland or the ocean liner environment at Manchester's Trafford Centre, although such places can of course be 'used' in different ways (see Chapter 7; and see Bryman, 1995; Fjellman, 1992, on Disney – the 'authentic' theme park!).

I have so far analysed the role of vision in the development of tourism. In particular from 1840 onwards tourism and photography came to be welded together and the development of each cannot be separated from the other. Both sets of practices remake each other in an irreversible and momentous double helix. From then we can say a 'tourist gaze' enters and makes the mobile, modern world (see Macnaghten and Urry, 1998: 180–5, Löfgren, 1999, for comparative material).

However, although the tourist gaze emerges in this general sense, it is clear that there have been rather different kinds of visual gaze that have been authorised by various discourses. These different discourses include *education*, as with the eighteenth century European Grand Tour and with many current study tour programmes; *health*, as with tourism designed to 'restore' the individual to healthy functioning often through staying in particular sites of bodily restoration (such as the Swiss Alps or Rotarua in New Zealand); *group solidarity*, as with much Japanese or Taiwanese tourism (see Shields 1990, on such group tourism at Niagara Falls); *pleasure and play*, as with 'ludic' tourism within all-inclusive Caribbean resorts only available for those who happen to be aged 18–30; *heritage and memory*, as with the development of indigenous histories, museums, recreated festivals, feasts, dances and so on (see Arellano, 2001, on the making of Inca heritage); and *nation*, such as with the increasingly profitable and autonomous notion of *Scotland – the brand* (McCrone, Morris and Kiely, 1995).

Moreover, these different discourses imply different socialities. With what in Chapter 1 I call the *romantic* gaze, solitude, privacy and a personal, semi-spiritual relationship with the object of the gaze are emphasised. In such cases tourists expect to look at the object privately or at least only with 'significant others'. Large numbers of strangers visiting, as at the Taj Mahal, intrude upon and spoil that lonely contemplation desired by western visitors (famously seen in the Princess Diana shot at the Taj; Edensor, 1998: 121–3). The romantic gaze involves further quests for new objects of the solitary gaze, the deserted beach, the empty hilltop, the uninhabited forest, the uncontaminated mountain stream and so on. Notions of the romantic gaze are endlessly used in marketing and advertising tourist sites especially within the 'west'.

By contrast what I call the *collective* tourist gaze involves conviviality. Other people also viewing the site are necessary to give liveliness or a sense of carnival or movement. Large numbers of people that are present can indicate that this is *the* place to be. These moving, viewing others are obligatory for the collective consumption of place, as with central London, Ibiza, Las Vegas, the Sydney Olympics, Hong Kong and so on (see Tester, 1994: 2, on Baudelaire's notion of *flânerie*: 'dwelling in the throng, in the ebb and flo, the bustle, the fleeting'). Indian visitors to the Taj Mahal are implicated in a communal witnessing with family or friends of a national monument (Edensor, 1998: 126). By contrast many seaside resorts in northern Europe and north America have lost the crowds necessary for the collective gaze – they have become sites of a lost collective gaze (see Walton, 2000).

However, beyond these two forms of the gaze, various writers have recently shown that there are other gazes, other ways in which places get visually consumed, both while people are stationary and through movement. These vary in terms of the socialities involved, the lengths of time taken and the character of visual appreciation. Thus first, there is the *spectatorial* gaze that involves the collective glancing at and collecting of different signs that have been very briefly seen in passing, at a glance such as from a tourist bus window (Urry, 1995a: 191). Then there is the notion of the *reverential* gaze used to describe how, for example, Muslims spiritually consume the sacred site of the Taj Mahal. Muslim visitors stop to scan and to concentrate their attention upon the mosque, the tombs and the Koranic script (Edensor, 1998: 127–8). An *anthropological* gaze describes how individual visitors scan a variety of sights/sites and are able to locate them interpretatively within an historical array of meanings and symbols. Some tour guides may themselves provide accounts that interpret sights/sites historically and inter-culturally (as in the case of Bali; see Bruner, 1995, on the anthropologist as tour-guide).

Somewhat related is the *environmental* gaze. This involves a scholarly or NGO-authorised discourse of scanning various tourist practices for their footprint upon the 'environment'. On the basis of such reflexivity it is then possible to choose that with the smallest footprint and then recommend that through various media to like-minded environmentalists (as with the UK-campaigning organisation, Tourism Concern; Urry, 1995a: 191). And finally, there is the *mediatised* gaze. This is a collective gaze where particular sites famous for their 'mediated' nature are viewed. Those gazing on the scene relive elements or aspects of the media event. Examples where such mediated gazes are found would include locations in Santa Monica and Venice Beach where many Hollywood films are set, the site of the Rover's Return pub from the soap opera *Coronation Street* (there are in fact three such 'pubs'), the village of Avoca in County Wicklow now overrun by *Ballykissangel* tourists and the Taj Mahal which is a setting for various 'masala' movies where particular scenes can be relived (Edensor, 1998: 127; Jeffries 1998, on the 'surreal side of the Street').

In each case it is important to note that there will always be other senses involved, albeit as subordinate in those tourist experiences organised through one or other of these gazes. Furthermore, I have so far considered the gaze from the perspective of the gazer. However, much tourism study is concerned with the consequences of being gazed upon, with for example working within a 'tourist honeypot' and being subject to a gaze somewhat similar to that within a panopticon (see Urry, 1992). Staged authenticity may have the effect of keeping out what may be deemed the intrusive eye while providing visitors what seems properly 'authenticated'. However, whether this is possible depends upon various determinants such as the relations of power within the 'host' community, the time-space characteristics of visitors and the kinds of gaze involved. For example, the least intrusive gaze may be the spectatorial since it is likely to be mobile and will soon pass by (although the endlessly anonymous traffic may itself be overwhelming). The anthropological gaze can be the most intrusive since tourists will insist staying for lengthy periods within the host community in order to get to know it 'authentically'. It might also be noted that local people can systematically view 'tourists' whose clothes, customs and cameras are matters of considerable entertainment, amusement and occasional disgust.

In the next section I consider how it is often 'bodies' themselves that are especially subject to the gaze, especially with the marked racial and gender inequalities that are involved. McClintock describes the extraordinary intertwining of male power with both colonised nature and the female body in the history of travel into and across the 'virgin' territories of the Empire (1995). The male look through a kind of 'porno-tropics' is endlessly voyeuristic. Thus an important determinant of the degree to which such a community feels itself under the empire of the gaze is not only the number of visitors but also their forms of mobility into, and through, the place of the 'locals'. In the rest of this chapter I consider this more general issue of mobility, in the next section with regard to its embodiment and in the final section in relationship to an intensely 'mobile culture'.

Embodying and Mobilising the Gaze

I have at times in this chapter referred to travel as *corporeal* travel. This is to emphasise something so obvious that it has often been forgotten (according to Veijola and Jokinnen, 1994, by most male theorists including myself!). It is that tourists moving from place to place comprise lumpy, fragile, aged, gendered, racialised bodies. Such bodies encounter other bodies, objects and the physical world multi-sensuously (see Ahmed, 2000, on the bronzing of the 'white' skin). Tourism always involves *corporeal* movement and forms of pleasure and these must be central in any sociology of diverse tourisms. In that sense the tourist gaze always involves relations between bodies that are themselves in at least intermittent movement.

Bodies moreover perform themselves in-between direct sensation of the 'other' and various sensescapes (Rodaway, 1994). Bodies navigate backwards and forwards between directly sensing the external world as they move bodily in and through it (or lie inertly waiting to be bronzed), and discursively mediated sensescapes that signify social taste and distinction, ideology and meaning. Such sensed and sensing bodies are concerned with various performativities. Bodies are not fixed and given but involve performances especially to fold notions of movement, nature, taste and desire, into and through the body. There are thus complex connections between bodily sensations and socio-cultural 'sensescapes' mediated by discourse and language (see Crouch, 2000, and Macnaghten and Urry, 2000b, on embodied leisure-scapes). This can be seen in the case of much of tropical travel such as to the Caribbean where early visitors were able to taste new fruits, to smell the flowers, to feel the heat of the sun, to immerse one's body in the moist greenery of the rainforest, as well as to see new sights (see Sheller, 2002).

The body senses as it *moves*. It is endowed with kinaesthetics, the sixth sense that informs one what the body is doing in space through the sensations of movement registered in its joints, muscles, tendons and so on. Especially important in that sense of movement, the 'mechanics of space', is that of touch, of the feet on the pavement or the mountain path, the hands on a rock-face or the steering wheel (Gil, 1998: 126; Lewis, 2001). Various objects and mundane technologies facilitate this kinaesthetic sense as they sensuously extend human capacities into and across the external world. There are thus various assemblages of humans, objects, technologies and scripts that contingently produce durability and stability of mobility. Such hybrid assemblages can roam countrysides and cities, remaking landscapes and townscapes through their movement. Examples of such mundane technologies implicated in movement include the car (see Sheller and Urry, 2000), the bike (see Rosen, 1993), the mountain boot (see Michael, 2000), the sailing boat (Matless, 2000), the snowmobile (Ingold and Kurttila, 2000), the personal stereo (Bull, 2000) and so on.

One effect of such mobile technologies is to change the nature of vision. The 'static' forms of the tourist gaze, such as that from the balcony vantage point, focuses on the two-dimensional shape, colours and details of the view that is laid out before one and can be moved around with one's eyes (Pratt, 1992: 222). Such a static gaze is paradigmatically captured through the still camera. By contrast, with what Schivelbusch terms a 'mobility of vision', there are swiftly passing panorama, a sense of multi-dimensional rush and the fluid interconnections of places, peoples and possibilities (1986: 66; similar to the onrushing images encountered on TV and film). There are a variety of *tourist glances*, the capturing of sights in passing from a railway carriage, through the car windscreen, the steamship porthole or the camcorder viewfinder (see Larsen, 2001). As Schivelbusch argues:

> the traveller sees ... through the apparatus which moves him through the world. The machine and the motion it creates become integrated into his visual perception; thus he can only see things in motion (cited Osborne, 2000: 168).

The nineteenth century development of the railway was momentous in the development of this more mobilised gaze. From the railway carriage the landscape came to be viewed as a swiftly passing series of framed panorama, a 'panoramic perception', rather than something that was to be lingered over, sketched or painted or in any way captured (Schivelbusch, 1986). Nietzsche famously noted that: 'everyone is like the traveller who gets to know a land and its people from a railway carriage' (quoted Thrift, 1996: 286). The development of the railroad had particular consequences on the very early development of tourism within the American frontier. Travellers made specific references to how the railroad annihilated space through its exceptional speed that was not fully noticed because of the unusual comfort of the railway carriage. The railway journey produced an enormous sense of vastness, of scale, size and domination of the landscape that the train swept through (Retzinger, 1998: 221–4). A contemporary declared in 1888 that the railroad ride was like 'an airline through the woods to the ocean' (Löfgren, 2000: 3).

Similarly the view through the car windscreen has also had significant consequences for the nature of the visual 'glance', enabling the *materiality* of the city or the landscape to be clearly appreciated (according to Larsen, 2001). Elsewhere I have elaborated some moments in the history of automobility, including in Europe inter-war motoring involving a kind of 'voyage through the life and history of a land' (Urry, 2000: ch. 3). The increasingly domesticated middle classes, comfortably and safely located in their Morris Minors 'began to tour England and take photographs in greater numbers than ever before' (Taylor, J., 1994: 122, and see 136–45, on the 'Kodakisation' of the English landscape). While in post-war US certain landscapes were substantially altered so as to produce a landscape of leisure '*pleasing* to the motorist ... using the land in a way that would "make an attractive *picture* from the Parkway"' (Wilson, 1992: 35; emphasis added). The state turned nature into something 'to be appreciated by the eyes alone' (Wilson, 1992: 37). The view through the car windscreen means that: 'the faster we drive, the flatter the earth looks' (1992: 33). More generally, Baudrillard suggests that deserts in the US constitute a metaphor of endless futurity, the obliteration of the past and the triumph of instantaneous time (1988: 6). Driving across the desert involves leaving one's past behind, driving on and on and seeing the ever-disappearing emptiness framed through the shape of the windscreen (Kaplan, 1996: 68–85). These empty landscapes of the desert are experienced through driving huge distances, travel involving a 'line of flight' into the disappearing future.

Nevertheless this corporeality of movement does produce intermittent moments of *physical proximity*, to be bodily in the same space as some landscape or townscape, or at a live event or with one's friends, family, colleagues, partner or indeed in the company of desired 'strangers' (all skiers, or all aged 18–30 and single, or all bridge players). Much travel results from a powerful 'compulsion to proximity' that makes it seem absolutely necessary (Boden and Molotch, 1994). Much work entails travel because of the importance of connection, of needing to meet, to encourage others, to sustain one's networks (Henley Centre website). To be there oneself is what is crucial in most tourism, whether this place occupies a key location within the global tourist industry or is merely somewhere that one has been told about by a friend. Places need to be seen 'for oneself' and experienced directly: to meet at a particular house of one's childhood or visit a particular restaurant or walk along a certain river valley or energetically climb a particular hill or capture a good photograph oneself. Co-presence then involves seeing or touching or hearing or smelling or tasting a particular place (see Urry, 2000: on the multiple senses involved in mobilities).

A further kind of travel occurs where a 'live' event is to be seen, an event programmed to happen at a specific moment. Examples include political, artistic, celebratory and sporting occasions, the last are especially 'live' since the outcome (and even the length) may be unknown. Each of these generates intense moments of co-presence, whether for Princess Diana's funeral, a Madonna concert, a World Expo or the 2000 Sydney Olympics. Each of these cannot be missed and they produce enormous movements of people at very specific moments in 'global cities' in order to 'catch' that particular mega-event live (see Roche, 2000). Roche describes the planned mega-events as 'social spatio-temporal "hubs" and "switches" that ... channel, mix and re-route global flows' (2000: 199). Such events are spatio-temporal moments of global condensation, involving the peculiarly intense 'localisation' of such global events within 'unique places due to the fact that they staged unique events'. These places therefore have the 'power to transform themselves from being mundane places ... into being these special "host city" sites' that come to occupy a new distinct niche within global tourism (Roche, 2000: 224).

Such co-presence nearly always involves travel over, and beyond, other places, to get to those visually distinct sites to watch a live event, to climb a particular rock-face, to wander 'lonely as a cloud', to go white-water rafting, to bungee jump and so on. These corporeally defined practices are found in specific, specialised 'leisure spaces', geographically and ontologically distant from work and domestic sites. Indeed part of the attraction of these places, where bodies can be corporeally alive, apparently 'natural' or rejuvenated, is that they are sensuously 'other' to everyday routines and places. Ring interestingly describes how the Alps were developed during the snineteenth century into such a specialised space where the English gentleman could apparently feel properly alive (2000: chs 4–6).

Such places involve 'adventure', islands of life resulting from intense bodily arousal, from bodies in motion, finding their complex way in time and space (see Frisby and Featherstone, 1997, on Simmel's 'adventurer'; and Lewis, 2001, on the rock-climbing 'adventurer'). Some social practices involve bodily resistance where the body physicalises its relationship with the external world. In the late eighteenth century development of walking as resistance, the 'freedom' of the road and the development of leisurely walking were modest acts of rebellion against established social hierarchy (Jarvis, 1997: chs 1 and 2 on 'radical walking'). Similarly, extreme 'adventure tourism' in New Zealand demonstrates forms of physical resistance to work and the everyday (see Perkins and Thorns, 1998). The hedonistic desire to acquire a bronzed body developed through resistance to the protestant ethic, women's domesticity and 'rational recreation' (see Ahmed, 2000). A similar resistance to the embodiment of the 'Protestant Ethic' can be seen in the growth of health spa travel where the body stays still and is subjected to exotic, pampered luxury treatments.

Crucial to analysing these performed, normally mobile bodies is the concept of 'affordance'. Gibson argues that people do not encounter a set of objective 'things' in the environment that may or may not be visually perceived (1986: ch. 8). Rather, different surfaces and different objects, relative to the particular human organism and its technologies, provide affordances. These are objective *and* subjective, both part of the environment and of the organism. Affordances stem from their reciprocity through people's kinaesthetic movement within their particular world. Affordances constrain behaviour along certain possibilities:

> there are a range of options ... implicit within a physical milieu and this implicit-
> ness is directly connected to the bodily capacities and limits of the [human]
> organism (Michael, 1996: 149).

Given certain past and present social relations, then, particular 'objects' in the environment afford possibilities and resistances, given that humans are sensuous, corporeal, technologically extended and *mobile* beings.

Examples of such affordances are a path that draws people to walk along it, a beach that invites one's skin to be tanned, a mountain that reveals a clear way of climbing it, a wood that is a repository of childhood adventures, and a museum that facilitates 'touching' the displays by the visually impaired moving through it. On the last of these Hetherington notes how museums are quintessentially places of seeing, of the 'making visible', of the tourist gaze (2000). They thus encounter enormous difficulties in providing affordances for the blind visitor. Touching the objects on display, the preferred alternative sense, makes objects 'tacky' and corroded so they no longer remain visually and physically the same. Given the way that much tourism is organised around various gazes, then the place of the visually impaired is unsettling within museums. But where other senses are significant, such as when listening to a concert, or physically climbing a mountain, or smelling perfume in a garden, then affordances are often denied to other categories of potential visitor.

So far I have regarded the body from the viewpoint of the body-viewer or body-mover. But tourism is often about the body-as-seen, displaying, performing and seducing visitors with skill, charm, strength, sexuality and so on. Desmond indeed notes how common live performance and bodily display are within tourism industries (1999). The moving body is often what gets gazed upon, as a 'spectacular corporeality' increasingly characterising global tourism. The performed body in dance has become common, such as Maori war-dances, Balinese dance ceremonies, Brazilian samba and Hula dancing in Hawaii.

These examples involve what MacCannell terms a 'reconstructed ethnicity' and a 'staged authenticity' (1999, 1973). In the Hula staging for bodily display, particular conceptions of the half-native, half-white female body are made available for visual consumption. Such dances appear to be 'real performances' and their attraction stems from the impression of an unmediated encounter, a genuine performance of an age-old tradition rather than something merely undertaken for the visitor. The performers in such dances become signs of what the tourist audience believes them to be.

And in some cases such dances are such powerful signifiers that the performances have become the dominant signifier of the culture in question. Thus with Maori and Hawaiian cultures the dance *is* the culture, swamping all other signifiers and being recognisable across the globe. Desmond has outlined the racial and gender history of the making of the female Hula dancer, from the early years of the last century to the current point where six million visitors a year are attracted to a naturalistic Eden signified by bodily displays of 'natural' female Hula dancers, a place-image globally recognised and endlessly re-circulated (1999: Part 1).

A Mobile World

The previous section has shown that there are therefore enormously powerful interconnections of 'tourism' and 'culture' in a mobile world (see Rojek and Urry in *Touring Cultures*, 1997). Not only do tourists travel but so too do objects, cultures and images. Increasingly there also appears to be a 'mobile culture' stemming from a 'compulsion to mobility'. Kaplan's *Questions of*

Travel well-captures such a culture of mobility (1996). Her extended 'family' was located across various continents. Travel and tourism was for her 'unavoidable, indisputable, and always necessary for family, love and friendship as well as work' (1996: ix). She was 'born into a *culture* that took the national benefits of travel for granted' as well as presuming that 'US citizens [could] travel anywhere they pleased' (Kaplan, 1996: ix). Implicit here is that one is *entitled* to travel since it is an essential part of one's life. Cultures become so mobile that contemporary citizens (not just Americans!) are thought to possess the rights to pass over and into other places and other cultures. Moreover, if household members are forever on the move then distinctions of home and away lose their power. Cultures imply and necessitate diverse and extensive forms of mobility. No other culture, though, matches the recent Hindu Kumbh Mela Festival in Allahabad in India on January 24th 2001. It was probably the largest number of people ever to have travelled to a single place within a short period of time; 30–50 million Hindus from all over the world went to the banks of the Ganges.

Indeed being part of any culture almost always involves travel. Culture-developing-and-sustaining-travel can take a number of different forms: travel to the culture's sacred sites; to the location of central written or visual texts; to places where key events took place; to see particularly noteworthy individuals or their documentary record; and to view other cultures so as to reinforce one's own cultural attachments.

The importance of travel to culture and how cultures themselves travel, can be seen from the nature of nationality. Central is the nation's narrative of itself. National histories tell a story, of a people passing through history, a story often beginning in the mists of time (Bhabha, 1990). Much of this history of its traditions and icons will have been 'invented' and result as much from forgetting the past as from remembering it (McCrone, 1998: ch. 3; Boswell and Evans, 1999). Late nineteenth century Europe was a period of remarkable invention of national traditions. For example in France, Jeanne d'Arc was only elevated from obscurity by the Catholic Church in the 1870s (McCrone, 1998: 45–6). *La Marseillaise* became the national anthem in 1879, Bastille Day was invented in 1880, in which year July 14th was designated for the national feast. More generally, the idea of 'France' was extended 'by a process akin to colonisation through communication (roads, railways and above all by the newspapers) so that by the end of nineteenth century popular and elite culture had come together' as a result of diverse mobilities (McCrone, 1998: 46). Key in this was the mass production of public monuments of the nation especially in re-built Paris, monuments that were travelled to, seen, talked about and shared through paintings, photographs, films and the European tourism industry.

This collective participation and the more general nation-inducing role of travel had been initiated with the 1851 Great Exhibition at London's Crystal Palace, the first ever national tourist event. Although the British population was only 18 million, six million visits were made to the Exhibition, many using the new railways to visit the national capital for the first time. In the second half of the nineteenth century similar mega-events took place across Europe with attendances at some reaching 30 million or so (Roche, 2000). In Australia a Centennial International Exhibition was held in Melbourne in 1888 and it is thought that two-thirds of the Australian population attended (Spillman, 1997: 51). Visitors from home and abroad confirmed Australia's achievements and characteristics.

More generally, since the mid-nineteenth century, travel to see the key sites, texts, exhibitions, buildings, landscapes, restaurants and achievements of a society has developed the cultural sense of a national imagined presence. Particularly important in the genealogy of nationalism has been the founding of national museums, the development of national artists, architects, musicians, playwrights, novelists, historians and archaeologists and the location of the nation's achievements within world exhibitions visited in often very large numbers (McCrone, 1998: 53–5; Kirshenblatt-Giblett, 1998; and Chapter 7).

The recent period has seen a global public stage emerging upon which almost all nations have to appear, to compete, to mobilise themselves as spectacle and to attract large numbers of visitors. This placement particularly operates through mega-events such as the Olympics, World Cups and Expos (Harvey 1996). These international events, premised upon mass tourism and cosmopolitanism, means that national identity is increasingly conceived of in terms of a location within, and on, a global stage. It is that staging which facilitates both corporeal and imaginative travel to such mega-events of the global order, especially the 'Olympics and Expos in the Growth of Global Culture' (Roche, 2000).

This connects to the changing nature of nationality (Maier, 1994: 149-50; McCrone, 1998). Once nationality was based upon a homogenous and mapped national territory, in which law was defined, authority claimed and loyalty sought within that territorial boundary. But now frontiers are permeable and much cultural life is interchangeable across the globe through extensive corporeal and imaginative travel. Thus 'territory is less central to national self-definition' and more important are specific places, landscapes and symbols including various kinds of consumption including food, drink and art (Maier 1994: 149; Lowenthal 1985). What are central then are various icons of a nation – icons that are also pivotal to that culture's location within the contours of global tourism, such as the central significance of gastronomy within France, currently the world's most popular tourist destination (see Csergo, 1997).

But such icons are continuously disputed. The power of national élites was, for example, powerfully contested in the intense debates over the Australian bicentennial held in 1988 (see Spillman, 1997: ch. 4). There was very strong Aboriginal opposition to the celebrations. They termed Australia Day, which was a huge tourist event, as 'Invasion Day'.

And more broadly there has been the proliferation of diverse, often localised, indigenous sociations seeking to save 'their particular history and heritage'. In Britain Samuel has documented the new democratic, familial, workerist, femininist, consumerist and domestic heritages that various sociations have saved, laid out for display, and sought to bring visitors in to see, touch, hear and remember (1994; see Macdonald, 1997, on Aros Gaelic heritage centre on the Isle of Skye). Former Welsh coal mining communities show the importance of 'experience' sites of vernacular heritage, as we saw in the previous chapter. There are various 'alternative heritage' tours – such as the Black Atlantic tour that visit sites connected to the transatlantic slave trade. Thus, the role of heritage and history has itself become a major issue. Questions of heritage, even where there is the commodification of history, makes 'history' central to the nature of given cultures and demonstrates that heritage cannot be divorced from the various 'techniques of remembering', many of which now involve tourist sites, festivals, events and so on (see Arellano, 2001).

Moreover, for many cultures much travel entails crossing national frontiers. Households in developing countries develop extensive mobility patterns when their incomes increase. The proliferation of 'global diasporas' extends the range, extent and significance of all forms of travel for far-flung families and households. It is said in Trinidad that one can really only be a 'Trini' by going abroad. Around 60 per cent of nuclear families have at least one member living abroad (Miller and Slater, 2000: 12, 36). Ong and Nonini also show the importance of mobility across borders in the case of the massive Chinese diaspora that is thought to be between 25–45 million in size (1997). Clifford summarises what has happened:

> Dispersed peoples, once separated from homelands by vast oceans and political barriers, increasingly find themselves in border relations with the old country thanks to a to-and-fro made possible by modern technologies of transport, communication, and labour migration. Airplanes, telephones, tape cassettes, camcorders, and mobile job markets reduce distances and facilitate two-way traffic, legal and illegal, between the world's places' (Cohen, 1997: 247).

Such diasporic travel is also rather open-ended in terms of its temporality. Unlike conventional tourism that is based upon a clear distinction of periods of 'home' and of 'away', the diasporic traveller often has no clear temporal boundaries as one activity tends to flow into the other, as Cwerner shows in the case of Brazilians living in London for quite indeterminate periods of time (2001).

In response to this array of processes recent commentators often now refer to the *nomadic* quality of contemporary social life. Thus du Gay *et al* interestingly describes the significance of the Sony Walkman:

> It is designed for movement – for mobility, for people who are always out and about, for travelling light. It is part of the required equipment of the modern 'nomad' ... it is testimony to the high value which the culture of late-modernity places on mobility (1997: 23–4; and see Bull's account of the soundscapes of the city, 2000).

Likewise Makimoto and Manners argue that we have entered a new nomadic age. Over the next decade, with digitisation, most of the facilities of home and the office will be carried around on the body or at least in a small bag, making those who can afford such objects 'geographically independent' (Makimoto and Manners, 1997: 2). They argue that such people will be 'free to live where they want and travel as much as they want' – they will be forced to consider whether they are settlers or really 'global nomads' (1997: 6). While for Bauman, the vagabond and the tourist are plausible metaphors for post-modern times: the vagabond, he says, is a pilgrim without a destination, a nomad without an itinerary; while the 'world is the tourist's oyster … to be lived pleasurably' (Bauman, 1993: 241). Both vagabonds and tourists move through other people's spaces, they both separate physical closeness from moral proximity, and both set standards for happiness and the good life. According to Bauman the good life has come to be thought of as akin to a 'continuous holiday' (1993: 243). There is thus no separate tourist gaze since according to Bauman this is simply how life is lived at least for the prosperous one-third within the new global order.

Feminist analysts have criticised the masculinist character of these metaphors that imply that there really can be ungrounded and unbounded movement. Yet clearly different people have very different access to being 'on the road', literally or metaphorically (Wolff, 1993). Moreover, Jokinen and Veijola demonstrate the deficiency of many nomadic metaphors that are 'masculinist' (1997). If these metaphors are re-coded as paparazzi, homeless drunk, sex-tourist and womaniser, then they lose the positive valuation that they have enjoyed within such a masculinist nomadic theory. Indeed the mobilities of some always presuppose the immobilities of others. The mobile tourist gaze presupposes immobile bodies (normally female) servicing and displaying their bodies for those who are mobile and passing by.

So finally, Morris recommends the metaphor of the motel for the nature of contemporary mobile life (1988). The motel possesses no real lobby, it is tied into the network of highways, it functions to relay people rather than to provide settings for coherent human subjects, it is consecrated to circulation and movement, and it demolishes the particular sense of place and locale. Motels 'memorialize only movement, speed, and perpetual circulation' – they 'can never be a true *place*' and each is only distinguished from the other in 'a high-speed, *empiricist* flash' (Morris, 1988: 3, 5). The motel, like the airport transit lounge or the coach station, represents neither arrival nor departure. It represents the 'pause' before tourists move on to the next stopping-point along the extraordinary routeways of a 'liquid modernity', leaving behind of course those immobilised bodies subject to high speed passing glances (there are, for example, 50,000 employees at Chicago's O'Hare airport: Gottdiener, 2001: 23; Morris 1988: 41). Globalisation has thus ushered in some momentous reconfigurations of the tourist gaze, both for the ever-mobile bodies intermittently pausing, and for the immobilised bodies that meet in some of these 'strange encounters' of the new world order. Such encounters involve exceptional levels of 'non-interaction', or urban anonymity especially within the 'walled cities' known as airports (Gottdiener, 2001: 34–5).

There has been a massive shift from a more or less single tourist gaze in the nineteenth century to the proliferation of countless discourses, forms and embodiments of tourist gazes now. In a simple sense we can talk of the globalising of the tourist gaze, as multiple gazes have become core to global culture sweeping up almost everywhere in their awesome wake. There is much less 'tourism' *per se* that occurs within specific and distinct kinds of time-space; there is what I have termed the 'end of tourism' in the more general 'economy of signs'.

Rather, there are countless mobilities, physical, imaginative and virtual, voluntary and coerced. There are increasing similarities between behaviours that are 'home' and 'away' (see Shaw, Agarwal, Bull, 2000: 282). Tourist sites proliferate across the globe as tourism has become massively mediatised, while everyday sites of activity get redesigned in 'tourist' mode, as with many themed environments. Mobility is increasingly central to the identities of many young people, to those who are part of diasporas and to many relatively wealthy retired people who can live on the move (see Desforges, 1998, on prosperous young people 'consuming the world'). And 'tourism reflexivity' leads almost every site – however boring – to be able to develop some niche location within the swirling contours of the emergent global order (see Martin Parr's stunning collection of *Boring Postcards*, 1999).

Elsewhere I discuss how notions of chaos and complexity can help to illuminate the unexpected, far-from equilibrium movements of social and physical processes that currently rage across the globe (see Urry, 2002). These movements have unpredictably elevated 'tourism', even as it de-differentiates from leisure, shopping, art, culture, history, the body, sport and so on, from the very margins to a central place within this emergent global order. And as it does so here and there pockets of disorder remain, of openings and gaps, memories and fantasies, movements and margins. (MacCannell, 2001, argues something similar in his notion of the 'second gaze'). One thing that is sure about the emergent global order is that it is only at best a contingent and temporary ordering that generates its massive and complex disordering.

Bibliography

Abercrombie, N. and Longhurst, B. (1998) *Audiences*. London: Sage.

Abercrombie, N. and Warde, A. *et al.* (2000) *Contemporary British Society*. Cambridge: Polity.

Adkins, L. (1995) *Gendered Work*. Buckinghamshire: Open University Press.

Adler, J. (1989) 'Origins of Sightseeing', *Annals of Tourism Research*, 16: 7–29.

Ahmed, S. (2000) *Strange Encounters*. London: Routledge.

Aglietta, M. (1987) *A Theory of Capitalist Regulation: the US Experience*. London: Verso.

Albers, P. and James, W. (1988) 'Travel photography: a methodological approach', *Annals of Tourism Research*, 15: 134–58.

Anderson, K. (1988) 'Cultural hegemony and the race-definition process in Chinatown Vancouver: 1880–1980', *Environment and Planning D: Society and Space*, 6: 127–49.

Arellano, A. (2001) *The Genesis of Inca Heritage*, PhD Dept of Sociology, Lancaster University (forthcoming).

Artley, A. and Robinson, J. (1985) *The Official New Georgians Handbook*. London: Ebury Press.

Ashworth, P. (1986) 'Nottingham-by-Sea', the *Guardian*, 21 June.

Atkinson, J. (1984) 'Manpower strategies for flexible organisations', *Personnel Management*, August: 28–31.

Augé, M. (1995) *Non-Places*. London: Verso.

Bagguley, P. (1987) *Flexibility, Restructuring and Gender. Changing Employment in Britain's Hotels*. Lancaster Regionalism Group Working Paper no. 24.

Bagguley, P. (1991) 'Gender and labour flexibility in hotel and catering', *Services Industries Journal*, 10: 737–47.

Bagguley, P., Mark-Lawson, J., Shapiro, D., Urry, J., Walby, S., Warde, A. (1989) 'Restructuring Lancaster', in Cooke, P. (ed.) *Localities*. London: Unwin Hyman. pp. 129–65.

Bagguley, P., Mark-Lawson, J., Shapiro, D., Urry, J., Walby, S., Warde, A. (1990) *Restructuring. Place, Class and Gender*. London: Sage.

Ball, R. (1988) 'Seasonality: a problem for workers in the tourism labour market', *Service Industries Journal*, 8: 501–13.

Barnes, J. (1999) *England, England*. London: Picador.

Barrett, F. (1989a) *The Independent Guide to Real Holidays Abroad*. London: *The Independent*.

Barrett, F. (1989b) 'Why the tour operators may face their last supper', *The Independent*, 7 November.

Barthes, R. (1972) *Mythologies*. London: Jonathan Cape.

Barthes, R. (1979) 'The Eiffel Tower', in *The Eiffel Tower and Other Mythologies*. New York: Hill & Wang. pp. 3–17.

Barthes, R. (1981) *Camera Lucida*. New York: Hill & Wang.

Bate, J. (1991) *Romantic Ecology: Wordsworth and the Environmental Tradition*. London: Routledge.

Baudrillard, J. (1983) *Simulations*. New York: Semiotext(e).

Baudrillard, J. (1985) 'The ecstacy of communication', in H. Foster (ed.) *Postmodern Culture*. London: Pluto. pp. 126–34.

Baudrillard, J. (1988) *America*. London: Verso.

Bauman, Z. (1987) *Legislators and Interpreters*. Cambridge: Polity.

Bauman, Z. (1993) *Postmodern Ethics*. London: Routledge.

Bauman, Z. (2000) *Liquid Modernity*. Cambridge: Polity.

Baxter, L. (1989) 'Nostalgia's booming future', *The Daily Telegraph*, 21 July.

Beckerman, W. (1974) *In Defence of Economic Growth*. London: Jonathan Cape.

Bell, D. (1976) *The Cultural Contradictions of Capitalism*. London: Heinemann.

Benjamin, W. (1973) 'The work of art in the age of mechanical reproduction', in T. Bennett (ed.) *Illuminations*. London: Fontana. pp. 219–54.

Bennett, T. (1983) 'A thousand and one troubles: Blackpool Pleasure Beach', in *Formations of Pleasure*. London: Routledge. pp. 138–55.

Bennett, T. (1986) 'Hegemony, ideology, pleasure: Blackpool', in T. Bennett, C. Mercer and J. Woollacott (eds) *Popular Culture and Social Relations*. Milton Keynes: Open University Press. pp. 135–55.

Bennett, T. (1988) 'Museums and "the people"', in R. Lumley (ed.) *The Museum Time-Machine*. London: Routledge. pp. 63–86.

Berger, J. (1972) *Ways of Escape*. Harmondsworth: Penguin.

Berman, M. (1983) *All that is Solid Melts into Air*. London: Verso.

Bhabha, H. (ed.) (1990) *Nation and Narration*. London: Routledge.

Blackpool in Focus (2000) *Tourism Data Economy Chapter*. Blackpool: Blackpool in Focus.

Blau, J. (1988) 'Where architects work: a change analysis 1970–80', in P. Knox (ed.) *The Design Professions and the Built Environment*. London: Croom Helm. pp. 127–46.

Boden, D. and Molotch, H. (1994) 'The compulsion to proximity', in R. Friedland and D. Boden (eds) *Now/Here: time, space and modernity*. Berkeley, CA: University of California Press. pp. 257–86.

Boorstin, D. (1964) *The Image: A Guide to Pseudo-Events in America*. New York: Harper.

Boswell, D. and Evans, J. (eds) (1999) *Representing the Nation: A Reader*. London: Routledge.

Bourdieu, P. (1984) *Distinction*. London: Routledge & Kegan Paul.

Brendon, P. (1991) *Thomas Cook: 150 Years of Popular Tourism*. London: Secker and Warburg.

British Hospitality Association (2000) *British Hospitality: Trends and Statistics*. London: British Hospitality Association.

Bruce, M. (1987) 'New technology and the future of tourism', *Tourism Management*, June: 115–20.

Bruner, E. (1994) 'Abraham Lincoln as authentic reproduction: a critique of postmodernism', *American Anthropologist*, 96: 397–415.

Bruner, E. (1995) 'The ethnographer/tourist in Indonesia', in M-F. Lanfant, J. Allcock, E. Bruner (eds) *International Tourism*. London: Sage, pp. 224–41.

Brunner, E. (1945) *Holiday Making and the Holiday Trades*. Oxford: Oxford University Press.

Bryman, A. (1995) *Disney and his Worlds*. London: Routledge.

Bryson, N. (1983) *Vision and Painting*. London: Macmillan.

BTA/ETB Research Services (1988) *Overseas Visitor Survey*. London: BTA/ETB Research Services.

BTA (2000) *Digest of Tourism Statistics. No 23*. London: British Tourism Authority.

Buck, M. (1988) 'The role of travel agent and tour operator', in B. Goodall and G. Ashworth *Marketing in the Tourism Industry*. London: Croom Helm. pp. 67–74.

Buck, N., Gordon, I., Pickvance, C. and Taylor-Gooby, P. (1989) 'The Isle of Thanet: restructuring and municipal conservatism', in P. Cooke (ed.) *Localities*. London: Unwin Hyman. pp. 166–97.

Bull, M. (2000) *Sounding Out The City*. London: Berg.

Burkart, A.J. and Medlik, S. (1974) *Tourism, Past, Present, and Future*. London: Heinemann.

Burton, R. (1989) 'Yorkshire tea and fat rascals', the *Guardian*, 25 March.

Butler, T. and Savage, M. (eds) (1995) *Social Change and the Middle Classes*. London: UCL Press.

Buzard, J. (1993) *The Beaten Track*. Oxford: Clarendon Press.

Cabinet Office (Enterprise Unit) (1983) *Pleasure, Leisure and Jobs. The Business of Tourism*. London: HMSO.

Cairncross, F. (1997) *The Death of Distance*. London: Orion.

Callan, R. (1989) 'Small country hotels and hotel award schemes as a measurement of service quality', *Service Industries Journal*, 9: 223–46.

Campbell, C. (1987) *The Romantic Ethic and the Spirit of Modern Consumerism*. Oxford: Basil Blackwell.

Campbell, M. (1989) 'Fishing lore. The construction of the "Sportsman"', *Annals of Tourism Research*, 16: 76–88.

Carlzon, J. (1987) *Moments of Truth*. Cambridge, MA: Ballinger.

Chandler, P. (2000) 'The UK Outbound Tour Operating Market – Changing Patterns of Distribution', *ETC Insights*, London: English Tourism Council.

Chivers, T. (1973) 'The proletarianisation of a service worker', *Sociological Review*, 21: 633–56.

Clark, P. (1983) *The English Alehouse: a Social History, 1200–1830*. London: Longman.

Clark, T.J. (1984) *The Painting of Modern Life*. London: Thames & Hudson.

Clarke, J. and Critcher, C. (1985) *The Devil Makes Work*. London: Macmillan.

Clifford, J. (1997) *Routes*. Cambridge, Mass: Harvard University Press.

Clift, S. and Carter, S. (eds) (1999) *Tourism, Travel and Sex*. London: Cassell.

Cloke, P. (1989) 'Land-use planning in rural Britain', in P. Cloke (ed.) *Rural Land-Use Planning in Developed Nations*. London: Unwin Hyman. pp. 18–46.

Cloke, P., Phillips, M., Thrift, N. (1995) 'The new middle classes and the social constructs of rural living', in Butler, T. and Savage, M. (eds) *Social Change and the Middle Classes*. London: UCL Press. pp. 220–38.

Cloke, P. and Perkins, H. (1998) 'Cracking the canyon with the awesome foursome: representations of adventure tourism in New Zealand', *Environment and Planning D. Society and Space*, 16: 185–218.

Cohen, E. (1972) 'Towards a sociology of international tourism', *Social Research*, 39: 164–82.

Cohen, E. (1979) 'A phenomenology of tourist types', *Sociology*, 13: 179–201.

Cohen, E. (1988) 'Traditions in the qualitative sociology of tourism', *Annals of Tourism Research. Special Issue*, 15: 29–46.

Cohen, R. (1997) *Global Diasporas*. London: UCL Press.

Colson, F. (1926) *The Week*. Cambridge: Cambridge University Press.

Cooper, R. (1997) 'The visibility of social systems', in K. Hetherington and R. Munro (eds) *Ideas of Difference: Social Spaces and the Labour of Division*. Oxford: Blackwell and Sociological Review. pp. 32–41.

Corbin, A. (1992) *The Lure of the Sea: the discovery of the seaside in the modern world. 1750–1840*. Cambridge: Polity.

Cosgrove, D. (1984) *Social Formation and Symbolic Landscape*. London: Croorn Helm.

Countryside Commission (1988) *Out in the Country*. Cheltenham: Countryside Commission.

Cowen, H. (1990) 'Regency icons: Marketing Cheltenham's built environment', in M. Harloe, C. Pickvance and J. Urry (eds) *Place, Politics and Policy. Do Localities Matter?* London: Unwin Hyman. pp. 128–45.

Craik, J. (1997) 'The culture of tourism', in C. Rojek and J. Urry (eds) *Touring Cultures*. London: Routledge. pp. 113–36.

Crang, M. (1999) 'Knowing, Tourism and Practices of Vision', in D. Crouch (ed.) *Leisure/Tourism Geographies*. London: Routledge. pp. 238–56.

Crang, P. (1994) 'It's showtime: on the workplace geographies of display in a restaurant in Southeast England', *Environment and Planning D. Society and Space*, 12: 675–704.

Crang, P. (1997) 'Performing the tourist product', in C. Rojek and J. Urry (eds) *Touring Cultures*. London: Routledge, pp. 137–54.

Crawshaw, C. and Urry, J. (1997) 'Tourism and the photographic eye', in C. Rojek and J. Urry (eds) *Touring Cultures*. London: Routledge, pp. 176–95.

Crick, M. (1985) '"Tracing" the anthropological self', *Social Analysis*, 17: 71–92.

Crick, M. (1988) 'Sun, sex, sights, savings and servility', *Criticism, Heresy and Interpretation*, 1: 37–76.

Crouch, D. (ed.) (2000) *Leisure/Tourism Geographies*. London: Routledge.

Csergo, J. (1997) 'La constitution de la spécialite gastronomique comme object patrimonial en France fin XVIIIe-XXe siecle en France', in D. Grange and D. Ponlot (eds) *L'esprit de lieux, le patrimoine et la cité*. Grenoble: Presses Universitaires de Grenoble.

Culler, J. (1981) 'Semiotics of Tourism', *American Journal of Semiotics*, 1: 127–40.

Cunningham, H. (1980) *Leisure in the Industrial Revolution*. London: Croom Helm.

Cwerner, S. (2001) 'The times of migration', *Journal of Ethnic and Migration Studies*, 27: 7–36.

Daniels, S. and Cosgrove, D. (1988) 'Introduction: iconography and landscape', in D. Cosgrove and S. Daniels (eds) *The Iconography of Landscape*. Cambridge: Cambridge University Press. pp. 1–10.

Davies, L. (1987) 'If you've got it, flaunt it', *Employment Gazette*, April: 167–71.

Deane, P. and Cole, W.A. (1962) *British Economic Growth, 1688–1959*. Cambridge: Cambridge University Press.

Debord, G. (1983) *Society of the Spectacle*. Detroit, IL: Black & Red.

Denison-Edson, P.W. (1967) 'Some aspects of a historical geography of Morecambe', BA dissertation, University of Cambridge.

Dent, K. (1975) 'Travel as education: the English landed classes in the eighteenth century', *Educational Studies*, 1: 171–80.

Dept of Employment (1971) *Manpower Studies No 10: Hotels*. London: HMSO.

Dept of Employment (1987) 'Historical supplement', *Employment Gazette*, February.

Dept of Transport (1988) *National Travel Survey: 1985/6 Report – Part 1. An Analysis of Personal Travel*. London: HMSO.

Desforges, L. (1998) '"Checking out the planet". Global representations/local identities and youth travel', in T. Skelton and G. Valentine (eds) *Cool Places*, London: Routledge. pp. 175–92.

Desmond, J. (1999) *Staging Tourism*. Chicago: University of Chicago Press.

Dicks, B. (2000) *Heritage, Place and Community*. Cardiff: University of Wales Press.

Douglas, M. (1973) *Natural Symbols; Explorations in Cosmology*. London: Barrie and Jenkins.

Du Gay, Hall, S., Janes, L., Mackay, H., Negus, K. (1997) *Doing Cultural Studies. The Story of Sony Walkman*. London: Sage.

Eco, U. (1986) *Travels in Hyper-Reality*. London: Picador.

Economic Development (n.d.) *'I've Never Been to Wigan, but I Know What It's Like'*. Wigan: Economic Development.

Eade, J. and Sallnow, M. (eds) (1991) *Contesting the Sacred. The Anthropology of Christian Pilgrimage*. London: Routledge.

Edensor, T. (1998) *Tourists at the Taj*. London: Routledge.

Edgar, D. (1987) 'The new nostalgia', *Marxism Today*, March: 30–5.

Ehrenreich, B. (1983) *The Hearts of Men*. London: Pluto.

Ehrenreich, B. (1989) *Fear of Falling*. New York: Pantheon.

Ellis A. and Heath, A. (1983) 'Positional competition, or an offer you can't refuse', in A. Ellis and K. Kumar (1983). *Dilemmas of Liberal Democracies*. London: Tavistock. pp. 1–22.

Ellis, A. and Kumar, K. (eds) (1983) *Dilemmas of Liberal Democracies*. London: Tavistock.

English Tourism Council (2000/2001) *ETC Insights*. London: ETC.

Enloe, C. (1989) *Bananas, Beaches and Bases*. London: Pandora.

ETAC (Education and Training Advisory Council) (1983) *Hotel and Catering Skills – Now and in the Future: Part H, Jobs and Skills*. Wembley: Hotel and Catering Industry Training Board.

Fainstein, S. and Judd, D. (eds) (1999) *The Tourist City*. Cornell: Yale University Press.

Farrant, S. (1987) 'London by the sea: resort development on the south coast of England, 1880–1939', *Journal of Contemporary History*, 22: 137–62.

Faulks, S. (1988) 'Disney comes to Chaucerland', *The Independent*, 11 June.

Featherstone, M. (1987) 'Consumer culture, symbolic power and universalism', in G. Stauth and S. Zubaida (eds) *Mass Culture, Popular Culture, and Social Life in the Middle East*. Frankfurt: Campus. pp. 17–46.

Feifer, M. (1985) *Going Places*. London: Macmillan.

Fevre, R. (1982) *Problems of Unbelief in the Sixteenth Century*. Cambridge, Mass: Harvard UP.

Finkelstein, J. (1989) *Dining Out. A Sociology of Modern Manners*. Cambridge: Polity.

Fiske, J. (1989) *Reading the Popular*. Boston: Unwin Hyman.

Fjellman, S. (1992) *Vinyl Leaves: Walt Disney World and America*. Boulder: Westview Press.

Fondersmith, J. (1988) 'Downtown 2040: making cities fun', *The Futurist*, March/April: 9–17.

Forster, E.M. (1955) *A Room with a View*. Harmondsworth: Penguin (orig. 1908).

Foster, H. (1985a) 'Postmodernism: a preface', in H. Foster (ed.) *Postmodern Culture*. London: Pluto. pp. ix–xvi.

Foster, H. (ed.) (1985b) *Postmodern Culture*. London: Pluto.

Foucault, M. (1970) *The Order of Things*. London: Tavistock.

Foucault, M. (1976) *The Birth of the Clinic*. London: Tavistock.

Frampton, K. (1988) 'Place-form and cultural identity', in J. Thackara (ed.) *Design after Postmodernism*. London: Thames & Hudson. pp. 51–66.

Franklin, S., Lury, C., Stacey, J. (2000) *Global Nature, Global Culture*. London: Sage.

Freeman, M. (1986) *Town-Centre Redevelopment: Architectural Styles and the Roles of Developers and Architects*. University of Birmingham Dept of Geography, Occasional Publication no. 20.

Frieden, B. and Sagalyn, L. (1989) *Downtown, Inc. How America Rebuilds Cities*. Cambridge, MA: MIT Press.

Frisby, D. and Featherstone, M. (eds) (1997) *Simmel on Culture*. London: Sage.

Gabriel, Y. (1988) *Working Lives in Catering*. London: Routledge.

Gershuny, J. (1987) 'The future of service employment', in O. Giarini (ed.) *The Emerging Service Economy*. Oxford: Oxford University Press. pp. 105–24.

Gibson, J. (1986) *The Ecological Approach to Visual Perception*. New Jersey: Lawrence Erlbaum.

Giddens, A. (1984) *The Constitution of Society*. Cambridge: Polity.

Gil, J. (1998) *Metamorphoses of the Body*. Minneapolis: University of Minneapolis Press.

Glancey, J. (1988) 'Hello campers', *Landscape*, July/August: 54–5.

Goodall, B. (1988) 'Changing patterns and structures of European tourism', in B. Goodall and G. Ashworth (eds) *Marketing in the Tourism Industry*. London: Croom Helm. pp. 18–38.

Goodwin, A. (1989) 'Nothing like the real thing', *New Statesman and Society*, 12 August.

Gottdiener, M. (2001) *Life in the Air. Surviving the New Culture of Air Travel*. Lanham, Mass.: Rowman and Littlefield.

Gottlieb, A. (1982) 'Americans' vacations', *Annals of Tourism Research*, 9: 165–87.

Grass, J. (1972) 'Morecambe: The People's Pleasure. The Development of a Holiday Resort, 1880–1902', MA dissertation, University of Lancaster.

Gratton, C. and Taylor, P. (1987) *Leisure Industries. An Overview*. London: Comedia.

Graves, R. (1965) *Majorca Observed*. London: Cassell.

Green, N. (1990) *The Spectacle of Nature*. Manchester: Manchester University Press.

Gregory, D. (1994) *Geographical Imaginations*. Cambridge, Mass.: Blackwell.

Gregory, D. (1999) 'Scripting Egypt: Orientalism and the cultures of travel', in J. Duncan and D. Gregory (eds) *Writes of Passage*. London: Routledge, pp. 114–50.

Greene, M. (1982) *Marketing Hotels into the 1990s*. London: Heinemann.

Guerrier, Y. and Lockwood, A. (1989) 'Core and peripheral employees in hotel operations', *Personnel Review*, 18: 9–15.

Hall, M. (1994) 'Gender and economic interests in tourism prostitution: the nature, development and implications of sex tourism in south-east Asia', in Kinnaird, V. and Hall, D. (eds) *Tourism: A Gender Analysis*. Chichester: John Wiley, pp. 142–63.

Halsall, M. (1986) 'Through the valley of the shadow', the *Guardian*, 27 December.

Hanna, M. (2000) 'Sightseeing Trends in 1999', *ETC Highlights*, London: English Tourism Council.

Harris, H. and Lipman, A. (1986) 'Viewpoint: A culture and despair: reflections on "postmodern" architecture', *Sociological Review*, 34: 837–54.

Harrison, B. (1971) *Drink and the Victorians*. London: Faber & Faber.

Hart, J. (1988) 'A package for Christmas', *Signature*, November/December: 18–19.

Hart, N. (1989) 'Gender and the rise and fall of class politics', *New Left Review*, 175: 19–47.

Harvey, D. (1987) 'Flexible accumulation through urbanism: reflections on "post-modernism" in the American city', *Antipode*, 19: 260–86.

Harvey, D. (1988) 'Voodoo cities', *New Statesman and Society*, 30 September: 33–5.

Harvey, D. (1989) *The Condition of Postmodernity*. Oxford: Blackwell.

Harvey, P. (1996) *Hybrids of Modernity*. London: Routledge.

Hattersley, R. (1989) 'A canny lad', *The Listener*, 19 January.

Hawkin, P., Lovins, A., Lovins, L.H. (1999) *Natural Capitalism*. London: Earthscan.

Hebdige, D. (1986–7) 'A report from the Western Front'. *Block 12*: 4–26.

Hebdige, D. (1988) *Hiding in the Light*. London: Routledge.

Heiman, M. (1989) 'Production confronts consumption: landscape perception and social conflict', *Society and Space*, 7: 165–78.

Heinich, N. (1988) 'The Pompidou Centre and its public: the limits of a utopian site', in R. Lumiey (ed.) *The Museum Time-Machine*. London: Routledge. pp. 199–212.

Hendry, J. (2000) The Orient Strikes Back. A Global View of Cultural Display. Oxford: Berg.

Hennessy, S., Greenwood, J., Shaw, G. and Williams, A. (1986) *The Role of Tourism in Local Economies: a Pilot Study of Looe, Cornwall*. Tourism in Cornwall Project, Dept of Geography, University of Exeter.

Hern, A. (1967) *The Seaside Holiday*. London: Cresset Press.

Hetherington, K. (2000) 'Museums and the visually impaired: the spatial politics of access', *Sociological Review*, 48: 444–63.

Hewison, R. (1987) *The Heritage Industry*. London: Methuen.

Hirsch, F. (1978) *Social Limits to Growth*. London: Routledge & Kegan Paul.

Hirschhorn, L. (1984) *Beyond Mechanization*. Cambridge, MA: MIT Press.

Hochschild, A. (1983) *The Managed Heart, Commercialization of Human Feeling*. Berkeley: University of California Press.

Holderness, G. (1988) 'Bardolatry: or, the cultural materialist's guide to Stratford-upon-Avon', in G. Holderness (ed.) *The Shakespeare Myth*, Manchester: Manchester University Press. pp. 1–15.

Hollingshead, K. (2000) 'The tourist gaze and its games of truth. An elaboration of the governmentality of Foucault via Urry', Millennium Conference: Tourism 2000, Sheffield, September.

Hooper-Greenhill, E. (1988) 'Counting visitors or visitors who count', in R. Lumley (ed.) *The Museum Time-Machine*. London: Routledge. pp. 213–32.

Horne, D. (1984) *The Great Museum*. London: Pluto.

Houston, L. (1986) *Strategy and Opportunities for Tourism Development*. Glasgow: Planning Exchange.

Hutcheon, L. (1986–7) 'The politics of postmodernism: parody and history', *Cultural Critique*, 5: 179–297.

Hutchinson, M. (1989) *The Prince of Wales: Right or Wrong?* London: Faber & Faber.

Hutnyk, J. (1996) *The Rumour of Calcutta*. London: Zed.

Ingold, T. and Kurttila, T. (2000) 'Perceiving the environment in Finnish Lapland', *Body and Society*, 6: 183–96.

Jakle, J. (1985) *The Tourist*. Lincoln: University of Nebraska Press.

James, N. (1989) 'Emotional labour: skill and work in the social regulation of feelings', *Sociological Review*, 37: 15–42.

Jameson, F. (1985) 'Postmodernism and consumer culture', in H. Foster (ed.) *Postmodern Culture*. London: Pluto. pp. 111–25.

Jamieson, B. (1989) 'Bass checks into the Penthouse Suite', *The Sunday Telegraph*, 27 August.

Januszczak, W. (1987) 'Romancing the grime', the *Guardian*, 2 September.

Jarvis, R. (1997) *Romantic Writing and Pedestrian Travel*. London: Macmillan.

Jay, M. (1993) *Downcast Eyes*. Berkeley: University of California Press.

Jeffries, S. (1998) 'Surreal side of the Street', the *Guardian*, October 2nd: Friday Review: 2–3.

Jencks, C. (1977) *The Language of Post-Modern Architecture*. New York: Academy.

Jenkins, S. (1987) 'Art makes a return to architecture', *The Sunday Times*, 15 November.

Johnson J. and Pooley, C. (eds) (1982) *The Structure of Nineteenth Century Cities*. London: Croom Helm.

Johnson, K. and Mignot, K. (1982) 'Marketing trade unionism to service industries: an historical analysis of the hotel industry', *Service Industries Journal*, 2: 5–23.

Jokinen, E. and Veijola, S. (1997) 'The disoriented tourist: the figuration of the tourist in contemporary cultural critique', in C. Rojek and J. Urry (eds) *Touring Cultures*. London: Routledge. pp. 23–51.

Jones, A. (1987) 'Green tourism', *Tourism Management*, December: 354–6.

Jordonova, L. (1989) 'Objects of knowledge: a historical perspective on museums', in P. Vergo (ed.) *The New Museology*. London: Reaktion. pp. 21–40.

Kadt, de, E. (1979) *Tourism: Passport to Development*. Oxford: Oxford University Press.

Kaplan, C. (1996) *Questions of Travel*. Durham, US: Duke University Press.

Key Note Report (1986) *Tourism in the UK*. London: Key Note Publications.

Key Note Report (1987) *Tourism in the UK*. London: Key Note Publications.

King, A. (1984) *The Bungalow*. London: Routledge.

Kinnaird, V. and Hall, D. (eds) (1994) *Tourism: A Gender Analysis*. Chichester: John Wiley.

Kirshenblatt-Gimblett, B. (1998) *Destination Culture. Tourism, Museums and Heritage*. Berkeley: University of California Press.

Klein, N. (2000) *No Logo*. London: Flamingo.

Knox, P. (1987) 'The social production of the built environment', *Progress in Human Geography*, 11: 354–77.

Knox, P. (1988) 'The design professions and the built environment in a postmodern epoch', in P. Knox (ed.) *The Design Professions and the Built Environment*. London: Croom Helm. pp. 1–11.

Krier, L. (1984) 'Berlin-Tagel' and 'Building and architecture', *Architectural Design*, 54: 87–119.

Kroker, A. and Cook, D. (1986) *The Postmodern Scene*. New York: St Martin's.

Landry, C., Montgomery, J., Worpole, K., Gratton, C. and Murray, R. (1989) *The Last Resort*. London: Comedia Consultancy/SEEDS (South East Economic Development Strategy).

Larkham, P. (1986) *The Agents of Urban Change*. University of Birmingham Dept of Geography, Occasional Publication no. 21.

Larsen, J. (2001) *Tourism Mobilities and the Tourist Glance: the 'Tourist Gaze' in Motion*. Dept of Sociology, Lancaster University, unpublished mimeo.

Lasch, C. (1980) *The Culture of Narcissism*. London: Sphere.

Lash, S. (1990) *Sociology of Postmodernism*. London: Routledge.

Lash, S. and Urry, J. (1987) *The End of Organized Capitalism*. Cambridge: Polity.

Lash, S. and Urry, J. (1994) *Economies of Signs and Space*. London: Sage.

Lawson, A. and Samson, C. (1988) 'Age, gender and adultery', *British Journal of Sociology*, 39: 409–40.

Lea, J. (1988) *Tourism and Development in the Third World*. London: Routledge.

Leadbetter, C. (1988) 'Power to the person', *Marxism Today*, October: 14–19.

Leidner, R. (1987) 'Scripting service work: case studies of fast food and insurance sales', *Society for the Study of Social Problems*, Chicago, August.

Lencek, L. and Bosler, G. (1998) *The Beach. The History of Paradise on Earth*. London: Secker and Warburg.

Lennon, J. and Foley, M. (2000) *Dark Tourism*. London: Continuum.

Lett, J. (1983) 'Ludic and liminoid aspects of charter yacht tourism in the Caribbean', *Annals of Tourism Research*, 10: 35–56.

Levitt, T. (1981) 'Marketing intangible products and product intangibles', *The Cornell HRA Quarterly*, August: 37–44.

Lewis, N. (2001) *The climbing body: choreographing a history of modernity*. PhD, Dept of Sociology, Lancaster University.

Ley, D. and Olds, K. (1988) 'Landscape as spectacle: world's fairs and the culture of heroic consumption', *Environment and Planning D: Society and Space*, 6: 191–212.

Lickorish, L.J. and Kershaw, A.G. (1975) 'Tourism between 1840 and 1940', in A.J. Burkart and S. Medlik (eds) *The Management of Tourism*. London: Heinemann. pp. 11–26.

Lodge, D. (1991) *Paradise News*. London: Secker and Warburg.

Löfgren, O. (2000) *On Holiday: A History Of Vacationing*. Berkeley: University of California Press.

Lowe, P. and Goyder, J. (1983) *Environmental Groups in Politics*. London: Allen & Unwin.

Lowenthal, D. (1985) *The Past is a Foreign Country*. Cambridge: Cambridge University Press.

Lumley, R. (ed.) (1988) *The Museum Time-Machine*. London: Routledge.

Lunn, T. (1989) 'How to swing unused talent into action', *The Sunday Times*, 20 August.

Lynch, K. (1973) *What Time is this Place?* Cambridge, MA: MIT Press.

Lynch, K. (1960) *The Image of the City*. Camb., Mass.: MIT Press.

MacCannell, D. (1973) 'Staged authenticity: arrangements of social space in tourist settings', *American Sociological Review*, 79: 589–603.

MacCannell, D. (1992) *Empty Meeting Grounds*. New York: Routledge.

MacCannell, D. (1999) *The Tourist*. New York: Schocken (orig. 1976).

MacCannell, D. (2001) 'Tourist agency', *Tourism Studies*, 1: 23–38.

Macdonald, S. (1995) 'Consuming science: public knowledge and the dispersed politics of reception among museum visitors', *Media, Culture and Society*, 17: 13–29.

Macdonald, S. (1997) 'A people's story: heritage, identity and authenticity', in C. Rojek and J. Urry (eds) *Touring Cultures*. London: Routledge. pp. 155–75.

Macnaghten, P. and Urry, J. (1998) *Contested Natures*. London: Sage.

Macnaghten, P. and Urry, J. (2000a) 'Bodies in the Woods', in *Bodies of Nature*, double issue of *Body and Society*, 6: 166–82.

Macnaghten, P. and Urry, J. (eds) (2000b) *Bodies of Nature*, double issue of *Body and Society*, 6: 1–202.

Maier, C. (1994) 'A surfeit of memory? Reflections of history, melancholy and denial', *History and Memory*, 5: 136–52.

Makimoto, T. and Manners, D. (1997) *Digital Nomad*. Chichester: John Wiley.

Mars, G. and Nicod, M. (1984) *The World of Waiters*. London: Allen & Unwin.

Marshall, G. (1986) 'The workplace culture of a licensed restaurant', *Theory, Culture and Society*, 3: 33–48.

Martin, B. (1982) *A Sociology of Contemporary Popular Culture*. Oxford: Blackwell.

Martin, B. and Mason, S. (1987) 'Current trends in leisure', *Leisure Studies*, 6: 93–7.

Matless, D. (2000) 'Action and noise over a hundred years: the making of a nature region', *Body and Society*, 6: 141–165.

Mawby, R., Brunt, P. and Hambly, Z. (2000) 'Fear of crime among British holiday makers', *British Journal of Criminology, Delinquency and Deviant Social Behaviour*, 40: 468–79.

McClintock, A. (1995) *Imperial Leather*. New York: Routledge.

McCrone, D. (1998) *The Sociology of Nationalism*. London: Routledge.

McCrone, D., Morris, A. and Kiely, R. (1995) *Scotland – the Brand*. Edinburgh: Edinburgh University Press.

McKay, I. (1988) 'Twilight at Peggy's Cove: towards a genealogy of "maritimicity" in Nova Scotia', *Borderlines*, Summer: 29–37.

McKellar, S. (1988) 'The enterprise of culture', *Local Work*, June: 14–17.

Mellor, A. (1991) 'Enterprise and heritage in the Dock', in J. Corner and S. Harvey (eds) *Enterprise and Heritage*. London: Routledge. pp. 93–115.

Mennell, S. (1985) *All Manners of Food*. Oxford: Blackwell.

Mercer, C. (1983) 'A poverty of desire: pleasure and popular politics', in T. Bennett (ed.) *Formations of Pleasure*. London: Routledge & Kegan Paul. pp. 84–101.

Merriman, N. (1989) 'Museum visiting as a cultural phenomenon', in P. Vergo (ed.) *The New Museology*. London: Reaktion. pp. 149–71.

Metcalf, H. (1988) 'Careers and training in tourism and leisure', *Employment Gazette*, February: 84–93.

Meyrowitz, J. (1985) *No Sense of Place. The Impact of Electronic Media on Social Behaviour*. New York: Oxford University Press.

Michael, M. (1996) *Constructing Identities*. London: Sage.

Michael, M. (2000) *Reconnecting, Culture, Technology and Nature*. London: Routledge.

Miller, D. and Slater, D. (2000) *The Internet*. London: Berg.

Mills, C.A. (1988). '"Life on the upslope": the postmodern landscape of gentrification', *Environment and Planning D: Society and Space*, 6: 169–89.

• Mishan, E. (1969) *The Costs of Economic Growth*. Harmondsworth: Penguin.

Mitchinson, A. (1988) 'New Society database. Holidays', *New Society*, 22 April.

Mitford, N. (1959) 'The tourist', *Encounter*, 13 (October): 3–7.

Mitter, S. (1986) *Common Fate, Common Road*. London: Pluto.

Morris, M. (1988) 'At Henry Parkes Motel', *Cultural Studies*, 2: 1–47.

Morton, A. (1988) 'Tomorrow's yesterdays: science museums and the future', in R. Lumley (ed.) *The Museum Time-Machine*. London: Routledge. pp. 128–43.

Munt, I. (1994) 'The other postmodern tourist: culture, travel and the new middle classes', *Theory, Culture and Society*, 11: 101–24.

Myerscough, J. (1974) 'The recent history of the use of leisure time', in I. Appleton (ed.) *Leisure Research and Policy*. Edinburgh: Scottish Academic Press. pp. 3–16.

Myerscough, J. (1986) *Facts About The Arts (1986 Edition)*. London: Policy Studies Institute.

Myerscough, J. (1988) *The Economic Importance of the Arts in Britain*. London: Policy Studies Institute.

NEDO (National Economic Development Office) (1986) *Changing Working Patterns*. London: NEDO.

NWTB (2000) *Sustaining Progress*, Wigan: North West Tourist Board Tourism Strategy.

Newby, H. (1982) *Green and Pleasant Land*. Harmondsworth: Penguin.

Newby, P. (1981) 'Literature and the fashioning of tourist taste', in D. Pocock (ed.) *Humanistic Geography and Literature*. London: Croom Helm. pp. 130–41.

Norman, P. (1988) 'Faking the present'. the *Guardian*, 10–11 December.

O'Rourke, P.J. (1988) *Holidays in Hell*. New York: Atlantic Monthly Review.

Ong, A. and Nonini, D. (eds) (1997) *Ungrounded Empires*. London: Routledge.

Osborne, P. (2000) *Travelling Light. Photography, travel and visual culture*. Manchester: Manchester University Press.

Ousby, I. (1990) *The Englishman's England*. Cambridge: Cambridge University Press.

Pahl, R. (1965) *Urbs in Rure. The Metropolitan Fringe in Hertfordshire*. London: LSE Geography Dept.

Papastergiadis, N. (2000) *The Turbulence of Migration*. Cambridge: Polity.

Parr, M. (1995) *Small World*. Stockport: Dewi Lewis Publishing.

Parr, M. (1999) *Boring Postcards*. London: Phaidon Press.

Parry, K. (1983) *Resorts of the Lancashire Coast*. Newton Abbot: David & Charles.

Pearce, P. and Moscardo, G. (1986) 'The concept of authenticity in tourist experiences', *Australian and New Zealand Journal of Sociology*, 22: 121–32.

Percy, S. and Lamb, H. (1987) 'The squalor behind the bright fast food lights', the *Guardian*, 22 August.

Perkin, H. (1976) 'The "social tone" of Victorian seaside resorts in the north-west', *Northern History*, II: 180–94.

Perkins, H. and Thorns, D. (1998) 'Gazing or performing: characterising the contemporary tourist experience: work in progress', Paper to World Congress of Sociology, Montreal, July-August.

Pevsner, N. (1970) *A History of Building Types*. London: Thames & Hudson.

Pfeil, F. (1985) 'Makin' flippy-floppy: postmodernism and the baby-boom PMC', in M. Davis, F. Pfeil and M. Spinker (eds) *The Year Left. An American Socialist Yearbook 1985*. London: Verso. pp. 263–95.

Phelps-Brown, E.H. (1968) *A Century of Pay*. London: Macmillan.

Pickvance, C. (1990) 'Council economic intervention and political conflict in a declining resort: the Isle of Thanet', in M. Harloe, C. Pickvance and J. Urry (eds) *Place, Politics, Policy. Do Localities Matter?* London: Unwin Hyman. pp. 165–86.

Pile, S. (1987) You'll have no fun rushing to the sun, *The Observer*, 16 May.

Pimlott, J. (1947) *The Englishman's Holiday*. London: Faber & Faber.

Pine, R. (1987) *Management of Technological Change in the Catering Industry*. Aldershot: Avebury.

Piore, M. and Sabel, C. (1984) *The Second Industrial Divide*. New York: Basic Books.

Pollard, S. (1965) *The Genesis of Modern Management*. London: Edward Arnold.

Pollert, A. (1988) 'The "flexible firm": fixation or fact', *Work, Employment and Society*, 2: 281–316.

Poon, A. (1989) 'Competitive strategies for a "new tourism"', in C. Cooper (ed.) *Progress in Tourism, Recreation and Hospitality Management* Vol. 1. London: Belhaven Press. pp. 91–102.

Poon, A. (1993) *Tourism, Technology and Competitive Strategies*, CAB International, Wallingford, Oxon.

Pratt, M. (1992) *Imperial Eyes*. London: Routledge.

Pressdee, M. (1986) 'Agony or ecstasy: broken transitions and new social state of working-class youth in Australia', occasional papers, South Australia College of Adult Education, Magill, S. Australia.

Punter, J. (1986–7) 'The contradictions of aesthetic control under the Conservatives', *Planning Practice and Research*, 1: 8–13.

Quick, R.C. (1962) *The History of Morecambe and Heysham*. Morecambe: Morecambe Times.

Raban, J. (1986) *Coasting*. London: Picador.

Retzinger, J. (1998) 'Framing the tourist gaze. Railway journeys across Nebraska, 1866–1906', *Great Plains Quarterly*, 18: 213–26.

Reynolds, H. (1988) '"Leisure revolution" prime engines of regional recovery'. *The Daily Telegraph* 2 December.

Richards, J. and MacKenzie, J. (1986) *The Railway Station*. Oxford: Oxford University Press.

Richards, J., Wilson, S., Woodhead, L. (eds) 1999. *Diana. The Making of a Media Saint*. London: I.B. Tauris.

Richter, C. (1987) 'Tourism services', in O. Giarini (ed.) *The Emerging Service Economy*. Oxford: Pergamon. pp. 213–44.

Ring, J. (2000) *How the English Made the Alps*. London: John Murray.

Ritzer, G. (1996) *The McDonaldization of Society*. Thousand Oaks, California: Pine Forge.

Robinson, H. (1976) *A Geography of Tourism*. Plymouth: Macdonald & Evans.

Rocca, T. (1989) 'Bardot scorns "Black tide of filth" in St Tropez', the *Guardian*, 10 August.

Roche, M. (2000) *Mega-Events and Modernity*. London: Routledge.

Rodaway, P. (1994) *Sensuous Geographies*. London: Routledge.

Rojek, C. (1988) 'The convoy of pollution', *Leisure Studies*, 7: 21–31.

Rojek, C. (1990) *Ways of Escape*. London: Macmillan.

Rojek, C. and Urry, J. (eds) (1997) *Touring Cultures*. London: Routledge.

Rose, M. (1978) *The Gregs of Styal*. Cheshire: Quarry Bank Mill Development Trust.

Rosen, P. (1993) 'The social construction of mountain bikes: technology and post-modernity in the cycle industry', *Social Studies of Science*, 23: 479–513.

Samuel, R. (1987a) 'History that's over', the *Guardian*, 9 October.

Samuel, R. (1987b) 'A plaque on all your houses', the *Guardian*, 17 October.

Samuel, R. (1994) *Theatres of Memory*. Verso, London.

Samuel, R. (1998) *Island Stories*. London: Verso.

Sasser, W. and Arbeit, S. (1976) 'Selling jobs in the service sector', *Business Horizons*, 19: 61–5.

Savage, M. (1988) 'The missing link? The relationship between spatial mobility and social mobility', *British Journal of Sociology*, 39: 554–77.

Savage, M., Barlow, J., Dickens, P., Fielding, T. (1992) *Bureaucracy, Property and Culture: Middle-Class Formation in Contemporary Britain*. London: Routledge.

Schama, S. (1995) *Landscape and Memory*. London: HarperCollins.

Schivelbusch, W. (1986) *The Railway Journey. Trains and Travel in the Nineteenth Century*. Oxford: Blackwell.

Scruton, R. (1979) *The Aesthetics of Architecture*. Princeton, NJ: Princeton University Press.

Selwyn, T. (ed.) (1996) *The Tourist Image*. Chichester: Wiley.

Shaw, G., Greenwood, J. and Williams, A. (1988) 'The United Kingdom: market responses and public policy', in A. Williams and G. Shaw (eds) *Tourism and Economic Development*. London: Belhaven Press. pp. 162–79.

Shaw, G., Agarwal, S., Bull, P. (2000) 'Tourism consumption and tourist behaviour: a British perspective', *Tourism Geographies*. 2: 264–89.

Sheller, M. (2002) *Consuming the Caribbean*. London: Routledge.

Sheller, M. and Urry, J. (2000) 'The city and the car', *International Journal of Urban and Regional Research*, 24: 737–57.

Shields, R. (1989) 'Social spatialization and the built environment: the West Edmonton Mall', *Environment and Planning D: Society and Space*, 7: 147–64.

Shields, R. (1990) *Places on the Margin*. London: Routledge.

Shoard, M. (1987) *The Land is Our Land*. London: Paladin.

Slattery, P. and Roper, A. (1986) *The UK Hotel Groups Directory: 1986–7*. London: Cassell.

Smith, D. (1988) 'A fine old stew in the kitchens', the *Guardian*. November 12th.

Smith, V. (1989) *Hosts and Guests. The Anthropology of Tourism*, Philadelphia: University of Pennsylvania Press, (first edition 1978).

Sontag, S. (1979) *On Photography*. Harmondsworth: Penguin.

Spang, L. (2000) *The Invention of the Restaurant*. Cambridge, Mass: Harvard University Press.

Special Projects Group, Lancaster City Council (1987) *Lancaster – Heritage City. Position Statement.* Lancaster: Lancaster City Council.

Spence, J. and Holland, P. (1991) *Family Snaps: the meanings of domestic photography.* London: Virago.

Spillman, L. (1997) *Nation and Commemoration.* Cambridge: Cambridge University Press.

Sprawson, C. (1992) *The Black Masseur.* London: Jonathan Cape.

Stallinbrass, C. (1980) 'Seaside resorts and the hotel accommodation industry', *Progress in Planning,* 13: 103–74.

Stamp, G. (1987) 'A right old Roman carry-on, *The Daily Telegraph,* 28 December.

Stauth, G. and Turner, B. (1988) 'Nostalgia, postmodernism and the critique of mass culture', *Theory, Culture and Society,* 2/3: 509–26.

SWET (Society of West End Theatres) (1982) *Britain at its Best: Overseas Tourism and the West End Theatre.* London: SWET.

Taylor, 1. (1988) 'Down beside the seaside' *Marxism Today,* October: 43.

Taylor, J. (1994) *A Dream of England. Landscape, Photography and the Tourist's Imagination.* Manchester: Manchester University Press.

Tester, K. (ed.) (1994) *The Flâneur.* London: Routledge.

Thomas, K. (1973) *Man and the Natural World: Changing Attitudes in England, 1500–1800.* London: Allen Lane.

Thompson, E.P. (1967) 'Time, work-discipline, and industrial capitalism', *Past and Present,* 38: 56–97.

Thompson, G. (1981) 'Holidays', Unit 11 of *Popular Culture and Everyday Life* (2). Milton Keynes: Open University Press.

Thompson, G. (1983) 'Carnival and the calculable: consumption and play at Blackpool', in T. Bennett (ed.) *Formations of Pleasure.* London: Routledge. pp. 124–36.

Thrift, N. (1989) 'Images of social change', in C. Hamnett, L. McDowell and P. Sarre (eds) *The Changing Social Structure.* London: Sage. pp. 12–42.

Thrift, N. (1996) *Spatial Formations.* London: Sage.

Towner, J. (1985) 'The Grand Tour: a key phase in the history of tourism', *Annals of Tourism Research,* 12: 297–33.

Towner, J. (1988) 'Approaches to tourism history', *Annals of Tourism History,* 15: 47–62.

Travel Alberta (n.d.) *West Edmonton Mall.* Edmonton: Alberta Tourism.

Turner, C. and Manning, P. (1988) 'Placing authenticity – on being a tourist: a reply to Pearce and Manning', *Australian and New Zealand Journal of Sociology,* 24: 136–8.

Turner, L. and Ash, J. (1975) *The Golden Hordes.* London: Constable.

Turner, V. (1973) 'The center out there: pilgrim's goal', *History of Religions,* 12: 191–230.

Turner, V. (1974) *The Ritual Process.* Harmondsworth: Penguin.

Turner, V. and Turner, E. (1978) *Image and Pilgrimage in Christian Culture.* New York: Columbia University Press.

UNDP (1999) *Human Development Report.* New York: UNDP and Oxford University Press

Urry, J. (1987) 'Some social and spatial aspects of services', *Environment and Planning D: Society and Space,* 5: 5–26.

Urry, J. (1988) 'Cultural change and contemporary holiday-making', *Theory, Culture and Society,* 5: 35–55.

Urry, J. (1990) 'The consumption of "tourism"', *Sociology,* 24: 23–35.

Urry, J. (1992) 'The Tourist Gaze "Revisited"', *American Behavioral Scientist,* 36: 172–86.

Urry, J. (1994) 'Time, leisure and social identity', *Time and Society,* 3: 131–49.

Urry, J. (1995a) *Consuming Places.* London: Routledge.

Urry, J. (1995b) 'A middle class countryside?', in Butler, T. and Savage, M. (eds) *Social Change and the Middle Classes.* London: UCL Press. pp. 205–19.

Urry, J. (1996) 'How societies remember the past', in S. Macdonald and G. Fyfe (eds) *Theorizing Museums.* Oxford: Sociological Review Monographs and Blackwells, pp. 45–65.

Urry, J. (2000) *Sociology Beyond Societies.* London: Routledge.

Urry, J. (2002) *Global Complexity.* Cambridge: Polity.

Uzzell, D. (1989) *Heritage Interpretation*. Vol. 2. London: Belhaven Press.

Valenzuela, M. (1988) 'Spain: the phenomenon of mass tourism', in A. Williams and G. Shaw (eds) *Tourism and Economic Development*. London: Belhaven Press. pp. 39–57.

Veijola, S. and Jokinen, E. (1994) 'The body in tourism', *Theory, Culture and Society*, 6: 125–51.

Venturi, R. (1972) *Learning from Las Vegas*. Cambridge, MA: MIT Press.

Vidal, J (1988) 'No room here for Mickey Mouse', *The Guardian*, 19 March.

Vulliamy, E. (1988) 'Squalid renaissance', the *Guardian*, 16 April.

Walter, J. (1982) 'Social limits to tourism', *Leisure Studies*, l: 295–304.

Walton, J. (1978) *The Blackpool Landlady*. Manchester: Manchester University Press.

Walton, J. (1979) 'Railways and resort development in Victorian England: the case of Silloth', *Northern History*, 15: 191–209.

Walton, J. (1981) 'The demand for working class seaside holidays in Victorian England', *Economic History Review*, 34: 249–65.

Walton, J. (1983) *The English Seaside Resort: A Social History, 1750–1914*. Leicester: Leicester University Press.

Walton, J. (1997) 'Seaside resorts and maritime history', *International Journal of Maritime History*, 9: 125–47.

Walton, J. (2000) *The British Seaside*. Manchester: Manchester University Press.

Walton, J. and Poole, R. (1982) 'The Lancashire wakes in the nineteenth century', in R. Storch (ed.) *Popular Culture and Customs in the Nineteenth Century*. London: Croom Helm. pp. 100–24.

Walvin, J. (1978) *Beside the Seaside*. London: Allen Lane.

Wang, N. (2000) *Tourism and Modernity*. Oxford: Elsevier.

Ward, M. and Hardy, D. (1986) *Goodnight Campers! The History of the British Holiday Camp*. London: Mansell.

Warde, A. (1988) 'Explaining gentrification and theories of consumption', mimeo, Dept of Sociology, Lancaster University.

Waterhouse, K. (1989) 'Wish you were here', *The Listener*, 12 January. Waterhouse, R. (1989) 'Town abandons trousers for sake of tourism', *Financial Times*, 8 July.

Waters, S. (1967) 'Trends in international tourism', *Development Digest*, 5: 57–61.

Wates, N. and Krevitt, C. (1987) *Community Architecture*. Harmondsworth: Penguin.

Welsh, E. (1988) 'Are locals selling out for a bowl of gruel?' *The Sunday Times*, 11 December.

Welsh, E. (1989) 'Unmasking the special agents', *The Sunday Times*, 26 February.

West, B. (1988) 'The making of the English working past: a critical view of the Ironbridge Gorge museum', in R. Lumley (ed.) *The Museum Time-Machine*. London: Routledge. pp. 36–62.

West, N. (2000) *Kodak and the Lens of Nostalgia*. Charlottesville: University of Virginia Press.

Whitaker, R. (1988) 'Welcome to the Costa del Kebab', *The Independent*, 27 February.

White, D. (1987) 'The born-again museum', *New Society*, 1 May: 10–14.

Whyte, W.F. (1948) *Human Relations in the Restaurant Industry*. New York: McGraw-Hill.

Wickers, D. (1987) 'Splashing out', the *Guardian*, 20 June.

Wickers, D. and Charlton, G. (1988) 'Oh, we do like to be by the seaside', *The Sunday Times*, 5 June.

Wiener, M. (1981) *English Culture and the Decline of the Industrial Spirit*. Cambridge: Cambridge University Press.

Williams, A. and Shaw, G. (1988a) 'Tourism and development: introduction', in A. Williams and G. Shaw (eds) *Tourism and Economic Development*. London: Belhaven Press. pp. 1–11.

Williams, A. and Shaw, G. (1988b) 'Western European tourism in perspective', in A. Williams and G. Shaw (eds) *Tourism and Economic Development*. London: Belhaven Press. pp. 12–38.

Williams, A. and Shaw, G. (1988c) 'Tourism: candyfloss industry or job creator?', *Town Planning Review*, 59: 81–103.

Williams, A., Shaw, G., Greenwood, J., and Hennessy, S. (1986) *Tourism and Economic Development: a Review of Experiences in Western Europe*, Tourism in Cornwall Project, Dept of Geography, University of Exeter.

Williams, I. (1988) 'Profits take a holiday', *The Sunday Times*, 30 June.

Williams, R. (1972) 'Ideas of nature', in J. Benthall (ed.) *Ecology. The Shaping Enquiry*. London: Longman, pp. 146–66.

Williams, R. (1973) *The Country and the City*. London: Paladin.

Williams, S. (1998) *Tourism Geography*. London: Routledge.

Wilsher, P. (1988) 'How they put sparkle back into cities', *The Sunday Times*, 15 May.

Wilson, A. (1988) 'The view from the road: nature tourism in the postwar years', *Borderlines*, 12: 10–14.

Wilson, A. (1992) *Culture of Nature*. Oxford: Blackwell.

Wolff, J. (1985) 'The invisible *flâneuse*: women and the literature of modernity', *Theory, Culture and Society*, 2: 37–48.

Wolff, J. (1993) 'On the road again: metaphors of travel in cultural criticism', *Cultural Studies*, 7: 224–39.

Wood, M. (1974) 'Nostalgia or never: you can't go home again', *New Society*, 7 November: 343–6.

Wordsworth, W. (1984) *The Illustrated Wordworth's Guide to the Lakes*. London: Book Club Associates.

Wouters, C. (1989) 'The sociology of emotions and flight attendants: Hochschild's *Managed Heart*', *Theory, Culture and Society*, 6: 95–124.

Wright, P. (1985) *On Living in an Old Country*. London: Verso.

WTTC (2000) *Summit for Economic Policymakers*. World Travel and Tourism Council. Vol. 1, No 1.

WTO (2000a) *Tourism Highlights 2000*. Madrid: World Tourism Organisation.

WTO (2000b) *Yearbook of Tourism Statistics 2000*. Madrid: World Tourism Organisation.

Younger, G. (1973) *Tourism: Blessing or Blight?* Harmondsworth: Penguin.

Zukin, S. (1991) *Landscapes of Power*. Berkeley: University of California Press.

Index

access to countryside, 87, 89
accommodation, 48, 49, 50
standard of, 52
adventure tourism, 155
advertising, 13, 14
'aesthetic-asceticism', 80–1, 86
affordances, 155–6
agriculture, 87, 88
effects of tourism on, 52
air travel, 5, 25
Airtours, 46
Albert Dock, Liverpool, 97, 101,
105, 109, 120
Alps, 147, 148, 155
Altes Museum, Berlin, 117
Alton Towers, 6, 33, 94
American Adventure, Peak District, 131
amusement parks, 33, 94
see also theme parks anthropological
gaze, 150–1
anticipation, of pleasure, 3, 13–14
Arbeit, S., 60–1
architecture
community, 114
modern, 111–12, 115
postmodern, 82, 87–8, 90, 111–17
vernacular, 87–8, 90, 114, 115
Arnold, M., 148
art galleries, 96
Artley, A., 113
arts/cultural tourism, 108, 137
Ash, J., 7–8
Ashworth, P., 23
Asian communities, 109, 139–40, 143
Association for Industrial
Archeology, 99
Atkinson, T., 70
attractions, development and growth of
new, 6, 146
audience participation, 77
aura, of cultural phenomena, 76, 78, 118
Australia, 158
authenticity, 75, 94, 118, 122–3, 131
quest for, 9–10, 12
staged, 9, 151

Aylesbury, 112
Ayton, R., 21

Bagguley, P., 69
Bali, 7–8, 51, 156
Ballykissangel tourists, 151
Bardot, B., 40
Barnes, J., 99–100
Barthes, R., 32, 43, 128
Bath, 113–14
Baudelaire, C., 126
Baudrillard, J., 77, 149, 154
Bauman, Z., 141, 160
Baxter, T., 27
Bayley, S., 120
beaches, 29, 36
Beamish Open Air Museum, Newcastle,
99, 119
Beatles, 109
Beckerman, W., 40
bed-and-breakfast, 48
Bell, D., 83
Benjamin, W., 76
Bennett, T., 33
Bentham, J., 134
Berman, M., 125, 126
Bettys tearooms, 73
Birchington, 29–30
Black Atlantic tour, 159
black Britons, 139
Blackpool, 21, 22–3, 24, 25, 26, 27,
31, 33
Blackpool Pleasure Beach,
6, 33
Blackpool Tower, 32
blaming, of tourists for economic/social
problems, 53
boarding houses, seafront, 22
bodies
grotesque, 29
mobility of, 151–6
bodily display, 156
Boorstin, D., 7
boulevards, Paris, 125–6
Bourdieu, P., 79, 80–2, 83, 85